THE ECHOING IDA COLLECTION

THE ECHOING IDA COLLECTION

EDITED BY

CYNTHIA R. GREENLEE

KEMI ALABI

JANNA A. ZINZI

FOREWORD BY

MICHELLE DUSTER

THE FEMINIST PRESS
AT THE CITY UNIVERSITY OF NEW YORK
NEW YORK CITY

Published in 2021 by the Feminist Press
at the City University of New York
The Graduate Center
365 Fifth Avenue, Suite 5406
New York, NY 10016

feministpress.org

First Feminist Press edition 2021

 This book was made possible thanks to a grant from New York State
Council on the Arts with the support of Governor Andrew M. Cuomo
and the New York State Legislature.

First printing January 2021

Cover art by Makeba KEEBS Rainey
Cover and text design by Drew Stevens

Library of Congress Cataloging-in-Publication Data
Names: Forward Together (Nonprofit organization). Echoing Ida, author. |
Alabi, Kemi, editor. | Greenlee, Cynthia R., editor. | Zinzi, Janna A.,
editor. | Duster, Michelle, writer of foreword.
Title: The Echoing Ida collection / [edited by] Kemi Alabi, Cynthia R.
Greenlee, Janna A. Zinzi ; foreword by Michelle Duster.
Description: First Feminist Press edition. | New York, NY : Feminist Press,
2021.
Identifiers: LCCN 2020027298 (print) | LCCN 2020027299 (ebook) | ISBN
9781558612839 (paperback) | ISBN 9781558612846 (ebook)
Subjects: LCSH: American literature--African American authors. | American
literature--Women authors. | American literature--21st century. |
Gender-nonconforming people's writings, American.
Classification: LCC PS508.N3 F67 2021 (print) | LCC PS508.N3 (ebook) |
DDC 810.9/896073--dc23
LC record available at https://lccn.loc.gov/2020027298
LC ebook record available at https://lccn.loc.gov/2020027299

PRINTED IN THE UNITED STATES OF AMERICA

We know, as Audre Lorde declared, our silence will not protect us. This book is dedicated to Black women, girls, and nonbinary kin who speak to get free—and to those who can't, not yet or never again. To all we came to know through their deaths or disappearances at the hands of perpetrators unknown or police or people unpunished, we hope this book helps answer Ida B. Wells's call: "The way to right wrongs is to turn the light of truth upon them."

Contents

FAMILY MATTERS

NAKED POWER

BEAUTY BREAKS

FOR THE KULCHA

BLACK LOVE AND BLACK FUTURES

ONWARD

Foreword

Michelle Duster

I grew up on the South Side of Chicago in what became a predominantly Black neighborhood. Both of my parents, Donald and Maxine Duster, especially my mother, were vigilant about making sure that I knew my heritage and history and that they were a source of pride. My mother went out of her way to find coloring books that had Black images. She took my brothers and me to the library on a frequent basis and found every available book with and by Black people. She encouraged us to decorate our rooms with magazine pictures of Black people. She hunted madly for Christmas ornaments that depicted Black culture; we colored Santa Claus and angels with brown markers. She wanted us to see ourselves; she wanted us to be proud of what we looked like and who we were as true citizens in this country who belonged here. My mother insisted that we deserved to be treated with respect and dignity. We were exposed to all kinds of music that was steeped in our cultural heritage—blues, jazz, gospel, and Negro spirituals. She was a very good dancer and tried her best to instill rhythm and fun into our household by blasting music and dancing around the house. When my mom started working as a teacher outside of the home on a consistent basis, one of our long-term babysitters was our next-door neighbor, who was from rural Mississippi. She was a contemporary of my grandmother and used to tell us stories of her experiences growing up picking cotton, using an outhouse, and living through racial oppression and terror.

We knew that we lived in a segregated city and avoided certain neighborhoods and sections that were full of racist white people—in fact, Dr. Martin Luther King Jr. remarked on the hostility he encountered in Chicago. But we navigated our way around white supremacy and racial intolerance throughout my childhood. I realized that my ancestors did not have the same choices and suffered incredible terror and injustice. And I learned more detailed information about the incredible life experiences that my ancestors endured while living in the apartheid South, with my most famous relative being my father's grandmother, my great-grandmother, Ida B. Wells.

Ida was born into slavery in 1862—three years before the Civil War ended. She grew up in Mississippi during Reconstruction, when formerly enslaved people had the first opportunity to become educated. The men could vote for the first time, own businesses, run for political office, and start institutions. But she also came of age during a time and place when Black women were expected to be deferential to men and were treated as second-class citizens to white people.

In 1884, my great-grandmother was physically removed from the ladies' coach of a train outside of Memphis because she refused to move to the "colored car" on her own. The humiliation she felt as an educated professional teacher who had legally purchased a first-class ticket but was considered not "good enough" to ride with white women was palpable. As she stated in her pamphlet *The Reason Why,* "White men pass through these 'colored cars' and ride in them whenever they feel inclined to do so, but no colored woman however refined, well educated or well dressed may ride in the ladies, or first-class coach, in any of these states unless she is a nurse-maid traveling with a white child."[1] She was so enraged that she sued the Chesapeake, Ohio and Southwestern Railroad Company for violating "separate but equal" policies because, as she argued, there was no equality between the ladies' coach and the colored car. She initially won her suit, only for it to be overturned in a higher court a few years later.

Ida also endured and documented terrorism that was waged against African Americans who wanted nothing more than equality in a country they had built and lived in for more than two hundred years. As Black people were being lynched across the country, their houses and businesses burned, and all kinds of other unbridled terror swept through their communities, Ida's voice rose above the lawlessness. After three of her enterprising friends who owned a grocery store were killed, she wrote editorials in her Memphis-based newspaper *Free Speech* to encourage Black people to use the little power they had against a terror state. She suggested boycotts of streetcars and white-owned businesses. She encouraged those who could to leave Memphis in search of a more equitable life elsewhere. Thousands left the city and moved to the Oklahoma Territory and other western states.

In addition to inflicting economic pain on the white establishment, Ida dared to counter the myth that Black men were lynched as punishment for raping white women. She knew that her friends were not guilty of that crime, so she investigated other lynchings to find out what was really happening. She wrote in her autobiography, *Crusade for Justice*, "The more I studied the situation, the more I was convinced that the Southerner had never gotten over his resentment that the Negro was no longer his plaything, his servant, and his source of income."[2] As a result of this revelation, she exposed the truth: that lynching was used as a form of terrorism in order to keep Black people in a second-class status.

In a daring piece Ida originally wrote in May 1892, she asserted, "Nobody in this section believes the old thread-bare lie that Negro men assault white women. If southern white men are not careful they will over-reach themselves and a conclusion will be reached which will be very damaging to the moral reputation of their women."[3] She was in Philadelphia when it was published, and a few days later, when she arrived in New York City, she learned that her printing press had been destroyed and a price put on her head. She lost everything except her determination, resourcefulness, and skill to keep spreading the truth about lynching and domestic terrorism.

Ida recognized that Black women did not have the same protections or considerations as white women. She wrote in her autobiography,

> I found that white men who had created a race of mulattoes by raping and consorting with Negro women were still doing so wherever they could, these same white men lynched, burned, and tortured Negro men for doing the same thing with white women; even when the white women were willing victims.[4]

So, my great-grandmother chronicled the violence experienced by the Black community as a whole during the late nineteenth century, as well as the lack of regard and protection that Black women faced. Over one hundred years later, we are still struggling to be socially and legally on par with white women. According to the Institute for Women's Policy Research's 2017 report, there are numerous disparities between white and Black women.[5] A few key findings include the fact that the median annual income for Black women is $34,000 versus $40,000 for white women. Furthermore, 84 percent of nonelderly Black women have health insurance versus 90 percent of white women, and nearly 25 percent of Black women live in poverty compared to 11 percent of white women. In addition, Black women are twice as likely to be imprisoned as white women.

Along with the real-life challenges that Black women contend with, we also need to combat the disproportionately negative way that we are portrayed in the news and opinion media coverage. In a 2017 study, Dr. Travis L. Dixon found that the media overwhelmingly depicts Black families as poor and dependent on welfare, Black fathers as absent, and Black families as disproportionately linked to criminality.[6] And when it comes to the depiction of Black women specifically, the prevailing stereotypes have been the comforting and reliable "mammy," the over-sexualized and promiscuous "jezebel," the loud-mouthed and angry "sapphire," and more recently, the indomitable "strong Black woman," who can take care of everything and has no need for companionship or support—none of which depict real Black women's lives in truthful ways. The danger, and challenge, for most Black women is to dispel and counter these stereotypes when navigating spaces outside of our culture. We also need to tell our own stories and take control over our own narratives.

My great-grandmother Ida B. Wells understood that we Black women—regardless of our status in life—need to chronicle our own stories. We need to be our own voices and have control over our own narratives, document and contextualize our own truths. Ida wrote articles for church publications and newspapers. She then went on to have part ownership of those newspapers because she knew that control over own voices was the way to have our stories told. When white women fought for the right to vote, they effectively excluded Black women from their suffrage organizations. As a result, our foremothers formed their own groups. My great-grandmother was one of the founders of the National Association of Colored Women in 1896 and the founder of the Alpha Suffrage Club in 1913. She and her contemporaries did not wait for permission and acceptance from white women to address their own issues and concerns. They took matters into their own hands and centered themselves. By chronicling the events of her time through the lens of Black people, Ida B. Wells created firsthand historical documents that we can read today to learn about stories and experiences from over 120 years ago.

Enter the Echoing Ida collective. Their articles, formed into a book for the first time here, continue in the legacy of my great-grandmother's work, capturing the multiple experiences of Black women, trans and cis, and nonbinary people living in the early part of the twenty-first century. We know that if we don't tell our stories, they most likely will not be told. And if they are told by someone else, they more than likely will not be told with the context and nuance that only we possess. We need to tell our stories for ourselves and future generations to affirm our humanity. We need to embrace ourselves in our true authenticity. We need to accept ourselves in all of our beauty and strength. Black women, trans and cis, and Black nonbinary people are just as multidimensional as any other group of people. We are individuals with a collective, shared history. And within that, we are one.

—Michelle Duster

July 2020

Notes

1. Ida B. Wells, "Class Legislation," in *The Reason Why: The Colored American Is Not in the World's Columbian Exposition: The Afro-American's Contribution to Columbian Literature*, ed. Robert W. Rydell (Champaign: University of Illinois, 1893), 17–22.
2. Ida B. Wells, *Crusade for Justice: The Autobiography of Ida B. Wells*, ed. Alfreda M. Duster, 2nd ed. (Chicago: University of Chicago Press, 2020), 61.
3. Ida B. Wells, "Lynch Law in All Its Phases," *Our Day: A Record and Review of Current Reform* 11 (January–February 1893): 333–47.
4. Wells, *Crusade for Justice*, 62.
5. Institute for Women's Policy Research, *The Status of Black Women in the United States*, June 2017, https://iwpr.org/wp-content/uploads/2020/08/The-Status-of-Black-Women-6.26.17.pdf.
6. Travis L. Dixon, *A Dangerous Distortion of Our Families: Representations of Families, by Race, in News and Opinion Media*, co-commissioned by Family Story and Color of Change, January 2017, https://colorofchange.org/dangerousdistortion/#full_report.

The Origin Story

Janna A. Zinzi

Picture it: It's 2011, and antiabortion advocates were doubling down on racist rhetoric targeting Black women. Billboards were popping up in urban centers like Chicago, New York, and Oakland, flagrantly claiming the most dangerous place for a Black child was the mother's womb. Reproductive justice advocates from across the country organized coordinated messaging denouncing the billboards and educating our communities. We would not be silent! But there was a dearth of Black women's voices in the media, and our perspectives were getting drowned out.

Mainstream media[1] coverage of reproductive health and rights has historically focused on a single "choice" framework or on legislation and litigation surrounding abortion and birth control. Reproductive justice, a framework founded by Black women, asserts that everyone should have the right to parent—or not to parent—a child. Everyone should be able to live and raise children in safe communities.

Systemic racism affects our reproductive health and rights beyond the construct of "choice," but this gets conveniently left out of the conversation. Reproductive health and rights reporting mostly feature a small pool of organizational spokespeople, primary healthcare providers, and legal analysts—so best believe they were overwhelmingly white, heterosexual, cisgender, middle- or upper-class women. Reproductive issues have always been framed from their lens and experience, so it's no surprise that we've heard our mamas, aunties, and cousins say that abortion is a "white women's issue."

The politically correct talking points would address the "disproportionate impact" of [insert issue] on Black women or women of color, but we were rarely speaking for ourselves. Often, the excuse (and a legitimate, unfortunate reality of journalism) was that reporters were on deadline and needed someone to talk to quickly. Most Black women and women-of-color-led organizations did not have well-staffed communications departments, let alone a staff member dedicated to communications, so larger organizations with more resources took advantage of this, leaving us out of the conversation.

Alicia Walters was a consultant working with the newly rebranded Forward Together (formerly Asian Communities for Reproductive Justice [ACRJ]) and a national multiracial coalition to organize a response to the racist antiabortion billboards. She was struck by the inequity in media coverage and lack of representation of Black women. Where were the experiences of the women doing work on the ground with deep connections to our communities? The specificity of how this campaign attacked Black families highlighted the need for more Black women spokespeople to discuss abortion, along with other social and political issues, using a reproductive justice lens. Our voices should be leading the conversation, not presented as an afterthought.

At the same time, the reproductive justice movement was also going through a difficult time. A lack of funding stretched Black-led reproductive justice organizations to capacity. There wasn't enough time, space, or funding to invest in media strategy or create a communications infrastructure when programming and organizing were foundational priorities. Yet we were in need of new ways of gathering with each other as Black women leaders, in need of recognition for who we were and what we were contributing, and in need of space to be innovative and experimental while building loving and supportive community where we could grow and learn. The idea was simple: to bring together Black women with deep experience and powerful perspectives on reproductive justice and provide the training and support to unleash their ideas on the world. Walters wanted to create a new vanguard of media mavens telling their stories and inventing new narratives.

Through her consulting work with Forward Together, Walters developed a strong and close relationship with Executive Director Eveline Shen. Shen's nurturing style of mentorship gave Walters the confidence to pitch her idea of creating the Black Women's Media Collective, a sort of media training incubator for Black women. Forward Together (then ACRJ) had been in the reproductive justice movement for over twenty years and showed an established commitment to racial justice. Under Shen's leadership, ACRJ released *A New Vision*,[2] a groundbreaking report explaining reproductive justice and how it connects and differs from reproductive rights and health. It was a natural partnership and extension of the long legacy of Black and Asian communities supporting each other. Walters asserts that it was a powerful allyship and "model for how we partner in each other's liberation." Shen had noticed the ways that Black women were getting attacked online for being vocal about their truths and understood the need for a sanctuary to develop their stories. Forward Together hired a new communications manager, Shanelle Matthews, a Black woman with a background in journalism and media studies. Matthews became a thought partner and collaborator supporting Walters in manifesting her vision.

The program started off as the Black Women's Media Collective, but the organizers felt there needed to be a stronger brand that spoke to people of our power, not simply a program. Walters wanted to be sure the brand was a reminder of those shoulders on which we stood; this work was built on the legacy of our ancestors and foremothers. After tossing around various names, they kept circling back to Ida B. Wells, wanting to weave in her name, spirit, and achievements.

We just came up with this idea that we weren't just her descendants but her echo. The vibration that she started lives in us and we are heeding her call. We hope to fulfill this call to expose the truth and the traumas of our society, and in doing so, to uplift so many people and communities as she did. We are inspired by how unapologetic she was, the way that her work was so obviously, naturally intersectional. Because that's how we live our lives, because that's who we are. She did it in a time when that was not common. And she didn't just give her writing and her expertise to somebody else to own and commodify, she owned it. And she recognized the importance of having a space where she was not controlled by somebody else's perspective or their bottom line. To do this as a community of Black women felt profound and powerful to me.

—Alicia Walters

Ida B. Wells is the kind of symbolic representation of this fellowship of this program. And in many ways, she began organizing and writing about lynchings in the spirit of wanting to share a message so that people would know what was going on with Black people. And we're doing the same thing in a different context in a different time. But it's the lineage of the work, right? So it's not starting new, it is picking up where she left off, echoing her work, and continuing to create the conditions in which people

*have the information that they need to be able to do something. One of her
quotes is that people must know before they can act. And that is, I think,
the spirit of Echoing Ida . . . that you are giving people the information
through values-based messaging to change their hearts and their minds.
To behave in different ways towards Black people and to make the commitment to eradicating anti-Blackness.*

—Shanelle Matthews

The first iteration of Echoing Ida consisted of a collective of six Black
women from around the United States that Walters and Matthews knew
from reproductive justice organizing and who were interested in media
and open to experimenting. The curriculum centered on the fundamen-
tals of getting their work into the media, such as writing compelling
op-eds, developing messages, and identifying narratives to shift. But
it turned out to be much more than writing and publishing articles; it
became a space for deep intimacy, trust, and community building. It
was clear from the start that everyone needed a support system of Black
women in the movement who nurtured each other's creativity. It's powerful to create with others who don't need you to justify your experiences
but challenge you to boldly express the underlying truths or challenge
you to be bolder in your truth telling. It was a refuge to be embraced
in our vulnerability of writing and sharing our stories, which are often
complex and personal. The Idas were talking weekly, offering each other
edits and feedback, sharing contacts, and bonding with every pitch perfected and piece published. We genuinely wanted to see each other win.

Walters worked over the next six years to build the program. An
organizer by training with an innate inclination toward communicating,
Walters cultivated relationships with online outlets that spoke to our
desired audiences, such as *Ebony*, a legendary African American publication, and the popular niche reproductive health news site, *RH Reality
Check* (now *Rewire News Group*). That gave the Idas the confidence and
experience to pitch and place pieces in dozens of other outlets, including
the *New York Times*, *Slate*, and *Bitch*. Walters and the Echoing Ida team
brought in expert Black women editors with decades of experience in
the journalism industry to mentor each Ida. They experimented with
how Idas could support organizations with underresourced or nonexistent communications infrastructures. Monthly webinars allowed Idas
from around the country to connect with each other while learning new

valuable skills, such as podcasting and investigative reporting, from other Black women experts. Forward Together supported annual writing retreats for in-person strategizing, brainstorming, and, yup, twerking. We created magic together online and offline.

With this spirit, the Idas have grown now into thirty-five members from the OGs to the new jacks. The network and circle continue to grow, reaching more of our people across movements and geography. We present together at conferences, uplift each other's projects, hype each other up when life gets tough, and protest arm in arm because, ultimately, our work is rooted in justice for all of us, especially those most impacted by white supremacy. Our mission was, and always will be, radical truth telling.

Reproductive justice ideas and analysis are more prevalent these days (although there is always more to do), and Echoing Ida has been a marked part of this movement. It exemplifies what is possible when other women of color support Black women's leadership. The program helped launch the careers of some of the thought leaders published in this book. It created an environment where Black women and nonbinary people could develop their voice and expertise. Echoing Ida allowed us to believe in our potential and cultivate our innate power. It created pathways for us to spread out beyond writing into podcasts and multimedia content creation. Idas shared their personal stories to help illustrate how reproductive justice shows up in the daily lives of Black folks around the world. The program visibilizes a wide range of Black women reproductive justice leaders in a coordinated and intentional way. Echoing Ida provides a replicable model for social movements and nonprofit organizations to better value voices of directly impacted leaders and support them to navigate media as an essential vehicle in the cultural narrative shift. It shifted media conversations about teen pregnancy and young parents, Black women's maternal health, and abortion. By telling their truths and breaking down what intersectionality actually looks like, the Idas are also providing a primer on reproductive justice for movement organizers who are pushing us all to think more inclusively.

At the time of this writing (August 2020), we've published over five hundred pieces across one hundred publications. We outchea! And it is only the beginning. The story of Echoing Ida is one of inspired vision, trust, risk, and love—one that we hope inspires Black people to create that which is calling them to be created, regardless of whether they think they have the skills or connections to do so. From our founder on down, we were not all professional writers. We were Black women with stories to tell and perspectives to share. And the world has benefited from our willingness to heed the call to tell our truths. This anthology honors the dedication to truth telling within Echoing Ida and among numerous Black and nonbinary people across the world in online and offline spaces. We are unfuckwitable. We are part of a movement, a growing wave of Black voices guided by our ancestors, like Ida B. Wells and countless women before and after her. We are carrying the torch and this legacy. We are answering the call to document our struggles and our joy and to preserve our history in our own words. Join us on this journey full of love, magic, and healing: snapshots of our own transformation as we continue to call for liberation.

Notes

1. "Reproductive Justice Media Reference Guide," Forward Together, accessed August 14, 2020, https://forwardtogether.org/tools/rj-media-guide-2014/.
2. Asian Communities for Reproductive Justice, *A New Vision for Advancing Our Movement for Reproductive Health, Reproductive Rights and Reproductive Justice* (Oakland, CA: 2005), https://forwardtogether.org/tools/a-new-vision/.

THE STRUCTURE AND THE STRUGGLE

Introduction

Kemi Alabi

"When workers are renovating a home," Alexandra Moffett-Bateau explains in her critical examination of the Ferguson uprising, "and something about the foundation or the structure itself is unsafe, they say that the building has lost its 'integrity.' What they mean is that the home can no longer stand on its own and can no longer be considered a safe or secure place to live."

The structure: The house white supremacy, cisheteropatriarchy, and capitalism built. A violent political, economic, and cultural system created to hoard power and resources, specifically among white, straight, cisgender men.

The struggle: attempting life within the structure as people never meant to survive it.

The structure has no integrity, and we're not safe inside. To understand the shape the structure takes, just look at the imprints it leaves on our bodies. To understand the struggle's breadth and depth, just follow our attempts to live life free from harm. As the humans it warps into mules and machines, goblins and ghosts, we know more about the structure than its keepers. Here are some notes: knowledge to both survive the struggle and dismantle the structure brick by brick.

Bianca Campbell takes us to a bookstore in Georgia to expose the ways "oppression can preoccupy our safe spaces, even in our minds." Quita Tinsley writes from the aftermath of the Charleston church massacre, charting routes to healing when our sites of refuge collapse. "It's my duty," Tinsley explains, "to ensure that as a community, we are centering the folks who are most marginalized." And our writers take that duty seriously, whether it's Ruth Jeannoel revealing Black girls' experiences with the school-to-prison pipeline, Moffett-Bateau centering Black LGBTQ people on African American Women's Equal Pay Day, or Raquel Willis turning #MeToo into #UsToo with the stories of Black trans survivors.

As Erin Malone shares in her 2016 election postmortem on rural America, when we erase whole people and experiences from the equation, we bypass the full problem—and reach for incomplete solutions. The intersections of race, gender, sexuality, class, ability, and more reveal everything we need to know about our home's integrity. Our lived experiences? Quality intel. Our struggles? Very real. And when we shout our truths together? The whole damn structure starts to shake.

The Violence Happening in Ferguson Is More Than Physical

Alexandra Moffett-Bateau

On Saturday, August 9, 2014, Michael Brown became one of several US Black men in recent weeks to die violently at the hands of a law enforcement officer. Within days, Ferguson, and along with it Black American hearts and minds everywhere, seemed to implode. I know mine did.

My Facebook, Twitter, and Google feeds were consumed with what was happening in Ferguson. All of my friends and loved ones were trying to process the crisis, express outrage, and grieve simultaneously. I couldn't think or feel anything else. It was an emotional paralysis that I've never experienced concurrently with such a large group of people before.

As the days went on, the National Guard was called, tear gas was used on nonviolent protesters, and I struggled to trudge through the overwhelm of watching my community be treated in a way that lacked compassion, empathy, or humanity.

Nearly a month later, I want to explore what multiple forms of violence—emotional, physical, bureaucratic, and spiritual—do to a group of people when they simultaneously converge on a community.

A big mistake that people tend to make when thinking and talking about violence is assuming that the term only refers to physically painful encounters. So when we have discussions about police brutality, state violence, or intrastate conflicts, we (understandably) tend to limit those conversations to, for example, young men being beaten on the street by a law enforcement officer, or the bombing of a school in Gaza, or the number of lives lost in Ukraine. Most people have been socialized to think about violence in terms of death and bodily pain.

As philosopher Vittorio Bufacchi argues, "The problem with adopting the notions of injury, harm or vigorous abuse as the groundwork from which to define the concept of violence" is that these terms and/or experiences may actually be the consequences of violence, and "not necessarily what constitutes the act of violence in itself."[1] What Bufacchi means by this is that the bodily harm we generally point to as being violent may actually be the symptom of a disease—in this case, other forms of violence—that we miss completely because we were so horrified (understandably so) by the physicality of what we thought was the initial act.

We may miss the violence of the police officer who said something to a young woman that completely destroyed her spirit prior to hitting her in the face. We may miss the destruction of a young man's spiritual altar in his home prior to being beaten brutally in the street after he reacted. We may miss that a woman's children were suddenly taken from her home a week before she was raped by a social worker.

While these examples are somewhat extreme, I am using them to get at a central point: physical, emotional, spiritual, and even bureaucratic harm can all enact different modes of violence, both on the community and the individual. Or, as Bufacchi argues, an act of violence occurs when the integrity or the unity of a subject (person or animal) or object (property) is being intentionally or unintentionally violated as a result of an action or an omission.

When considering how emotional, spiritual, or bureaucratic violence could function otherwise, it is useful to think more carefully about our understanding of integrity. When workers are renovating a home and something about the foundation or the structure itself is unsafe, they say that the building has lost its "integrity." What they mean is that the home can no longer stand on its own and can no longer be considered a safe or secure place to live.

It is useful to think of a loss of integrity due to violence within an individual or within a community in the same way. When a person's lived experience illustrates that their "home" (actual or metaphorical) is no longer safe or secure, then a loss of integrity or, in Bufacchi's terms, a violation occurs. This violation of the perception of one's interior self or community can have consequences that deeply affect an individual's ability to live their life, in addition to paralyzing their movement within their neighborhood, their city, or even the world.

In this sense, then, the very act of racism and/or the impact of structural racism on individuals and the groups of which they are a part can be considered a violent act. I consider the violence that was experienced by the people of Ferguson when their governor imposed a mandatory cur-few to be bureaucratic violence. I consider the attempt of mainstream media to malign protesters as looters, villains, and criminals to be emo-tional violence. I consider the multiple deaths and shootings of Black men and women across the country to be both physical and emotional violence. I consider the failure of the Ferguson Police Department to arrest Darren Wilson after the shooting death of Michael Brown to be a form of spiritual violence that has a devastating and completely debili-tating effect on Black communities across the United States.

All of these examples are instances in which individuals and com-munities have been met with a series of structures that fundamentally distrust and disempower them. It is through this lack of trust and the systematic dismantling of individual and community-wide power that violation occurs. Whether the loss of integrity happens within the mind or the body, it often has a very physical manifestation in the lived expe-riences of the victim.

So what is the impact of the simultaneous convergence of physical, emotional, spiritual, and bureaucratic violence in a single town on a single community? You have Black Americans in Ferguson and around the country who are paralyzed by fear, overwhelmed, and expressing a righteous rage—all of which cannot and should not be doused with sim-ple, superficial, or temporary solutions. You have an entire community of people who are more afraid for their safety than they have been in a lifetime. But you also have a community that is adamant that they will be the last generation to feel this fear.

Notes

1. Vittorio Bufacchi, *Violence and Social Justice* (London: Palgrave Macmillan, 2007), 40.

Originally published on Rewire.News *on September 4, 2014.*

Powerless in the Face of White Supremacy and a Gun

Bianca Campbell

While out shopping in Georgia at my favorite bookstore, the same day the Emanuel AME Church reopened its doors after white supremacist Dylann Roof murdered nine Black Christians during Wednesday night Bible study, a white man in camouflage entered the store, openly carrying a gun on his hip.

In my home state, we'd recently allowed licensed individuals to bring their guns into bars, churches, and college campuses, all for the sake of "safety." Yet in this moment, at the bookstore, I realized that such gun control laws only ensure that certain people feel safe, while others who do not wish to own a gun are left feeling powerless.

This tense moment was still too soon. Too soon after Charleston, after the deaths of Eric Garner and Rekia Boyd—and even too soon after Emmett Till. Too soon after cops in Georgia attacked Kenya Harris until she miscarried.

Too soon because I haven't processed the constant surveillance and prosecution I experience as a dark-skinned Black person navigating a society where I can be tried and executed in the streets without a jury.

The gun-toting man had a wide-shouldered build and was probably shorter than me once he took off his combat boots. Looking back, I probably could have taken him on in a fair fight. Lord knows, I've fought men bigger than him before.

The bookstore employee, who will go down in history as my favorite bookstore employee ever, immediately said to the man, "Whoa, that's a gun! That makes me uncomfortable."

Anywhere you stood in the store, you could hear his reply: "Well, it shouldn't be a problem so long as I don't feel threatened." The way his voice trailed off as his eyes panned the room froze me temporarily. I tucked myself behind a bookshelf where I could still see and hear what was happening. He also said he had an open-carry license—as if that would make us feel safe.

And then to change the subject, as if carrying a gun in a bookstore is no big deal, he shared that he had been scoping out the bookstore for some time but only just decided to come in. I popped my head over a bookshelf to lock eyes with the bookstore employee. We widened our gaze and raised our eyebrows at each other to nonverbally confirm that this situation was indeed absurd.

But what troubled me the most about the situation as it was happening was the realization that our legislative system was working as intended in that moment.

Long before I walked in to buy a copy of *Octavia's Brood* so that I could think about a world where my body is free through activism-driven science fiction, the system set things up with discriminatory gun control laws. (The book is a fiction anthology known in movement work as a recognition that working toward a free, accessible, and just world is comparable to sci-fi imaginings of new worlds and new ways of being that could eventually become reality.)

The idea of openly carrying a gun to protect myself has never been a realistic option—only when I'm imagining myself as Storm from *X-Men* dismantling oppressive systems with Black feminist thunderstorms and a small silver Glock just in case. In reality, if the cops saw me with a gun, a bag of Skittles, or even a loosey cigarette, they would probably shoot me and ask questions about my permit later. As a Jamaican American whose parents had to navigate the country's unjust immigration system, I've almost always known that papers and permits don't save dark-skinned people.

And so now, Georgia's open-carry policy, the Second Amendment of the US Constitution, and the whole foundation of America's justice system works as it was always intended: allowing certain people to feel safe at the expense of others existing in fear. I was without arms and face-to-face with a man who may or may not have wanted to kill me—a man who had the freedom to make that decision without repercussions.

As he approached me in a corner of the store, my heart raced as I thought about the families of the victims and the nine people who were being put to rest in Charleston. I kept thinking about Tywanza Sanders, who jumped in front of a bullet to defend his aunt Susie Jackson. I wondered if I could drum up that courage. I wondered if Cynthia Hurd was as frozen as I was. "She was not a victim," her brother said in the public remarks he made days after her murder. "She was a Christian. She was a soldier. She was a warrior." I wondered if elder Ethel Lance felt as caught off guard by how someone could pray with you and then unload seventy rounds of bullets into innocent people. I thanked the employee, a fellow woman of color, repeatedly in my head for maintaining calm in that moment of uncertainty. The man and I stood for a moment side by side browsing titles like *Does Your Mama Know?* It was a split second. Then I darted away to the middle of the store in three wide steps.

After he burrowed his nose into every corner of the bookstore, all he bought were two button pins with probably the most unpolitical messaging on them. I didn't get to see them, but I know the store carries some very alluring pins of cats. Maybe he got those? At the counter, he showed the employee his Harry Potter tattoo. He made uncomfortable comments about how the tattoo reminds him of seeking truth and justice against liars loud enough for all of us to hear. He talked about his "no good" ex. He said "open carry" ensures that his son respects him.

"Do you need a bag?" the bookstore employee interrupted, making it clear it was time for him to go.

Once he left, the rest of us still in the store let out a communal, belly-deep sigh. One customer noticed that, subconsciously, all the books they had collected to purchase were about men and violence. "They take up so much space," the customer said with regard to the man who had just left and the bundle of books in their arms.

Oppression can preoccupy our safe spaces, even in our minds.

My fellow customer's comment allowed all of us in the store to laugh and begin the process of grasping what had just happened.

I don't know why he came in armed. I don't know what his intentions were. I don't want to know. I want to know a world where I don't have to be caught up in fear in the first place. I want a world where none of us feel the need to carry a gun. A world where the Confederate flag and a CVS aren't more important to our political leaders than seven burning churches, the countless dead at the hands of militarized police, and those empowered with the false hubris of white supremacy. (Around the same time that Roof committed mass murder against innocent Black people, other white supremacists were burning down several Black churches. What should have felt like a critical moment in US history was dismissed by mass media in favor of mentioning recent events at CVS and the anger white supremacists were feeling over mass actions to remove the confederate flag from state institutions.)

People like me, and hopefully you, are trying to make that world a reality in the here and now. Bree Newsome, for example, took the Confederate flag down from the South Carolina statehouse with her bare hands. Emanuel AME Church reopened its doors when I'm sure domestic terrorists and other right-wing extremist groups were hoping they'd stay closed. Not only are these activists not giving in to the pressure, but they're reminding all of us that the world we're fighting for uses love to overpower violence. Sanders's five-year-old niece, just by virtue of her surviving the shooting by playing dead, is proof of Audre Lorde's prophesizing.

No, we were never meant to survive, Lorde, and so whenever we end up doing so, we are being revolutionary, perhaps even futuristic.

Originally published on Rewire.News *on July 2, 2015.*

Healing in the Midst of Tragedy: How Can Black Folks Keep Surviving in the Face of Constant Trauma?

Quita Tinsley

The church has always been a huge part of my life. Before I joined the junior choir, I would sit in the choir stand with my mom, not even tall enough for my little head to be above the pew. I would sing along to the classic gospel songs that I knew by heart. I always made a point to remember the scripture of the week for our youth pastor and to know all the books of the Bible for our Bible study teacher. I was the youth superintendent of Sunday school and a junior usher. The church gave me a platform to grow into a role of leadership, which is so rare for little Black girls. Church is where I discovered my love of music. Church is the place where I found the most solace while going through depression in my adolescent years. Growing up in the church shaped the way I navigate the world and understand myself.

When I got the news of the Charleston massacre, it shook me to my core. Even though it wasn't my former church or my family, it felt like it was because the possibility of it being my church and family seemed so real and close to home. And with all of the invalid excuses that people use to try to justify the racist genocidal traumas that Black folks face, I couldn't fathom how folks could excuse this. And my heart grew even heavier with the news of eight Black churches burning down in the following days. I kept asking myself, "How could someone violate these safe places and commit such violent acts?"

I know and understand church is not a safe place for many of us, but historically for Black folks, church has been a sanctuary, free of the white gaze. It has been a place for Black folks to be free and be in community with each other. I think of the elders in my family and how churches served as their first schools because of the racist history of the education system in this nation. I think of the history of the church I grew up in, which spans almost two hundred years. I think of how I partially grew into myself inside the walls of my church and how much of a safe and sacred place I found it to be.

And as I try to navigate my own grief and trauma, I wonder how we as a community can come together for healing when our physical spaces are constantly violated and are no longer safe. Our neighborhoods, schools, churches, and homes cannot protect us from the violence of white supremacy. And as we try to heal from one trauma, we are updated on another attack, all while navigating the microaggressions and blatant oppression in our everyday lives.

As I write this, I come on the heels of attending the Movement for Black Lives Convening. And while it was a short trip, it was so powerful in all its glory. And all of the beauty of that experience was tarnished by the violent attack of Cleveland RTA police, another example of Black people building safe spaces for ourselves and having racist institutions work to tear them down.

It's hard not to feel hopeless when thinking about the countless others around the world who are experiencing deep and murderous oppression while also living in our own oppression at the same time. In order to keep moving forward, I must remind myself not only of the fragility but also the resiliency of my people, and I must remember not to further isolate myself when I'm hurting. I have to turn to community. We must take care of each other.

Checking in with people has been a tool that I use to engage in community healing. I try my best to send emails and/or texts to family and friends just to see how they are doing. And even if I'm contacting someone for a specific reason, I still try to check in on how they are doing both mentally and physically. Sometimes it becomes routine for me to ask the people I talk to often, "What's up?" or "What are you doing?" when initiating a conversation with them. But lately, I challenge myself to ask folks how they are doing instead. I want to provide folks an opportunity to let me know how they are truly feeling. Whether they want to let me know things are tough, and they need support in feeling better, or they just got some really awesome news and want to share it. It's my duty to check in with the community because we aren't robots that just do things; we have feelings and emotions.

But checking in isn't just about seeing how others are doing. It's also about me checking in with people and letting them know how I'm doing. Let's be honest. Society teaches marginalized folks that the trauma and hurt we experience isn't valid, and we have to continue every day like nothing has happened to us. And for me, that looks like saying, "I'm fine" or "good," when in reality, I'm severely hurting. To shift that, I have to be committed to letting the people who care about me know when I need help. I received the news of the Charleston massacre as I was landing in Detroit for the Allied Media Conference, where I was expected to attend the conference as though a massacre hadn't just taken place. Black folks attending the conference and facilitating workshops provided space for each other, which helped me work through some of my own feelings.

Many of the experiences of Black people, whether they be personal or community based, cause us actual grief. We are constantly grieving the lives of people we do or do not know and the possibility of it being us. We have to provide space for ourselves and other Black folks to express that grief, no matter how it takes form. We have to remind ourselves that folks can be angry, afraid, and/or sad. These feelings and others are not mutually exclusive. We have every right to be angry, and we shouldn't police others who are angry. Black rage is real and should be validated in the ways that emotions that mirror sadness and/or fear would be.

I also try to remember to honor our happiness and joy. It's not uncommon on the internet and in real life for folks to shame people who are partaking in things simply for entertainment versus being serious about "real" issues. We shouldn't feel guilty for feeling happiness or joy in the midst of tragedy. Watching folks dance and sing at the Allied Media Conference and the Movement for Black Lives Convening brought me a joy that helped heal some of my own trauma. Being able to laugh, smile, dance, and connect with other Black people brings a deep happiness to my core—the kind of happiness that helps me make it another day. It is not only important to feel these things but also to document them with photos and videos. We must be reminded of the joy that is still possible.

I also try to hold myself and others accountable, especially when it comes to the lives and experiences of Black women, Black queer folks, Black trans folks, Black gender nonconforming folks, Black people who are incarcerated, Black working-class folks, and other Black people who are further marginalized. How can they heal when they are not only experiencing trauma from the larger society but also at the hands of those within their community? It's my duty to ensure that, as a community, we are centering the folks who are most marginalized.

This quote by Assata Shakur can often be heard from Black folks organizing around this nation:

> It is our duty to fight for our freedom. It is our duty to win. We must love each other and support each other. We have nothing to lose but our chains.

In my opinion, sometimes we get so focused on fighting to win our freedom and lose our chains that we forget to take care of each other along the way. We must remember to love and care for each other as Black folks because there is no winning without it.

Originally published on The Body Is Not an Apology *on October 13, 2015.*

What Black Lives Matter Organizers Are Doing to Fight White Supremacy at Every Level

Shanelle Matthews

The banter on the 2016 presidential campaign trail was not unlike that of election years past in that it was full of nasty, backhanded, gender-based undercuts aimed at delegitimizing opponents and drawing out emotional responses at the ballot box. Noticeably different from previous year's strategies, however, was the Trump campaign's deliberate courting of one of America's oldest and biggest threats to a civil and just world: white supremacists.

To garner votes and stoke antiestablishment flames, Trump latched on to the ideology of white supremacy and incentivized violence on the campaign trail. He encouraged his supporters—some of whom carried the banner of Nazism and Klansmanship—to physically harm people, promising at a February 2016 rally to "pay for the legal fees" of anyone who got violent with anti-Trump protesters.[1] He used political dog whistles to signal a twenty-first-century ideological war—one that has also included hate speech and deadly violence.

The deadly 2017 white supremacist rally in Charlottesville, Virginia, made visible what many organizers and activists have been warning since the 2016 campaign season: Donald Trump promised more death, disenfranchisement, and deportations—and now he's delivering on that promise. The violence he will inflict in office through policy and the permission he gives for others to commit acts of violence are just beginning to emerge.

The good news is that we're not helpless; there are many things we can all do to fight white supremacy. Some of these things are changes we can make to our everyday lives, while others are issues that need to be addressed on a systemic national scale. But we need to know exactly where to begin—and what brand of white supremacy we're dealing with at every turn.

It's important to remember that white supremacy is not just people in hoods, nor can it be reduced to only people who are poor, rural, and white. White supremacy is a web of violent and abusive behaviors bolstered by white nationalists, racist elected officials, violent police and law enforcement, corporate money, and you. Yes, you. And me too. White supremacy is an insidious spectrum ideology, so most of us perpetuate it, even if we don't mean to.

If we want to win this battle, we need to open our eyes to all the symbiotic ways white supremacy touches each and every one of our lives and then come up with the best course of action to fight it.

Organize Courageous Conversations

Black Lives Matter and the Movement for Black Lives more broadly are working across geographical and issue areas to call attention to white supremacy and build sustainable, resourced movements to significantly reduce it. For some of the most explicit brands of ideological white supremacy—like that espoused by the white supremacist who plowed into anti-racist protesters in Charlottesville, killing local activist Heather Heyer—organizers are taking the fight to their own backyards, organizing people in local communities, having courageous conversations with people who would not otherwise have courageous conversations with us, or encouraging our allies to have those conversations in our stead. For example, take a cue from the Dream Defenders, a Florida-based organizing collective that hosted a Day of Dinners and asked people to "open their hearts and homes to start a new conversation about the country we want and a future worth fighting for."

The same organizing we've been doing for decades is being replicated all over the country. Organizing that includes building and convening member-led organizations where everyday people can strategize together about how to build power for ourselves. Organizing that holds the officials we elect to office accountable for their decisions. Organizing that demands a just and fair society for us all. Building the kind of people power we need to organize our country into a safe place for Black people—one that leads with inclusivity and a commitment to justice, not intimidation and fear.

In other ways, we are challenging white supremacy by helping bring democracy within reach. Organizers from Greensboro to St. Louis are creating opportunities for civic engagement: some organizers are running for political office themselves and others pushing candidates to use the Movement for Black Lives's Vision for Black Lives policy platform. Anyone in the United States can send this platform to their legislators and ask them to use it to drive change through their campaigns.

Additionally, Black organizers are training to make ideological interventions through the media to help transcend barriers to empathizing with and understanding Blackness and the plight of Black communities in America. For example, through Channel Black, organizers are supplementing tried-and-true, on-the-ground organizing tactics with media interventions, like correcting misinformation about what the movement is and what we stand for and putting members of the movement front and center. By increasing the diversity of faces and opinions debating issues that impact America's most oppressed, we are reducing racial bias and prejudicial treatment by law enforcement, vigilantes, and everyday people.

Pressure Elected Officials

A less explicit, but equally devastating, brand of white supremacy involves our elected officials willfully ignoring systems of oppression that directly, and often physically, harm people of color. Elected officials knowingly harmed thousands of Flint, Michigan, residents by giving them a water supply tainted by lead and other poisons, which killed a dozen and left many others with lead poisoning and lifelong chronic illness; years later, officials still refuse to take responsibility. In response, organizations like Color of Change[2] are using digital organizing and campaigns to mobilize everyday people and put pressure on decision makers.

The importance of these efforts cannot be underscored enough. We must reckon with the anti-Blackness of America's history that led to this political moment. And we must get justice for those hurt along the way. You can pressure your elected officials by showing up to their committee meetings, flooding their voicemails and emails with your questions and concerns (and kudos when they're deserved), and by supporting organizations that hold them accountable with your dollars and time.

Presidential hopeful Kamala Harris and Stacey Abrams are giving Black people and other people of color hope for a political experience that is dignified and allows us to see ourselves, our families, and our values reflected. However you feel about the electoral process, having policy makers who are eager to make important interventions in Congress is critical to ensuring that white supremacists have less—not more—power.

Demand Justice

Police brutality and violence and bias within the criminal justice system are the brand of white supremacy that most people ignore, either because solutions feel intimidating and out of reach or because the assumption of security is too comfortable to question. Every year, people are killed by law enforcement, correctional officers, immigration thugs, security guards, and violent vigilantes. And every time an enforcement officer or vigilante kills someone they're meant to protect and is acquitted, that is white supremacy in action. All of America must take responsibility for and contend with our deadly policing system. All of us.

This political moment may feel new, but we've been here before. There isn't a difference between the so-called alt-right and neo-Nazis and racist confederates of the days when Black people were chattel slavery; we are talking about the same exact thinking. And as long as it has existed, Black organizers and their allies have been here to combat it. The question is, are we the same nation that ignored the erection of Confederate soldier statues and prisons built to incarcerate African Americans[3] at five times the rate of whites, or are we different? Are you different?

Notes

1. Tim Dickinson, "Why Not to Vote for Trump, From A to Z," *Rolling Stone*, September 26, 2016, https://www.rollingstone.com/politics/politics-features/why-not-to-vote-for-trump-from-a-to-z-124703/.

2. "Lead Poisoning in Flint, Michigan," Color of Change, accessed August 14, 2020, https://act.colorofchange.org/sign/lead-poisoning/.

3. Lauri Jo Reynolds and Stephen F. Eisenman, "Tamms Is Torture: The Campaign to Close an Illinois Supermax Prison," *Creative Time Reports*, May 6, 2013, https://creativetimereports.org/2013/05/06/tamms-is-torture-campaign-close-illinois-supermax-prison-solitary-confinement/.

Originally published on Bustle *on August 15, 2017.*

Urban and Rural America Are Connected by Economic Refugees Like Me

Erin Malone

In the aftermath of the 2016 election, there was a flurry of finger-pointing and anxiety on the part of progressives about how we could have lost to Trump, with many pundits trying to make sense of the result. One common narrative was that "we" urban liberals in blue enclaves lived in a bubble and had no idea what "they," the struggling working class of Middle America, were facing. It was the idea of the Big Sort: America is getting increasingly divided as we self-segregate into ideologically polarized regions.

You could easily place me in the urban, coastal, progressive bucket. I am one of the millions of small-town kids from the middle of the country who have settled on a coastal blue island. I live in New York, and my career has taken me through three bastions of liberalism: academia, labor unions, and nonprofits. I'm an ardent Black Lives Matter activist. My story doesn't fit neatly into this idea of "we" and "they," however, and it challenges a narrative that can cause us to write off communities that could be organized.

I grew up in Tamms, a tiny Illinois town at the confluence of the Mississippi and Ohio Rivers. Front Street, the old main drag, now has just one tiny post office amid a cluster of buildings that have been abandoned for decades. The per capita income is $11,131 as of the 2000 census. My stepfather moved us there from a Washington, DC, suburb in 1993 after military downsizing forced him to leave. With a new family and small parting stipend from the US Army, he was looking for a family-friendly place where he could stretch a dollar. Both he and my mom had roots in Illinois. He had fond memories of spending childhood summers in his grandparents' quaint rural town. Days there were spent ripping and running with cousins through the countryside and nights lying awake and listening to the sounds of train whistles and cicadas—a welcome escape from the harshness of his home in inner-city Chicago in the 1960s.

When we moved there, though, the town was already years into decline. A civil rights uprising in 1967 and the ensuing white flight from the county seat of Cairo accelerated an economic descent that began with railroads replacing the river industries in the 1930s. Tomes could be written about Cairo—a Midwestern town that is actually further south than Richmond, Virginia—its violent civil rights history and ensuing decline. But I grew up in nearby Tamms. We arrived at a particularly difficult time. Most of the region was underwater, having been recently battered by the Great Flood of 1993. My stepdad eventually found work at a Procter & Gamble factory assembling diapers, and my mom found work successively at the local laundromat, as a home care worker, and as a teacher's aide. We went from the working poor to the middle class.

The new hope for the town's economic turnaround in my youth came from President Clinton's 1994 crime bill. Hoping to get some of the funding from the bill's heavy investment in prisons, Tamms entered a bid to be the site of a new maximum-security prison. "Home of the First Super Max" was added to "A Good Place to Live" on the sign that welcomed people into Tamms. Residents were promised jobs, state funding, and an increased flow of people coming in and out for work. When the bid came through, not one local person was trained or hired, and the town's residents saw no revenue, just an increase in their utility bills. The prison was off the highway, so there was no need for workers to stop in the town, and most prisoners held there had long been abandoned by their families and got no visitors. An extended campaign in Chicago against human rights violations and death penalty executions at the supermax shut the prison down in 2013.[1]

Growing up in Tamms, I wanted nothing more than to leave. In 2000, I went away to college in Champaign, Illinois, followed by graduate school in San Diego, and finally settled in Brooklyn. If you'd asked me back in the spring of 2016, I might have agreed with the idea that people self-segregate into cultural and political identities by geography. I believed that until my mom fell ill, and I had to go home for the first time in five years.

I got a call at 2 a.m. from my brother. My mom had to be rushed to the emergency room; he'd found her on the floor catatonic. I needed to go home. I fell back into my old home-going routine, preparing myself to walk that fine line between hometown hero and class turncoat. I practiced saying "yes ma'am," "no sir," and "God bless you." I made an extra effort to stop cursing. I was careful to pick out clothes that were nice but not too flashy. I'd need an outfit for church, but my judgment of what was appropriate was long gone. My routine could easily support an argument for the Big Sort.

Once at home, I learned that her prognosis wasn't good. If she survived, she might face brain damage and severe physical impairment. She might need home care. My brain raced. She didn't have great health insurance. I couldn't put her on mine. I realized I might need to go home often. I might even need to move home. I wondered where I would find work. I wondered where I would live. There wasn't room in the house, and there were no properties for rent.

My mother was in a medically induced coma for the first few days, but her prognosis started looking better. It turned out to be meningitis, and with heavy doses of antibiotics, she'd recover. To keep occupied between visiting hours, I looked through my Facebook friends list to see who I could reconnect with. Classmate after classmate had left just like me—first for school and then even further afield to find work: Atlanta, Houston, Chicago, St. Louis, Memphis, Miami.

When I talk about "my hometown," I'm actually referring to a collection of about seven small towns with populations under one thousand that all went to the same school: Tamms, Olive Branch, Elco, Hodges Park, Sandusky, Unity, and Thebes. Most of these towns are pretty racially homogenous, with Tamms being the only one that really had both Black and white residents. I filtered my Facebook friends by my high school to see what my old classmates were up to. It was pretty clear from my newsfeed who was able to make a life here and who had to leave.

The farmers' sons and daughters stayed; so did children of local shop owners. Though there are plenty of struggling white folks (some parts of the movie *Winter's Bone* look familiar to me), the local economy runs in kinship networks, and folks look out for their own. The kids who became our local elected officials were all white. They shared idyllic photos of their families in cornfields and daughters in local beauty pageants. The Black girls were largely all far from home now, posting about trying to get back for a birthday or church event but noting they probably wouldn't be able to because they couldn't get the time off of work. The

Black boys—the ones who were alive and not in jail—were mostly still back home, talking about trying to stay on their grind and turn their situation around.

I got off of Facebook and decided to walk through the town with my little brother. I asked him, Are the streets emptier than when we were kids? Are there more abandoned houses than I remember? It seems like there are folks struggling with addiction; has the meth problem gotten bad? The local park is pretty empty for a weekend; where are the kids? He told me that they'd cut back on a lot of youth programming at our church because there weren't many kids there anymore—folks my age mostly having moved away and not adding a new generation to the congregation.

I don't think people in cities understand how bleak rural poverty can be. One difference between the urban poverty I see in my gentrifying Brooklyn neighborhood and what I experienced back home is that kids regularly see people who are richer than them. It might invoke in them anger or insecurity, but they can see people living the lives they dream of. In rural America, it can be hard to imagine anything different than what you grow up with. The lack of hope hangs like a cloud over the town. "I just need to get away from here" is a refrain I grew up with and still regularly see on my news feeds. I always knew I'd need to leave home to build a life for myself. I didn't question it.

Walking through my hometown, it was clear. Though we may adopt the worldviews of our new homes, we aren't moving to cities and coasts because we are bohemians looking for like-minded people or better cultural fit. We move to cities because that's where jobs are—where we can build lives and support our families from afar. We are economic refugees, fleeing the bleakness of our birthplaces brought on by years of economic policies and practices that have devastated our communities. I followed a path that millions of people of all ethnicities have tread for almost a century, following the opportunities promised on the radio, in the movies, on TV, and now online. Leaving in our wake shrinking towns populated only with children and the elderly—an entire generation vanished. Making blue counties bluer and red counties redder.

I remembered how painful that geographic, economic, and cultural transition was for me. I only saw my family one time per year because that was how often I could afford to get home. I arrived at college with the $100 my parents gave me (the last bit of financial assistance I ever got from them). That $100 wasn't enough to cover even one of my books. And I felt out of place both with the Black kids from Chicago and the white kids from downstate.

I remember the shame and stigma I encountered for being from rural America. I learned terms like "backwater," "flyover state," and "bumble-fuck." Eventually, I started saying them too to distance myself from my supposedly backward origins. I worked to shake the stigma by becoming more cosmopolitan. I started to travel, and I learned other languages, but the shame is still there. I feel it when I hear a grad school friend doing a postdoc in some small town talk about it like it's hell on earth. Or when I get a backhanded compliment like, "I can't believe you're from a small town; you seem so sophisticated." I know I'm not the only one either. A fellow union organizer from a small town near mine immediately took me under her wing when I came on staff. I've found a kinship with small-town kids in big cities. I find joy in comparing graduation sizes and trading stories of our small towns' quirks—like the fact that hunting season was an excused absence at my school—as our city friends listen in, bewildered.

But the greatest pain is how I grew apart from my family. I remember the guilt I felt at my brother's graduation when it hit me that I missed his whole childhood. He was seven when I left, and I'd only been home a handful of times after moving away to college. I joke now that it took me longer to get home from graduate school in San Diego than it took me to get to China. I would fly to Chicago because I couldn't afford to rent a car to drive down from St. Louis, and there was no public transportation to Tamms. I'd need to crash on a friend's couch because I usually missed the train down south. I'd take the six-hour train ride to Carbondale and wait overnight there for my mom to pick me up. The ride up from Tamms was forty miles on a dark highway with no street-lights. There were deer, and my mom couldn't risk hitting one and losing her transportation.

After a while, I just stopped going back. Conversations became strained. I grew closer to folks really different from the ones I grew up with—atheists and immigrants and queer folks. I learned the world wasn't just Black and white. That there were even many types of Black folks from something called the African diaspora. And some of these folks became my new family—united by proximity and ideals, instead of blood.

My mother, thankfully, made a full recovery after weeks in the hospital; however, the fear evoked by going back home and by my mom's illness stayed with me. I faced the realization that my home in New York was as much the result of economic forces as of personal choice and that however much I wanted to be close to my mom, an entire economic system stands between us.

My story of being at once Black and a woman who made the journey from rural to urban, conservative-leaning to left-leaning, and working class to middle class gives me a unique perspective on this historical moment. I feel like I have work to do. To fight back against the idea that the rural working class and the urban progressive are mutually exclusive sets and that both are white and male. To help folks in cities understand the reality of my folks back home. To share stories with family about how their fates are connected to those of my immigrant and queer chosen family here. To find ways to fight the despair and hopelessness in both places and build bonds between the disaffected in Tamms and the hopeless on my block in Bed-Stuy who've both been abandoned by our political and economic systems.

One of my coworkers often says that in our advocacy work, when we ascribe the story of dying towns and lack of opportunity only to the white working class, it confuses the problem. To think that progressives in cities are only out-of-touch liberal elites will lead us to the wrong solutions.

I'm less interested in reaching and changing the minds of Trump voters. When I look at my old classmates who voted for him, they aren't the folks suffering in my community. They are folks who have some version of the American dream: They have stable jobs, own homes, and take yearly vacations. They see the people in my town who are truly struggling, both Black and white, as takers, abusing the system and living off the middle class's taxes. As roughly 43 percent of eligible voters didn't vote, leading to Hillary winning the popular vote and Trump winning with fewer votes than 2012 Republican nominee Mitt Romney, I think we're better served focusing our attention elsewhere.[2]

It's important to remember that Trump didn't win people earning less than $50,000 a year, most of whom voted for Hillary.[3] But I can't really claim that Hillary won the poor and working class. Many of the 43 percent of folks who didn't vote in this election are people like those in my hometown. There are people all across this country who don't vote at all because they rightfully don't see how it will make a difference in their lives. I want to reach folks like my brother who desperately want to work but have no real options. I want to reach the folks who have dreams—to be an artist, a musician, a judge, an entrepreneur—that seem unachievable because there are no models and no pathways.

I'm not sure what the next steps are, but I know they will require addressing the lack of opportunity in communities like the one I came from. I call on the small-town kids in big cities across the country to join me in figuring this out. It won't be easy. There are real economic and personal barriers to getting home, and we have challenges like media deserts and Facebook algorithms that prevent us from sharing our realities from afar.[4] Still, we must try to reconnect with and advocate for our hometowns in whatever ways we can. The time is now.

Notes

1. Laurie Jo Reynolds and Stephen F. Eisenman, "Tamms Is Torture: The Campaign to Close an Illinois Supermax Prison," *Creative Time Reports*, May 6, 2013, https://creativetimereports.org/2013/05/06/tamms-is-torture-campaign-close-illinois-supermax-prison-solitary-confinement/.

2. Christopher Ingraham, "About 100 Million People Couldn't Be Bothered to Vote This Year," *Washington Post*, November 12, 2016, https://www.washingtonpost.com/news/wonk/wp/2016/11/12/about-100-million-people-couldnt-be-bothered-to-vote-this-year/; Will Drabold, "How Donald Trump Won Fewer Votes than Romney or McCain—but Still Won the Election," *Mic*, November 9, 2016, https://www.mic.com/articles/159032/how-donald-trump-won-fewer-votes-than-romney-or-mc-cain-but-still-won-the-election.

3. Jeremy Slevin, "Stop Blaming Low-Income Voters for Donald Trump's Victory," *TalkPoverty*, November 16, 2016, https://talkpoverty.org/2016/11/16/stop-blaming-low-income-voters-donald-trumps-victory/.

4. Tom Grubisich, "Despite Many New Local News Sites, 'Media Deserts' Are a Stubborn Reality," *StreetFightMag*, June 26, 2014, https://streetfightmag.com/2014/06/26/despite-many-local-news-sites-media-deserts-are-a-stubborn-reality/; John Herrman, "Inside Facebook's (Totally Insane, Unintentionally Gigantic, Hyperpartisan)

Political-Media Machine," *New York Times*, August 24, 2016, https://www.nytimes.com/2016/08/28/magazine/inside-facebooks-totally-insane-unintentionally-gigantic-hyperpartisan-political-media-machine.html.

This article was originally published by The Nation *magazine on November 16, 2016, and is republished here with permission.*

Equal Pay Day for (Some) African American Women

Alexandra Moffett-Bateau

It's an interesting thing: despite being a professor of political science and spending a good chunk of my time studying inequity in the lives of Black American women, I had no idea that Equal Pay Day for African American Women was this month, on August 22.

What is Equal Pay Day for African American Women, you may ask? It's the estimated date that the average Black woman would have to work until to earn the same annual income that men (inclusive of all races) earned in 2013. According to the National Women's Law Center, Equal Pay Day for women overall is April 8, and for Latino women, it doesn't come until November.

So, what does this dearth in pay along race and gender lines mean in practice? Well, in terms of raw numbers, according to a 2013 report by the Center for American Progress,

> Women on average earn 77 cents for every dollar a man earns for comparable work—a gender wage gap of 23 percent. Women of color suffer from an even more severe gap. According to the National Partnership for Women and Families, African American women and Latinas in the United States are paid $18,817 and $23,298 less than non-Hispanic white men yearly, respectively. That's 64 cents and 55 cents for every dollar a man earns.[1]

I have to admit, after looking at the numbers, I was surprised. Not only does the wage gap between men and women inclusive of all races remain sizable but also the gaps within gender and between racial groups are astonishing. The reality that African American women make 64 cents for every dollar men make has devastating consequences not only for Black communities but also for the US economy at large. When an entire segment of the population is disenfranchised in this way, regardless of education or opportunity, it creates inequalities around basic needs (like healthcare, housing, and childcare) that become entrenched within the economy.

The number of policy reports that have been written about this issue is staggering. Just about every liberal-leaning policy organization has written a piece about the lack of pay equity in the United States. Most of these reports are doing the good work of pushing for additional policy, executive and congressional alike. But one has to wonder, if pay discrimination was outlawed decades ago, is another executive order really going to fix it? In April of 2014, President Barack Obama signed into law an executive order meant to "prevent workplace discrimination and empower workers to take control over negotiations regarding their pay."[2] Given that the wage gap continues to exist, the impact of the executive order was limited.

Don't get me wrong, doing something is better than nothing; as the Civil Rights Act of 1964 showed us, policy with teeth can push the country into much-needed political and social reform. But the most recent executive order to prevent workplace discrimination is no such piece of policy.[3] Especially when, in Oklahoma, you can still lose your job, or be kicked out of school, simply for *appearing* to be gay.[4] What's the point of federal policy if states can completely gut it (as was the case with elements of Obamacare)?[5]

Indeed, July 16 wasn't Equal Pay Day for *all* African American women. When the data is further disaggregated by race, sexuality, and gender, the stakes that are at issue are made more clear.[6]

Lesbian women of color struggle even more with issues of pay inequity, high poverty, unemployment rates, and discrimination. Working gay and transgender people of color still earn less than their heterosexual and white gay and transgender counterparts, but lesbian women of color struggle even more severely. The average Latina lesbian couple earns $3,000 less than Latino opposite-sex couples. Black lesbian couples face an even greater economic disparity, earning $10,000 less than Black same-sex male couples. Black same-sex couples significantly lag behind white same-sex couples with median incomes of $41,500 compared to $63,500.

Furthermore, lesbian couples of color experience high rates of poverty and unemployment. In 2012, the poverty rate for Black lesbian couples was 21.1 percent; for Latina lesbian couples, the rate was 19.1 percent; for Native American lesbian couples, the rate was 13.7 percent; and for Asian Pacific Islander lesbian couples, it was 11.8 percent. These numbers stand in stark contrast to white lesbian couples, who had poverty rates of only 4.3 percent.

The combination of homophobia, racism, sexism, and classism keeps lesbians of color entrenched in poverty. The pay gap between lesbian of color couples and heterosexual couples means that it is nearly impossible for their wages to keep up with the rate of inflation in the United States—Black lesbian couples earn, on average, $10,000 less than Black same-sex male couples.

In short, Black lesbians are hypermarginalized within their race, gender, and sexual orientation. The rates of poverty and unemployment for Black lesbians means that we must think more critically about policy and legislation that would improve the quality of life across *all* marginalized groups.

In a post–Defense of Marriage Act world, a closely held secret is how little marriage legislation has meant for the lived realities of Black LGBTQ people, particularly Black trans and lesbian people. While winning the right to marriage was an important victory for many across the nation, the poverty rate for Black lesbian couples is 21.1 percent, compared to a white lesbian poverty rate of 4.3 percent. Organizations that purport to be concerned about the entire LGBTQ population should be incensed.

Without a living wage, Black women continue to go without access to housing, healthcare, childcare, or quality education. An important start to addressing this issue would be raising the minimum wage to a living wage across the United States. Next, instead of demolishing public housing, we should create low-income housing that offers a healthy and self-sustaining environment for the individuals who live there, and reinvest in public works programs that would rebuild key infrastructure in our cities. With these solutions, we can provide important work and training opportunities for the unemployed across the country, as well as rebuild major cities, whose roads, public buildings, and other infrastructure have been crumbling for decades.

We must continue to raise our voices against inequality within the United States and around the world. It is critical that as a nation we become committed to making sure that everyone is paid a living wage in accordance with their skills, training, and experience. By bringing attention to the wage gap and the disenfranchisement that stems from it, we can improve the lives of not only Black women but of people everywhere.

Notes

1. Sophia Kerby, "How Pay Inequity Hurts Women of Color," Center for American Progress, April 9, 2013, https://www.americanprogress.org/issues/economy/reports/2013/04/09/59731/how-pay-inequity-hurts-women-of-color/.
2. Lilly Ledbetter and Cecilia Munoz. "Taking Action in Honor of Equal Pay Day," White House of President Barack Obama, April 8, 2014, https://obamawhitehouse.archives.gov/blog/2014/04/08/taking-action-honor-national-equal-pay-day.
3. Ledbetter and Munoz, "Taking Action."
4. Arturo Garcia, "OK College Expels Woman One Semester from Graduation over Her Same-Sex Marriage," *Rawstory: US*, July 11, 2014, https://www.rawstory.com/2014/07/ok-college-expels-woman-one-semester-from-graduation-over-her-same-sex-marriage/.
5. Jazmine Walker, "What Happened to the 'Affordable' Part of the Affordable Care Act?," *Rewire.News*, July 15, 2014, https://rewire.news/article/2014/07/15/happened-affordable-part-affordable-care-act/.
6. Kerby, "How Pay Inequity."

Originally published on Rewire.News *on July 22, 2014.*

#UsToo: We Must Expand the Conversation on Sexual Violence

Raquel Willis

The reemergence of the #MeToo campaign and the reclamation of its inception by Just BE Inc. founder and activist Tarana Burke speaks to a larger problem within the conversation on sexual harassment and violence. The experiences of famous, wealthy, cisgender, heterosexual, and able-bodied white women like Rose McGowan and Alyssa Milano are constantly prioritized, while those of more marginalized people are invisibilized. Within such a biased and capitalistic culture, it's no surprise celebrities have been able to spark a collective discussion on these issues in ways that an average Black woman with limited access, like Burke, possibly never would have been able to.

Our society often doesn't believe that the sexual violence that happens to folks who fall outside of the McGowan-Milano script is as important or worthy of discussion. There's a continued obsession with cisgender white women's purity[1] that places their safety at the crux of these conversations. Historically, other women were seen as having even less agency over their bodies. Enslaved Black women were routinely sexually exploited by white male and female slave owners. And to a lesser extent, ill-intended white women (postslavery) have been able to use their privilege in these conversations to further violence against marginalized people. Remember Emmett Till?

I've often felt like I couldn't discuss my experiences with sexual harassment and assault because I've witnessed the difficulty that even cisgender women face when they disclose. My transgender, queer, and Black identities render my claims even less believable in a society that views me as inherently deviant. And as a Black trans woman, there is a distinct way in which my body and the desires I have for it have been coded within society. Just a few generations ago, I could have been arrested simply for not wearing enough articles of clothing corresponding to the gender I was assigned at birth. In fact, two moments that sparked the current LGBTQ+ Movement—Compton's Cafeteria Riots and the Stonewall Riots—transpired because of how gender nonconforming and transgender people were profiled by law enforcement.

There's even the instance of Frances Thompson,[2] a formerly enslaved Black trans woman who endured the Memphis Riots of 1866. She was raped along with Lucy Smith, a cisgender roommate, and testified before a congressional committee. In *Sex, Love, Race: Crossing Boundaries in North American History*, author Martha Hodes makes a profound declaration: "Ultimately Thompson's transvestism was such a powerful tool for conservatives not because Thompson was represented as bizarre or unique, but rather because her image resonated so strongly with the pre-existing conservative discourse attributing dishonorable gender and sexuality to all African American women."

This dismissal of trans women and femmes who speak up about sexual violence and harassment is the result of centuries-old heteronormative, patriarchal beliefs about identity. Due to flawed ideas on why trans women and femmes transition, we are often confronted with comments like, "Welcome to womanhood," or "Well, you got the attention you wanted," as if the desire to be respected in our identities means the sexism that we face is justified. These mindsets demean us and devalue our experiences through victim blaming while also reinforcing the idea that identifying with womanhood and femininity means that stripping people of their agency is fair game.

Trans and gender nonconforming people are rarely given the space to discuss our own experiences with sexual violence, partly due to damaging notions of us being predators or the idea that we're not desirable enough for anyone to commit such actions against us. Both of these ideas are far from the truth. In the 2015 US Transgender Survey, 47 percent of trans folks reported having been sexually harassed at some point in their lives. Our transness and gender nonconformity often make us even more of a target to others.

We are lacking nuance when we paint sexual harassment and violence as only happening to a certain kind of woman at the hands of a certain kind of man. These issues go much deeper than the "a woman versus a man" formula. We must grapple with patriarchy as a system and how it negatively impacts everyone.

Where trans women and femmes have been able to insert a sliver of awareness into the public discourse about our experiences, trans men and transmasculinity are discussed even less. The idea that masculinity automatically makes you a perpetrator of sexual violence ignores the fact that many men and masculine folks have stories of their own. (It also ignores that women and femmes are capable of committing sexual violence.) Nonbinary and other gender nonconforming folks are altogether ignored. That's the problem with the binary; it ignores that gender-based issues are always more complex than what's on the surface. We can center the discussion on women and nonbinary folks while still acknowledging what happens to people of other genders.

Further, the state has routinely been ineffective at preventing sexual violence and protecting survivors. According to the Rape, Abuse & Incest National Network, 75 percent of sexual assaults go unreported for many reasons, including fear of retaliation from the perpetrator, not seeing the instance as important enough, and largely out of the belief that police won't actually help.

For instance, Ky Peterson, a Black trans man in Georgia, was incarcerated after being attacked and raped while walking home in October 2011. While Peterson was defending himself, his rapist was killed. Peterson had already had negative experiences with the police in prior instances of sexual violence, so he had no reason to believe they would heed his cry for help. Peterson is currently serving a twenty-year sentence for this act of self-defense.

Once on the inside, harassment and rape are regularly seen as par for the course for trans folks in prisons and detention centers. In July 2017, Eyricka King, a Black transgender woman, garnered attention online after a video of her mother, Kelly Harrison, went viral.[3] In it, she discussed King's treatment while incarcerated at the Franklin Correctional Facility in New York. Placed in solitary confinement, King was repeatedly threatened, attacked, and denied medical care. These attacks, by both inmates and guards, included sexual violence. But King's important story isn't considered when we have a limited scope of these issues.

It is up to everyone to raise consciousness about sexual violence to another level. It's clear that a president who loves "pussy grabbing" and an administration committed to moving justice further out of reach for survivors won't do it for us.

Personally, the #MeToo campaign has affected me deeply. Some folks have called the campaign ineffective and have said that it doesn't do enough to combat rape culture. Others have voiced how problematic it is that people are called to relive some of their darkest moments publicly with little to no guarantee of how they will be supported. These critiques are valid; however, storytelling continues to be one of the greatest tools to transform culture and ourselves.

Notes

1. Jennifer Loubriel, "4 Racist Stereotypes White Patriarchy Invented to 'Protect' White Womanhood," *Everyday Feminism*, July 10, 2016, https://everydayfeminism.com/2016/07/protect-white-womanhood/.
2. Hannah Rosen, "'Not That Sort of Women': Race, Gender, and Sexual Violence during the Memphis Riot of 1866," in *Sex, Love, Race: Crossing Boundaries in North American History*, ed. Martha Hodes (New York: New York University Press, 1999), 267–86.
3. Justin Moran, "Trans Woman Eyricka King Attacked & Denied Medical Treatment in New York Prison," *Out*, July 13, 2017, https://www.out.com/news-opinion/2017/7/13/trans-woman-eyricka-king-attacked-denied-medical-treatment-new-york-prison.

Originally published on INTOMore.com *on October 23, 2017.*

The School-to-Prison Pipeline Affects Girls of Color, but Reform Efforts Pass Them By

Ruth Jeannoel

A six-year-old Black girl named TT was suspended and sent home because she poked a boy with an eraser.

When I asked her what happened, TT told me that the boy was bothering her and wouldn't stop even after she asked him, so she poked him with an eraser. TT was subsequently suspended from school for two days.

As the mother of a kindergartener, I am very familiar with this type of age-appropriate childish misbehavior. As an organizer for Power U Center for Social Change, a grassroots organization based in Miami, the fact that another student of color was harshly and unfairly punished for age-appropriate behavior also did not surprise me. TT was just one of many girls who fall victim to zero tolerance and school push out every day.

As most education advocates know, zero-tolerance policies shut the doors of academic opportunity to students of color by funneling them into the juvenile and criminal justice systems. The combination of overly harsh school policies and the growing role of law enforcement in schools has created a school-to-prison pipeline in which punitive measures, such as suspensions, expulsions, and school-based arrests, are increasingly used to deal with student misbehavior. What many education advocates aren't talking about, however, are the gender dynamics at play in this phenomenon.

A report by the African American Policy Forum (AAPF), *Black Girls Matter: Pushed Out, Overpoliced and Underprotected*, outlines how girls of color face much harsher school discipline than their white peers but are simultaneously excluded from current efforts to address the school-to-prison pipeline. The report states that nationally, Black girls are six times more likely to get suspended than their white counterparts. In comparison, Black boys are three times more likely to get suspended than their white counterparts.[1]

Despite the statistics, there are no initiatives like the My Brother's Keeper program—a five-year, $200 million program initiated by President Obama to support boys of color—to engage and nurture young women of color. Even though Black girls are criminalized and brutalized by the same oppressive system, rarely does their brutalization make national news.

Consider the 2014 case of seventeen-year-old high school student Brittany Overstreet in Tampa Bay, Florida. According to local news reports, she was "accused of becoming combative and aggressive toward school administrators" when they wanted to search her bag for mace. During a struggle with the officer, the teenager was slammed twice on the ground, which resulted in a concussion and her jaw being fractured in two places. She was handcuffed, suspended for ten days, and faced criminal charges. She did not have mace in her purse.

In the current movement to dismantle the school-to-prison pipeline, girls like Brittany are often an afterthought. As a Black woman, I experience the intersection of race and gender every day: I see the ways in which Black girls are subjugated simultaneously by patriarchy, white supremacy, and heterosexism. Worse yet, we are also expected to be strong and indestructible, an attribute that is also detrimental because Black girls are perceived as being more socially mature and self-reliant,[2] and thus they receive less attention in school.

In my work, I have often found that when Black girls struggle with trauma and other unmet needs, they only receive attention from school staff when their behavior leads to punishable offenses, particularly in school districts like Miami that rely on harsh discipline and zero tolerance. Despite gendered vulnerabilities, such as sexual victimization,[3] pregnancy,[4] and significant familial responsibilities that many Black girls experience, they are socialized to hold in their pain and their trauma.

When girls cry for help, both explicitly and implicitly through misbehavior, school officials should immediately engage them. This is a great opportunity to build relationships with students, helping them see the harm that was caused and teaching them how to address their problems. This simple solution is known as restorative justice, a nonpunitive way of addressing conflict and building relationships that shifts the culture of our schools and holds not only students but also public officials and teachers accountable.

In addition to restorative justice, the aforementioned AAPF report also outlines interventions to address the various challenges facing girls of color, including developing programs that identify signs of sexual victimization; advancing programs that support girls who are pregnant, parenting, or otherwise assuming significant familial responsibilities; and improving data collection to better track discipline and achievement by race/ethnicity and gender for all groups.

Policy makers should take heed of these recommendations and commit to an approach to dismantling the pipeline that takes into account how race, gender, and other forms of bias can intersect to exacerbate discrimination faced by individuals. As a mother of two Black girls, I want schools to be a place where they can learn without the threat of being pushed out or excluded, where they can speak up without being silenced, and where their needs, hopes, and dreams are heard and valued.

Notes

1. Kimberlé Williams Crenshaw, Priscilla Ocen, and Jyoti Nanda, *Black Girls Matter: Pushed Out, Overpoliced and Underprotected* (New York: African American Policy Forum, 2015), 18–19, https://static1. squarespace.com/static/53f20d90e4b0b80451158d8c/t/54dcc1ece4b001 c03e323448/1423753708557/AAPF_BlackGirlsMatterReport.pdf.
2. Crenshaw, Ocen, and Nanda, *Black Girls Matter*, 12.
3. Terrell Jermaine Starr, "STUDY: More Than Half of Black Girls Are Sexually Assaulted," *NewsOne*, December 2, 2011, https://newsone. com/1680915/half-of-Black-girls-sexually-assaulted/.
4. Teresa Wiltz, "Racial and Ethnic Disparities Persist in Teen Pregnancy Rates," Pew Charitable Trusts, March 3, 2015, http://www. pewtrusts.org/en/research-and-analysis/blogs/stateline/2015/3/03/ racial-and-ethnic-disparities-persist-in-teen-pregnancy-rates.

Originally published on the Guardian *on June 11, 2015.*

The Right to (Black) Life

Renee Bracey Sherman

Today marks three years since Michael Brown was killed in Ferguson, Missouri, by a police officer. That's three years that his mother, Lesley McSpadden, has mourned her son.

Ms. McSpadden and other mothers of Black people slain by police have become emblems of the movement against racialized police violence. But they represent something bigger: the heartbreaking dilemmas Black women face at every point in the motherhood journey.

Many American women live under a fog of critique about our choices when it comes to our reproductive health and motherhood. But this is especially true for Black women.

If we choose to have an abortion, we are cast as villains by antiabortion campaigns that tap into the trauma of our country's racial history. Outside of clinics, I often hear protesters shout racial slurs and say things like "unborn Black lives matter" when Black people walk past them.

In addition, Black women are ostracized for having children "too young" and for having kids that society deems "illegitimate."

Then, regardless of the life we provide for our children, if they are killed by police officers, our parenting decisions will inevitably be criticized.

From conception until death, damned if we do and damned if we don't.

With access to women's reproductive healthcare under attack and low-income families and women of color disproportionately affected, many advocates have rightly been concerned that Black women are particularly vulnerable.

Yes, it's essential that Black women have the choice about whether to conceive and give birth. But this choice, without the ability to protect a child from violence, rings hollow. That's why it's important to understand that the fight for reproductive justice and the fight to end police brutality go hand in hand.

State violence and control, whether through racist policing, the criminal justice system, or the welfare system, are issues at the core of reproductive justice. They are fundamentally about whether you, or the state, have control over your own body and destiny.

The movement for reproductive justice, a human rights framework created by women of color in 1994, is not only about the ability to decide if, when, and how to become a parent. It's also about the ability to survive, and perhaps even thrive, in your own body. It's about the right to abortion care, of course, and to healthy pregnancies free of shame. And reproductive justice is about the ability to raise children to become adults.

But we can't make these choices if we ourselves aren't safe. Not only do Black women have to worry about police brutalizing their children, but we also have to fear this violence ourselves.

Charleena Lyles was pregnant when she was shot and killed by the police in her Seattle home, in front of her children, after she called them for help after a robbery. Korryn Gaines, fearing for her and her children's lives, was shot and killed after she armed herself when Baltimore County police officers came to her home to serve her with an arrest warrant. Over a dozen Black women were raped and terrorized by Oklahoma City officer Daniel Holtzclaw, who preyed on them because he thought no one would care about Black women.

The impact of this discrimination and inequality begins early. The American College of Obstetricians and Gynecologists writes that "racial bias is an issue that affects our patients, either directly by subjecting them or their families to inequitable treatment, or indirectly by creating a stressful and unhealthy environment."[1]

Instead of working to create solutions to end police violence, antiabortion politicians and the countless people who have criticized bereaved Black mothers argue over whether the deceased—someone's child—was an "angel" or not. They ask whether his father was involved enough and whether his mother taught him right from wrong.

They scrutinize every parenting decision and ignore the structural issues that force those decisions. They don't engage with the challenges we face in a racist society that limits our ability to survive.

It's heartbreaking to make the life-changing decision to carry a pregnancy to term only to bury your baby because police officers killed him while he was playing in a park or while she was sleeping on a couch.

Far too often, compassion for Black lives doesn't extend beyond the womb or to the Black women carrying that womb. Too few tears are shed for the people killed by police violence. Reproductive justice is about the resolve to raise our families on our own terms, safely. This is the fight for the right to life.

Notes

1. "ACOG Statement of Policy on Racial Bias," The American College of Obstetricians and Gynecologists, February 2017, https://www. acog.org/clinical-information/policy-and-position-statements/ statements-of-policy/2017/racial-bias.

Originally published in the New York Times *on August 9, 2017.*

BIRTH JUSTICE ... AND YES, THAT INCLUDES ABORTION

Introduction

Cynthia R. Greenlee

Among the Idas are mothers, future parents, aunties, people who don't want children, people who can't have them, young parents, and those who've been pregnant but have never borne children.

Some of us have had babies in hospitals where our opinions didn't matter. Our friends and relatives have too. We know that as antiabortion propaganda smears Black birthing people by saying that their wombs are the "most dangerous place for a Black baby," our healthcare systems are not safe.

We are not afraid to say the word "abortion." And you shouldn't be either. We have had them and don't regret them. We have had them with support or without others' support.

We lead the movements to tell our stories about birth, abortion, and struggles to access quality care because hiding essential healthcare is not an option (and abortion *is* healthcare) and our healthcare system is itself unhealthy. In this section, you see the power of story. Renee Bracey Sherman, founder of the nonprofit We Testify, is a pioneer of public abortion storytelling for social and political change. Elizabeth Dawes Gay co-led the Black Mamas Matter Alliance, one of the nation's leading organizations sounding the alarm about how many Black people die or suffer serious injury in childbirth. Shanelle Matthews is an expert communication strategist for Black liberation movements, crafting messages that make it into protest and policy. But here she tells her own story.

Our stories are both individual experiences and collective ones. Have you had a healthcare provider "compliment" how articulate you are while you're in the exam room? Or developed preeclampsia during pregnancy? Or insisted, like the Greatest of All Time tennis player Serena Williams, that you are not well, and doctors need to pay attention?

We are the best judges of what we need.

Who Should You Listen to on Abortion?
People Who've Had Them

Renee Bracey Sherman

Across literature and social media, there's the #OwnStories movement. Simply put, people—especially those who have been marginalized and are vulnerable to silencing—must be able to narrate their own lives and control their stories and how they are used. Renee Bracey Sherman made a strong case for the right to represent one's self in this editorial for the New York Times.

When I arrived at the clinic in Washington, I looked for the young woman I was waiting for. Her body was covered with tattoos of birds and stars. She hugged me with a warm smile and introduced me to her boyfriend. He didn't look at me. In fact, he didn't look me in the eye for the five hours we sat together in the waiting room.

I assumed it was out of shame until I noticed the white supremacist tattoos on his shaved head, neck, forearms, and knuckles. As a Black woman, I was scared of him. Yet I felt a bond. They had driven several hours from Virginia to avoid the numerous restrictions on abortions there. He was returning from jail. She already had a child and wasn't ready for another. I knew the feeling well.

She asked for an abortion doula because she wanted unconditional support, no matter what she decided. She wanted me, a total stranger, to reinforce her trust in herself. After she went to the procedure room, her boyfriend and I went outside—me to make a call, him to smoke. In the elevator down, he finally spoke: "Thank you."

When I had an abortion, I was nineteen and alone. Though I was pretty sure my parents would have supported my decision, I didn't want to take the risk. So I kept it a secret. My boyfriend at the time dropped me off at the clinic, unwilling to go inside. I walked through the bomb-proof door, and a kind Orthodox Jewish nurse took care of me. She held my hand as the sedation filled my veins and offered me saltine crackers and Coca-Cola when I woke up in the recovery room.

These are the realities of abortion.

The need to terminate a pregnancy knows no political affiliation nor religious faith. I've hugged, cried with, and held the hands of hundreds of people who've had abortions, many of whom never thought they would. All were thankful that someone was there to provide care, sit with them when they were alone, and hold their hair as the nausea took over. All felt the stigma and shame society thrusts on them.

The abortion debate rages on, but the voices of those who've actually had abortions are ignored. Few people try to understand our lives. And we are never asked the most simple but important question: Why did you do it?

That's intentional. It's easier to strip us of our rights when we're not treated as humans; when political candidates, like Donald Trump, say we deserve "some form of punishment"; when elected officials vote to define abortion as "murder"; and when people call us killers.[1] Language matters, and it leads to violence. Abortion providers, and people who share their stories, including me, have received thousands of threats.[2]

But nearly one-third of American women are estimated to have an abortion by forty-five, according to the Guttmacher Institute, a research group that supports abortion rights. Sixty-two percent of us are people of color. A majority are religious. We're trying to make ends meet and can't afford to expand our families at that particular time.

When we are denied abortions, we are three times as likely to end up below the federal poverty line, compared with those who are able to get the abortions they want. About two-thirds of people who have abortions are parents who want to give the children they already have the best life. Ninety-five percent of women surveyed don't regret their decisions, and it doesn't affect our mental health.

The reproductive justice movement doesn't work only for abortion rights.[3] Led by women of color, it also ensures that everyone is able to decide if, when, and how to grow their families. When I became pregnant, I considered what life as a parent would look like. Would I be able to earn enough to make my child healthy lunches? Would I be able to finish my own education? It's unfair to deny access to abortion care while simultaneously degrading the social services needed to raise children.

Adoption is posed as the perfect option, and it's great for those who choose it, but it isn't a solution for those who don't want to be pregnant or can't risk pregnancy.

In states like Indiana, Georgia, Tennessee, and Virginia, elected officials are willing to imprison people for administering their own abortions because they simply couldn't afford care nearby. Vice President Mike Pence is a man so obsessed with abortion that as governor of Indiana, he signed every antiabortion bill that crossed his desk, including mandating funerals after abortions and requiring medically unnecessary ultrasounds.[4] He also awarded millions of taxpayer dollars to fake pregnancy centers.[5]

Antiabortion policies like these aim to bring about an end to abortion, but history has shown us there's no such thing. Abortion will continue. The only question is whether it will be safe or unsafe.

The crux of the issue is not whether you would have an abortion yourself. It's whether you would stand in the way of someone else's decision. Everyone loves someone who has had an abortion, though we may not know it.

We need politicians who protect our decisions to create our families and support us as we do it—or don't. We also need people willing to sit in the clinic with us, without judgment.

I hope I provided the same unconditional kindness for the young woman with the tattoos that the Orthodox Jewish nurse offered me a decade earlier and that she will pass it on to someone else.

The voices of people who've had abortions should be central to the conversation. The question is, will you listen?

Notes

1. Matt Flegenheimer and Maggie Haberman, "Donald Trump, Abortion Foe, Eyes 'Punishment' for Women, then Recants," *New York Times*, March 30, 2016, https://www.nytimes.com/2016/03/31/us/politics/donald-trump-abortion.html.; Reid Wilson, "Oklahoma House Declares Abortion Murder," *The Hill*, May 9, 2017.
2. "Violence Statistics & History," National Abortion Federation, accessed February 21, 2019, https://prochoice.org/education-and-advocacy/violence/violence-statistics-and-history/.

3. Renee Bracey Sherman, "What the War on Reproductive Rights Has to Do with Poverty and Race," *YES! Magazine*, May 25, 2016.

4. Laura Bassett, "Mike Pence Has Led the Fight against Reproductive Rights for Half a Decade," *HuffPost*, July 20, 2016, https://www.huffpost.com/entry/mike-pence-reproductive-rights-abortion_n_5787cc73e4b0867123e036a1.

5. Shari Rudavsky, "State Awards $3.5 Million Contract to Antiabortion Organization for Pregnancy Services," *Indianapolis Star*, October 12, 2015, https://www.indystar.com/story/news/2015/10/13/state-awards-35-million-contract-anti-abortion-organization-pregnancy-services/73819882/.

Originally published in the New York Times *on May 20, 2017.*

The Road to *Roe*: Paved with Bodies of Women of Color and the Legal Activism of African Americans

Cynthia R. Greenlee

January 22, 1973, was a landmark day. The US Supreme Court released its decision to legalize abortion nationwide in the case of Roe v. Wade. *Years later, the day is marked by marches, the recognition that abortion rights won decades ago can be lost today, and calls to honor the people who fought then, the people who died or were hurt because they had to seek dangerous illegal care, and the people who provided safe BUT illegal care. The* Roe *anniversary is an occasion for remembering, but as now-historian Ida Cynthia R. Greenlee pointed out when she was studying as a graduate student, it's also an occasion for forgetting the very real contributions of Black Americans to the abortion rights movement.*

Every year when the anniversary of *Roe v. Wade* rolls around, I am troubled by the loud silences in our triumphant tales of struggle. Our pro-choice creation myths—including true stories about twenty-six-year-old Sarah Weddington (the Texas attorney and primary counsel in the *Roe v. Wade* case) facing the Supreme Court, the Jane Collective of Chicago referring women to safe abortion care in the sixties, and countless women who died from unsafe abortions—are largely narratives without the voices and contributions of African Americans.

As a history doctoral student who researches African Americans and abortion, the story I tell is quite different.

I frequently hear variations on these themes: "abortion is a white feminist thing," "Black people are against abortion," or "abortion is Black genocide." When these ideas surface, I remind their proponents that almost a third of all US abortions are currently performed on Black women. (Statistics from 2008 reported that 37 percent of abortions performed annually in this country are on Black women, who have the nation's highest rate of unintended pregnancy.)[1]

56

But the story must go further back in time. Indeed, for much of American history, abortion was strongly associated with African Americans. During slavery, people of African descent were believed to have special knowledge of botanicals, such as cottonseed, tansy, and rue, that could cause abortion. (Some herbal remedies suspected of causing abortion were called "Negro remedies." Tansy, rue, and other botanicals, such as pennyroyal and cedar berries, were thought to be used by enslaved women to induce pregnancy loss.)[2] Slave owners and doctors suspected that bondswomen curbed their births through abortions.

Historians can't prove that definitively, and certainly, poor healthcare, inadequate diet, and overwork set the stage for female slaves' infertility and reproductive complaints. But we do know that after slavery, white commentators traveled to the South and lamented that the Black birth rate seemed to be slowing, sometimes blaming abortion. In effect, they were nineteenth-century forerunners to Black nationalists who claimed abortion was a form of "race suicide." Whether enslaved women practiced "reproductive resistance" has long been the subject of debates among historians. Slavery historian Eugene Genovese firmly rejected this idea, while Deborah Gray White and Jennifer Morgan have noted that slaves attempted to control their own fertility in many ways and that the poor health and nutrition of enslaved women and infants also likely played a role in pregnancy loss or miscarriage, which can be indistinguishable from abortion.

And we do know that immediately before *Roe* legalized abortion in 1973, the overwhelming majority of the women who died from illegal abortions in New York City were Black and/or Latina. (A study from the 1960s said that abortion complications from 1960 to 1962 caused 25 percent of white maternal deaths, 49 percent of Black ones, and 65 percent of Latina fatalities in New York City.)[3] The human cost of making abortion illegal is evident in *Jet* magazine, once the most influential chronicle of the Black middle class. It often detailed the deaths of Black women, such as twenty-nine-year-old Josephine Fuller of Washington, DC; the former beauty queen bled to death at home and left behind four children in 1953.[4]

The doctor who performed Fuller's procedure—also Black—was charged in her death. While abortion opponents often charge abortion providers with conspiring to create a Nazi-style "final solution" for Blacks, African Americans provided abortions to Black and white women. (For an antiabortion example comparing Nazism, slavery, and abortion, see http://www.blackgenocide.org/abortion.html.) These providers ran the gamut from licensed physicians, healers who drew on herbs and community traditions, midwives, and untrained quacks. Notably, while the whites-only American Medical Association pushed the criminalization of abortion in the late 1800s, the all-Black National Medical Association did not take a stand either way on banning abortion. Yet Black providers often felt the combined sting of law enforcement and racism during the illegal era between the 1880s and 1973: Chicago's Dr. T.R.M. Howard was charged repeatedly, and when Columbia, South Carolina, physician Benjamin Everett allegedly performed an abortion on a white woman in 1916, prosecutors asked the woman what she was doing at "a nigger house."[5]

But the road to *Roe* was paved not just with the bodies of women but also with the legal activism of African Americans. We can't talk about *Roe* without nodding to the 1970 *Abramowicz v. Lefkowitz* case that triggered the liberalization of New York State's abortion law before Weddington's date with the justices.[6] On the legal team was Florynce Kennedy, the National Organization for Women cofounder who argued pointedly—and for the first time in any legal case—that changing the state's abortion law was not merely a matter of physicians' right to practice but also women's rights.[7] Kennedy gathered women's abortion stories at her kitchen table, but there were also other Black power brokers at the metaphorical table.

Noted civil rights attorney Napoleon Williams was an assisting counsel, and Percy Sutton—a former Freedom Rider, Manhattan borough president, and Apollo Theater investor—signaled his support. Civil rights and reproductive rights were not mutually exclusive.

In the 1960s and early 1970s, the first generation of Black women elected to statewide office put reforming abortion laws on the legislative agenda—even in red states. In 1967, Dr. Dorothy Brown of Tennessee—a surgeon who ran back and forth between the hospital and general assembly—introduced an unsuccessful bill to allow abortion in cases of rape and incest.[8] While that initiative ultimately cost Brown her seat, Missouri Rep. DuVerne Calloway was elected in 1962 and cosponsored a failed abortion reform in 1971 but held office until 1982.[9]

Their voices echo today in the efforts of Black women state legislators, such as Virginia delegate Charniele Herring, who led the charge against her state's proposal to require unnecessary "transvaginal" ultra-sounds before abortions.[10] They also echo in the grassroots mobilization of historically Black colleges in Mississippi, whose students' votes helped defeat the state's dangerously sweeping personhood amendment in 2011. And they echo in the work of Black abortion providers who challenge new abortion restrictions and serve in remote and underserved locations.

As a historian, I amplify these echoes as reminders that the abortion movement was never monochromatically white. We can ill afford these silences at a time when women's actions during pregnancy—whether choosing home birth, drug use, or merely delivering a stillborn child—are criminalized. These silences cannot persist when keeping abortion legal and accessible is a constant struggle. And as antichoice factions assert that the most dangerous place for Black children is in their mothers' wombs, we must acknowledge that these battles are waged on the terrain of Black women's bodies. And that's a terrain I'm not willing to cede.

Notes

1. Susan A. Cohen, "Abortion and Women of Color: The Bigger Picture," *Guttmacher Policy Review* 11, no. 3 (2008), https://www.guttmacher.org/sites/default/files/article_files/gpr110302.pdf.
2. Sharla Fett, *Working Cures: Healing, Health, and Power on Slave Plantations* (Chapel Hill: University of North Carolina Press, 2002), 60–83.
3. Barbara Winslow, *Shirley Chisholm: Catalyst for Change* (New York: Avalon Publishing, 2013), 158.
4. "Hold Doctor in DC Socialite's Abortion Death," *Jet*, April 9, 1953, 18.
5. Cynthia R. Greenlee, "T.R.M. Howard: Civil Rights Rabble-Rouser, Abortion Provider," *Dissent*, May 16, 2013, https://www.dissentmagazine.org/blog/t-r-m-howard-civil-rights-rabble-rouser-abortion-provider.
6. Reva Siegal, "*Roe*'s Roots: The Women's Rights Claims That Engendered *Roe*," *Boston University Law Review* 90 (2010): 1875–1907, https://digitalcommons.law.yale.edu/cgi/viewcontent.cgi?article=2137&context=fss_papers.
7. Sherie Randolph, *Florence "Flo" Kennedy: The Life of a Black Feminist Radical* (Chapel Hill: University of North Carolina Press, 2018), 168–85.

8. Natelege Whaley, "Black Women and the Right for Abortion Rights: How This Brochure Sparked the Movement for Reproductive Freedom," NBCNews.com, March 25, 2019, https://www.nbcnews.com/news/nbcblk/black-women-fight-abortion-rights-how-brochure-sparked-movement-reproductive-n983216.

9. John Grinstead, "Legislative Summary," *The Examiner*, February 15, 1971, 2.

10. Alexa Epitropoulos, "Charniele Herring Rises the Democratic Ranks," *Alexandria Times*, February 8, 2018, https://alextimes.com/2018/02/charnieleherring.

Originally published on Rewire.News *on January 23, 2013.*

Whitewashing Reproductive Rights:
How Black Activists Get Erased

Renee Bracey Sherman

Black History Month is a time for the celebration of heritage. It's twenty-eight days that our ancestors' stories and struggles are shared in schools, media, and communities. But, as with most Black culture and histories, it's been appropriated, mangled, and spoon-fed to us without the rich flavor and spice. Bland.

Over the past few decades, we have seen conservatives distort our legacies of struggle, erase the disproportionate impact of their policies, and co-opt our victories—remember conservative radio host Glenn Beck's attempt to reclaim the civil rights movement from those who have "distorted" it? More recently and preposterously, the Christian right and some groups on the left have been whitewashing Black history in the movement for women's autonomy—even using it and our children against us without our full consent. They've rewritten history to the point that many believe our ancestors were fervently antiabortion and still would be today. We've allowed them to change the legacy of our leaders, and it's time we take it back. It's time we tell our own stories.

Abortion for Black women has always been a revolutionary rejection of patriarchy, white supremacy, and forced systems of oppression. The great scholars Patricia Hill Collins and Angela Y. Davis have explained that throughout slavery and into the twentieth century, self-abortion through herbal remedies, hangers, hatpins, and pencils were a way out of slavery and poverty. Some of our ancestors fought hard to refuse to carry the children of their master-rapists and rear another generation of slaves, even when it meant that "barren" women were deemed worthless chattel and sold between plantations. From generation to generation, stories and recipes were passed down to ensure that women weren't forced to carry pregnancies they never desired or weren't able to carry healthily. As many powerful women raised children in the worst conditions imaginable, there were also those who refused.

Antiabortion activists think themselves clever when they compare abortion to slavery, but reams of historical records prove their narrative to be rooted in quicksand. They have ignored the stories of men and women being raped, beaten, starved, and worked literally to death and the reverberating effects of that most inhumane of institutions. It is indeed preposterous to assert that a free Black woman deciding her own fate as her ancestors have done for centuries (including within the context of slavery) is a perpetrator of the crimes from which she continues to suffer.

Black women have been a part of the workforce since our arrival on these shores. But as our elders joined the ranks of laborers during World War I, they found a great need for access to birth control and abortion. In her 1998 book, *When Abortion Was a Crime*, historian Leslie J. Reagan writes that hospitals and the medical establishment, already mainly white-serving, sought to disenfranchise midwives and keep them from providing abortions while community doctors set up clinics to help families access then-illegal abortion care. In Detroit, Dr. Edgar Bass Keemer Jr. provided abortions from 1938 through the 1950s, ensuring that Black women had access to safe abortion care regardless of their income. Whether contraception or abortion, men and women in the Black community have always banded together to provide for the needs of our own.

During the civil rights movement, economic justice and equality were central to organizing—and Martin Luther King Jr. knew that family planning was key to achieving them. Many activists today say that King would be "pro-life," but we have stories and his own words to the contrary. In 1966, Planned Parenthood honored him for his work in opening access to family planning methods; his wife, Coretta Scott King, accepted the award on his behalf. King explained that because Black workers were often relegated to low-wage jobs, limiting family size was important to economic success. "For the Negro," he said, "intelligent guides of family planning are a profoundly important ingredient in his quest for security and a decent life." The day she accepted the award, Coretta Scott King said she was "proud to be a woman."

As Black feminists from the seventies onward sought to expand racial, gender, and economic equality for women of color, they found themselves being left out of mainstream conversations about equal pay and reproductive rights. Their stories were left untold in a women's rights movement led by mainly white women. Tired of being silenced and fueled by an international movement for human rights, they began the reproductive justice movement to bring to light the fact that communities of color lack access to basic healthcare and pregnancy options, including the opportunity to raise our children with dignity. They demanded that our stories be heard, and their demands still affect how we think about policy today.

Despite centuries with a boot on our necks, Black women embody a legacy of boldness that has been crucial to social change throughout history. Whether undermining slavery's use of our bodies or speaking unabashedly about the threats to our bodily autonomy today, Black women have long been leaders in the struggle for our bodies, our children, and our lives. Yet whether the focus is on effort or impact, we are often left out of today's story. Despite the fact that Black women consistently deliver pro-choice Democratic politicians, white women often split their votes with antichoice Republican candidates; mainstream postelection framing says that "women" made the difference in the election, erasing our hard work and voices. Pundits like to cite that the wage gap for women is 77 cents to a man's dollar but forget to note that it's 64 cents for Black women and 55 cents for Latinas. Ignoring this income gap while the government is simultaneously cutting food assistance and access to family planning methods erases actions that hurt women of color the most.

We need the audacity of our ancestors now. We have too much knowledge and too many resources to continue to have the narrative reshaped and our realities ignored before our eyes. The Black community has historically supported bodily autonomy and access to safe and legal abortion. Our history proves that we have led the way in the abortion and reproductive justice movement, and we are influential in policy now. It's high time we ensure that our influence is accurately reflected and that we celebrate it. This Black History Month, while right-wing pundits will undoubtedly try to co-opt our legacy in service of their agenda, I plan to read up on my history and share those stories from the rooftops. I refuse to allow my ancestors to be silenced and erased, or my own reality and contributions to be ignored, because as Zora Neale Hurston told us, "If you are silent about your pain, they'll kill you and say you enjoyed it."

This first appeared in Salon, *a website located at https://www.salon.com, on February 25, 2014.*

What My First Pregnancy Taught Me about Birth Justice

Ruth Jeannoel

After discovering I was pregnant for a second time, I had concerns that my previous cesarean section would keep me from having a vaginal birth. But what I learned after speaking with medical professionals and reading up on vaginal birth after cesarean (VBAC) is that it is possible with the appropriate resources.

I also came to realize that the medical community needs to do more to support women of color, particularly Black women, who must confront a number of hurdles in order to have a VBAC.

All across the country there, has been an injection of #BlackLivesMatter in our decades-long Black liberation movement. Reproductive justice, including birth justice, is a critical part of those efforts. Birth justice includes making sure Black moms have full control of their own health and birth process through proper childbirth education and community resources.

It was around 9:30 p.m. on October 22, 2008, when I began to have contractions, and I went to the hospital. I was about thirty-two weeks into my first pregnancy, which was well before my "safe period" of thirty-seven weeks, which in 2008 was described as the stage when the fetus has fully developed. (The "safe period" has since changed to thirty-nine weeks.) Within six hours of labor, I developed preeclampsia, which is a pregnancy condition affecting as many as 8 percent of all pregnancies and can be deadly for Black women.[1]

At about 10:30 p.m., the doctors explained I would need an emergency cesarean or else I could lose the little one I had been carrying.

I was scared: at the age of twenty-one, I had to have major surgery.

The nurses quickly changed my gown, gave me an epidural, and moved me from my hospital room to surgery. I kept thinking about how I didn't want any of this because I wanted to give birth naturally and without any pain relief medication, but it sounded so urgent. It sounded like I needed to really have a cesarean for both my safety and the health of my baby.

And so on October 22 at 11:59 p.m., I had a C-section.

C-section rates are declining in the United States, but Black women continue to have them more frequently than their white counterparts. According to 2014 data from the Centers for Disease Control and Prevention, the cesarean delivery rate "declined for non-Hispanic white women for the fifth consecutive year, down 2% from 32.0% in 2013 to 31.4% in 2014 and 4% from the 2009 peak. Rates declined 1% for both non-Hispanic black (from 35.8% to 35.6%) and Hispanic women (32.3% to 31.9%). For the second year in a row, non-Hispanic white women had the lowest cesarean delivery rate; non-Hispanic black women continued to have the highest rate."[2]

Throughout my pregnancy, I saw a midwife at a birth center who ultimately was not with me when I developed preeclampsia and had to go under the knife. I felt disempowered because everything happened so fast, and it seemed as if all of the decisions were made for me.

After the surgery, my family and close friends were glad that the baby and I were both safe. But beneath their concern for our safety, I could see there was an underlying stigma around having a cesarean birth. Even though the C-section was not planned, I would get looked down on as if I weren't "woman enough" because I didn't have a vaginal birth. I felt ashamed and didn't know how to share my birth story because, in a way, I had lost decision-making control over it. I was unprepared to deal with the stigma that was attached to having a C-section.

A couple years after having my first child, I began to have a different understanding of what reproductive justice is and began to reflect more on what it would look like in my own life. The SisterSong Women of Color Reproductive Justice Collective describes reproductive justice as "the human right to have children, not have children, and parent the children we have in safe and healthy environments."[3]

During that period between my two pregnancies, after having more conversations with other mothers and hearing different birth stories, I began to understand that what I was attempting to deal with wasn't about vaginal birth versus cesarean birth; it was about women having the bodily autonomy to make their own decisions.

I told myself that if I ever got pregnant again, I would make sure that I had all the necessary information to ultimately decide how my birth went: I would do everything in my power to have a vaginal birth. For example, had I known in advance that I may be susceptible to pre-eclampsia, I would have looked into methods to lower the risks of complications, like a low-dose aspirin regimen.[4]

While telling everyone who asked (or didn't) that I would have a vaginal birth, I ran into several myths. The main one was that you can't have a vaginal birth after a C-section. It just didn't make sense to me because I knew that birthing was a natural process, meaning that I needed to trust my body and know that every pregnancy was different and that my body could handle a vaginal birth.

I began reading and asking my ob-gyn about vaginal births, and she described the risks and benefits of having a VBAC and emphasized that it was very possible. And she, of course, was right.

As research from the National Institutes of Health explains, "VBAC is a reasonable and safe choice for the majority of women with prior cesarean."[5] The American College of Obstetricians and Gynecologists agrees, adding that "most" women with one prior cesarean and "some" women with two prior cesareans are candidates for VBAC.[6]

The main problem a woman seeking to have a VBAC might encounter, I found during my research, was a potential uterine rupture. However, a report published in the *Obstetrics & Gynecology* medical journal found

> despite increased rates of VBAC attempt and VBAC failure among black women as compared with other racial groups, black women are significantly less likely to experience a uterine rupture. It is unclear whether this discrepancy in magnitudes of risks and benefits across race associated with VBAC trials is attributable to selection bias or inherent racial differences.[7]

My research helped me to better understand that the risks associated with a VBAC weren't as high as I'd thought.

When I found out that I was pregnant five years later, I moved forward with my plan to have a VBAC. By that time, I had moved to another state, and VBACs were not as common or accessible in Florida as they were in Massachusetts.

I quickly learned that not every ob-gyn I encountered performs VBACs. In South Florida, I had only three doctors to choose from. With help from my doula, I was able to find the right one and a hospital where VBACs were an option.

Unfortunately, in Black communities, not everyone will have access to doctors who do VBACs. Because of the higher risk of uterine rupture, many hospitals, especially in low-income communities of color, are not able to make this accommodation. Also, I found that doctors often do not promote VBACs; therefore, many women who may want to have one may not know that such an option exists.

In 2014, at thirty-seven weeks, I was able to have a successful VBAC and give birth to my second born. I was proud of myself that I was able to have a vaginal birth under my own terms in a hospital room with an amazing team of doctors.

It's important to dispel the myth that you can't have a vaginal birth after a previous C-section. Doctors and the medical community have a responsibility to make sure that all women have the appropriate information to make an informed decision over their bodies. It will always be a woman's right to choose how she wants to have her child and where she wants to have her child if her local hospital doesn't offer the services she requires.

Notes

1. Steven Reinberg, "Give Aspirin to All Pregnant Women at Risk of Preeclampsia: US Experts," *US News & World Report*, September 8, 2014, https://health.usnews.com/health-news/articles/2014/09/08/give-aspirin-to-all-pregnant-women-at-risk-of-preeclampsia-us-experts.

2. Brady E. Hamilton et al., "Births: Final Data for 2014," *National Vital Statistics Report* 62, no. 12 (December 2015): 1–64, https://www.cdc.gov/nchs/data/nvsr/nvsr64/nvsr64_12.pdf.

3. "What Is Reproductive Justice," SisterSong, accessed August 14, 2020, https://www.sistersong.net/reproductive-justice/.

4. Martha Kempner, "Panel Recommends Low-Dose Aspirin Regimen for Women at Risk of Preeclampsia," *Rewire.News*, April 9, 2014, https://rewire.news/article/2014/04/09/panel-recommends-low-dose-aspirin-regimen-women-risk-preeclampsia/.

5. Jeanne-Marie Guise et al., "Vaginal Birth after Cesarean: New Insights," *Evidence Report, Technology Assessment* 191 (March 2010): 1–397, https://pubmed.ncbi.nlm.nih.gov/20629481/.

6. Laurie Barclay, "ACOG Issues Less Restrictive Guidelines for Vaginal

Birth after Cesarean Delivery," Medscape, July 22, 2010, https://www.
medscape.com/viewarticle/725597.

7. Alison G. Cahill et al., "Racial Disparity in the Success and
    Complications of Vaginal Birth after Cesarean Delivery," *Obstetrics and
    Gynecology* 111, no. 3 (March 2008): 654–58, https://pubmed.ncbi.nlm.
    nih.gov/18310368/.

Originally published on Rewire.News *on May 24, 2016.*

Serena Williams Could Insist That Doctors Listen to Her. Most Black Women Can't.

Elizabeth Dawes Gay

Some cultural moments are just made for Ida insight. And when tennis star Serena Williams shared her near-death experience after childbirth, Elizabeth Dawes Gay jumped into action. She knew the statistics, knew how common it is for Black women to have complications before, during, and after labor. But she also knew that, as scary and potentially tragic as Williams's story was, it was an opportunity to underline that, in the United States, celebrity, money, and the best healthcare possible cannot ensure a Black woman a healthy or happy birth.

The world got to learn a little bit more about pro-tennis player Serena Williams's experience giving birth to baby girl Alexis Olympia through her January 2018 interview with *Vogue* magazine. That little bit is now shining a big spotlight on the American healthcare system and the hurdles and dangers women face bringing life into the world.

Williams delivered Alexis Olympia by emergency C-section after the baby's heart rate declined. All was well until the next day when Williams felt short of breath. She immediately brought this to the attention of her care providers and requested a computed tomography (CT) scan because of her history of pulmonary embolism—that is, blood clots in her lungs—but they thought her pain medication was making her confused. Nonetheless, she was able to insist on a CT scan and get an accurate diagnosis and appropriate treatment.

Williams is an international superstar, a sports phenom, and on track to set a new record for Grand Slam victories. But for all her celebrity and status, she is still a Black woman in America. And as such, her birthing experience can't be separated from the birthing experiences of so many Black women in America, who are far more likely than white women to suffer serious complications or die as a result of childbirth. When discussing Williams's maternal health emergency, it's vital to address the role played by racism and racial discrimination—a requirement to sustainably address the United States' growing maternal health problem.

Black women are nearly four times more likely to die from pregnancy and childbirth than white women, and they are also more likely to experience severe maternal morbidity, such as a heart attack, hemorrhage, sepsis, or blood clots like Williams did, regardless of their level of education or income.[1] In fact, data from the New York City Department of Health show that Black college-educated women were more likely than white women who hadn't completed high school to experience adverse maternal health outcomes.

Knowledge and money aren't enough to save Black women because racism trumps all.

Denying that fact or failing to mention it when the opportunity presents itself, hinders meaningful progress on maternal health in the United States, where maternal mortality is rising instead of declining as it is in the rest of the developed world. We won't go far in solving the American maternal health problem without first acknowledging and then addressing how racism—both inside and outside the healthcare setting—harms Black moms.

Racial discrimination within the healthcare setting is a modern problem built on the legacy of slavery, reproductive oppression, and control of medicine and Black bodies. It's important to remember that the white medical establishment worked hard to eliminate Black midwives through smear-messaging campaigns claiming they were "dirty" and by passing laws restricting their practice. Today, racial discrimination in clinical care presents in a variety of ways. Research has shown that implicit racial bias may cause doctors to spend less time with Black patients and that Black people receive less-effective care. Doctors are also more likely to underestimate the pain of their Black patients. And anecdotes of disrespect and mistreatment abound.

To those familiar with this history and research, the fact that Williams's doctors didn't initially take her calls for care seriously isn't surprising. Williams knew her history with blood clots and knew what she was experiencing, but her providers weren't inclined to trust her. How many other Black women have died or nearly died because their providers refused to listen to them or because these women didn't have the power to insist?

Beyond that, racism outside of the clinical setting is a much broader problem that influences health even before people can interact with the healthcare system. Black people experience chronic stress resulting from exposure to overt and covert racism and microaggression, which can range from something as basic as intentionally avoiding eye contact to the extreme of being harassed, abused, or killed by police. And racist policies—like those dictating where our children go to school, whether we can vote, how clean the water in our communities needs to be, who patrols our neighborhoods, and on and on—create structural inequalities that disadvantage Black people and set us up to fail.

The chronic stress arising from racial discrimination and racist policies targeting those both Black and female takes a toll on the body and disrupts the normal biological processes necessary for optimal health. Decades of research has established a link between stress and health, specifically the negative health consequences of living while Black in America, regardless of socioeconomic status.

Nation contributor Dani McClain described for the magazine her experience dealing with this knowledge while pregnant with her daughter. She wrote, "You might think that I don't need to worry: I eat a healthy diet; I don't have high blood pressure or diabetes. I am not poor; I have private insurance and a master's degree. I started prenatal appointments at 10 weeks and haven't missed one. But I'm under no illusion that my class privilege will save me."[2]

Dani also shared that she stopped watching the news during her last trimester—the accounts of police violence against Black bodies were just too much. She wasn't wrong in doing so. Research by Dr. Fleda Mask Jackson found a connection between perceived police violence and depressive symptoms among pregnant Black women. The risk of depressive symptoms was higher in those pregnant Black women who also already had a male child. Yet much of the discourse from care providers and public health professionals has neglected to explicitly name the role of racial discrimination and systemic oppression in Black maternal outcomes.

California is considered a leader in maternal health because it has succeeded in reducing maternal mortality for all moms in the state, mostly through enhanced safety protocols that help hospitals manage emergencies during labor and delivery and provide higher-quality care. The maternal mortality rate declined from 10.9 deaths per 100,000 live births in 2000 to 7.3 deaths per 100,000 live births in 2013. Despite these gains, the maternal mortality rate for Black women in California is 26.4 deaths per 100,000 live births. When Dr. Elliott Main, medical director of the California Maternal Quality Care Collaborative, was asked in a November 2017 interview about ongoing disparities in maternal health, he failed to explicitly mention racism or racial discrimination, focusing instead on differential treatment and resources at hospitals where Black women give birth.

As a public health professional, I have attended dozens of conferences, meetings, and briefings on maternal health. I have often been disheartened to hear public health leaders and researchers neglect to explicitly call out the role of racism in maternal health, even when asked about it directly. Providers, researchers, and public health professionals are more inclined to point to the high prevalence of chronic diseases, such as high blood pressure and diabetes, and to the epidemic of obesity in the Black community. This places the onus for large-scale change on individuals rather than the systems that we know cause harm. Nor does it acknowledge how racial oppression contributes to the overrepresentation of chronic disease and illness among Black people.

To advance maternal health in the United States, we have to address our race problem, and that starts by naming it. We must acknowledge that racial discrimination affects Black mothers, even those as celebrated as Serena Williams. Williams acknowledged the outpouring of stories that followed her going public with her own, writing on Facebook, "I didn't expect that sharing our family's story of Olympia's birth and all of [the] complications after giving birth would start such an outpouring of discussion from women—especially Black women—who have faced similar complications and women whose problems go unaddressed." She encouraged women to "continue to tell those stories. This helps. We can help others." That's the first step, yes—but providers, researchers, and public health experts also need to hear our stories and acknowledge the role of racism.

Notes

1. Elizabeth A. Howell et al. "Site of Delivery Contribution to Black-White Severe Maternal Morbidity Disparity," *American Journal of Obstetrics & Gynecology* 215, no. 2 (August 2016): 143–52, http://dx.doi.org/10.1016/j.ajog.2016.05.007.
2. Dani McClain, "What It's Like to Be Black and Pregnant When You Know How Dangerous That Can Be," *The Nation*, March 6, 2017, https://www.thenation.com/article/archive/what-its-like-to-be-black-and-pregnant-when-you-know-how-dangerous-that-can-be/.

This article was originally published by The Nation *magazine on January 18, 2018, and is republished here with permission.*

Choice Under Fire: Issues Surrounding African American Reproductive Rights

Renee Bracey Sherman

While driving through Memphis, Tennessee, last spring, Cherisse Scott passed antiabortion billboards, paid for by Prolife Across America, which stated, "Dad's princess #♥beat at 18 days" next to the smiling face of a Black infant. Scott, founder and CEO of SisterReach, an Atlanta-based nonprofit committed to supporting reproductive autonomy for women and girls, launched a campaign to remove the billboards from the city's Black communities, claiming the ads are a racist attempt to create division between Black men and women. "They are inflammatory and racist," Scott tells *Ebony*. "They were put up to make us invisible and dismiss why we have to have abortions."

According to the Guttmacher Institute, nearly one in four cisgender women will have an abortion by age forty-five.[1] Research shows Black women make up one-third of American women who have abortions, although they are only 13 percent of the US female population.[2] Black women are disproportionately more likely to have an abortion, a fact the Guttmacher Institute attributes to the lack of consistent access to quality contraception and healthcare. The US Department of Health and Human Services reports that Black women are also three to four times more likely than white women to die from pregnancy-related causes.[3] For some, access to contraception and safe abortion care can mean the difference between life and death.

In response to Prolife Across America's campaign, SisterReach erected its own billboards to highlight the need for access to quality schools, healthcare, transportation and safe neighborhoods. "We're pushing back to change the narrative," states Scott. "We don't need outsiders to tell us about our lives." She says this mission is not only about abortion; it's also about ensuring that Black women can raise their families with dignity, with a living wage, and without fear of violence.

Yamani Hernandez, executive director of the National Network of Abortion Funds, believes it is important to fully understand how abortion fits into Black women's lives. A 2010 report from the Insight Center for Community Economic Development found that single Black women have a median wealth of $100, compared to $41,500 for white women.[4] "Given the wealth disparities Black women face, it's even more important that they have the freedom and agency to decide whether and when they become parents," she explains.

A recent study from the University of California supports Hernandez's theory; women who sought an abortion but were turned away due to the state's gestational limits were three times as likely to be living in poverty two years later than those who were able to access the procedure.[5] Researchers say this is reflective of the economics of abortion, with the Guttmacher Institute finding three-quarters of women citing the inability to afford a child and the impact it would have on the children they already have as reasons for wanting an abortion.[6] Data reveals that over 60 percent of women seeking abortions had at least one child, with more than 30 percent already parenting more than two children. Hernandez says the ability to access abortion care could "mean securing economic sustainability to become the parent they want to be and have the families they want to have."

A 2013 poll conducted by Belden Russonello Strategists LLC found that 80 percent of African Americans believe abortion should be legal and accessible, regardless of personal stances on the issue, with the opinions remaining favorable among weekly church attendees and conservatives.[7] Rev. Emma Akpan, a North Carolina–based member of the African Methodist Episcopal Church, feels this is why faith leaders must move away from talking about abortion in a stigmatizing way because it isn't representative of what communities actually believe. "That rhetoric is dangerous because women who may need an abortion will one day sit in our pews. It leads them to believe that they are sinful to request an essential piece of reproductive health care."

Of course, not everyone supports our right to choose. Ryan Bomberger of the Radiance Foundation, an organization that creates antiabortion multimedia ads targeted at the Black community, believes there is no lack of access to contraception for Black women and that abortion, not police brutality, is the civil rights issue of today. He says he also believes heterosexual families and "truth" are the "best weapons" against poverty, not access to abortion. Bomberger and many Republican politicians support crisis pregnancy centers, some of which have been found to distribute incorrect medical information in order to convince women not to seek abortions. Recently, California took action to regulate crisis pregnancy centers and curb the spread of falsehoods.

The Other Issues

Scott says she's open to working with antichoice legislators to ensure that pregnant Black women have access to healthcare, housing, and food, but she feels her hands are tied by legislation, such as Tennessee's Fetal Assault Law, which criminalizes pregnant women who are found with illegal drugs in their systems. Rather than receiving rehabilitation, they are sent to prison, Scott explains. "How are we creating a healthy and safe environment for people when they are scared to walk through the doors of a hospital or doctor's office?" asks Monica Raye Simpson, executive director of SisterSong, a reproductive justice organization based in Atlanta. "This does not promote family values. Instead, it further perpetuates the dismantling of the Black family, which weakens our communities."

For many advocates, the fight for reproductive rights also extends to standing up for women behind bars. Pregnant prisoners often lack access to proper care and are legally shackled during labor in over twenty-five states. "This practice is barbaric and inhumane and should be abolished," says La'Tasha Mayes, executive director of New Voices for Reproductive Justice. "Anti-shackling is a baseline [in the fight for healthcare] for pregnant incarcerated women," notes Mayes, whose organization fights for pre- and postnatal service, abortion, and contraceptive care for imprisoned individuals. The Sentencing Project found that 1 in 19 Black women is likely to be incarcerated, compared with 1 in 118 white women.[8] In addition, the American Medical Association says that between 5 and 10 percent of women are pregnant when they enter correctional facilities.[9]

Of slogans such as "Black Lives Matter, Beginning in the Womb," Mayes says, "It is absolutely shameful that during a transformative movement to liberate Black people in this country, those who oppose the human rights of Black women to control our own bodies seek to co-opt [protest language, such as] #BlackLivesMatter while attempting to undermine the reproductive justice movement."

Bomberger disagrees: "We extolled the truth that Black lives mattered long before the dishonest and propaganda-ridden hashtag movement."

Laying Down the Laws

Abortion is being restricted at record levels. Majority Republican legislatures continue to pass targeted regulation of abortion providers (TRAP) laws, which force clinics to undergo expensive construction changes—including widening hallways and upgrading procedure rooms to hospital standards fit for open-heart surgery—or shut down. Abortion opponents say the laws are designed to make abortion safer, yet research shows complications take place in less than 1 percent of the pregnancy terminations.

In 2013, parts of House Bill (HB) 2, Texas's TRAP law, went into effect, shuttering some clinics and banning abortion after twenty weeks. Although opponents of HB 2 have taken their case to the Supreme Court, its effects are already being felt: In 2012, Texas had forty-one abortion providers, and depending on how the Court rules, they could have fewer than ten.

Legislatures are also making accessing abortion at remaining clinics increasingly difficult. Currently, twenty states require waiting periods of either twenty-four or seventy-two hours, which forces patients to make multiple trips to the clinic. "We found that poor women and those living more than twenty miles from a [Texas] clinic were significantly more likely to say it was difficult to get to these extra, unnecessary visits, and one-third of the women reported the waiting period had a negative effect on their emotional well-being," says Daniel Grossman, MD, of his research at Ibis Reproductive Health. At present, seventeen states mandate counseling, some of which require physicians to educate patients on long-term mental health issues and disseminate medically inaccurate information linking abortion to breast cancer.

Four states—Mississippi, North Dakota, South Dakota, and Wyoming—have only one abortion provider, and more states are slated to join that list. Advocates say the right to abortion is meaningless without access, something many Black women may soon lose, if they haven't already.

Fighting Back

For nearly forty years, the Hyde Amendment has prohibited Medic-aid recipients, military personnel, and others who receive their health insurance through the government from accessing abortions by ban-ning federal funds from covering it. The EACH Woman Act, introduced by Congresswoman Barbara Lee (D-Calif.), seeks to end all abortion-coverage bans. "The EACH Woman Act will get us closer to a day when the right to an abortion is not only a right in words but in reality," offers Hernandez. Fifteen states allow state Medicaid funds to cover abor-tion, but if clinics continue to close, advocates believe it may not matter because the ability of a woman to terminate her pregnancy has already been decimated in many states.

As more clinics close and access dwindles, advocates point to the hypocrisy of pro-life politicians allowing Black families to live in poverty. "If they truly cared for Black lives, they would be present for all issues that impact Black people," says Simpson. "They would invest their money and time building relationships with grassroots communities instead of exploiting and shaming people for their human right to self-determine."

Notes

1. "Induced Abortion in the United States," Guttmacher Institute, September 2019, https://www.guttmacher.org/fact-sheet/induced-abortion-united-states.
2. Guttmacher Institute, "Induced Abortion."
3. "Pregnancy Mortality Surveillance System," Centers for Disease Control and Prevention, last modified February 4, 2020, https://www.cdc.gov/reproductivehealth/maternal-mortality/pregnancy-mortality-surveillance-system.htm.
4. "Women, Race and Wealth," Insight Center, accessed August 14, 2020, https://insightcced.org/women-race-and-wealth/.
5. Diana Greene, "Turnaway Study," ANSIRH, accessed August 14, 2020, https://www.ansirh.org/research/turnaway-study.
6. Guttmacher Institute, "Induced Abortion."

7. Belden Russonello Strategists LLC, *African American Attitudes on Abortion Contraception and Teen Sexual Health*, February 2003, http://www.brspoll.com/uploads/files/African-American%20Attitudes%20on%20Abortion%20Contraception%20and%20Teen%20Sexual%20Health.pdf.

8. Ashley Nellis, *The Color of Justice: Racial and Ethnic Disparity in State Prisons* (Washington, DC: The Sentencing Project, 2016), https://www.sentencingproject.org/wp-content/uploads/2016/06/The-Color-of-Justice-Racial-and-Ethnic-Disparity-in-State-Prisons.pdf.

9. Jennifer G. Clarke and Rachel E. Simon, "Shackling and Separation: Motherhood in Prison," *Virtual Mentor* 15, no. 9 (2013): 779–85, https://journalofethics.ama-assn.org/article/shackling-and-separation-motherhood-prison/2013-09.

Originally published on Ebony *on November 2, 2015.*

The Story That's Taken Ten Years to Tell: On Abortion, Race, and the Power of Story

Shanelle Matthews

"Are you in college?" The doctor could tell from my face I wasn't at all interested in having a conversation. "You speak well. I mean, you're articulate."

The wrinkles in my forehead deepened. I wrung my fingers tightly around the scratchy blue exam gown and briefly thought about the woman who had worn it before me: What was she like? I looked at him, desperately wanting to not have to actually speak, wishing he could just read my mind.

"Yes. I'm in college," I responded shortly. I was really thinking, "That's none of your business and really, is this the time to make small talk? When your elbow is deep in my vagina?" But I was grateful for him, so I frowned and looked away.

The room didn't feel particularly uncomfortable. I mostly gazed at the ceiling tiles, counting square by square. Occasionally, I peeked down. Over the long sheet that draped across my knees, I could see my feet, not really manicured, resting awkwardly in the titanium stirrups, straddling the doctor's full head of curly hair.

"We're just about done."

I sighed out a breath of relief. My abortion was almost over.

My abortion experience isn't the kind that might be featured in a Lifetime movie. By that I mean, I was eighteen, technically an adult. I consented to having sex, although I had never learned how to really protect myself. I lived in California, which is a state that provides emergency Medicaid for women who need financial assistance to help cover the costs of abortion care. The circumstances in which I found myself were not particularly difficult but only because at the time I didn't know any better.

I was six months out of high school, a full-time student-athlete living away from home. I was privileged enough to be going to college and receiving some scholarship money to do so. One day during practice, I found myself violently ill. Workouts were hard and often induced vomiting but not like this. I counted the days since my last period and realized I might be pregnant.

I was dating my teammate, who was several years older than me. He was sexually experienced, and while I wasn't a virgin, I had dated mostly women and had not been very sexually involved with men. He said he'd used protection. I believed him.

Upon receiving my pregnancy test results at the student health center, the nurse searchingly said, "Congratulations?" Her quizzical tone confused me. I gave her the side-eye and told her that I was on the track team and wouldn't be celebrating this pregnancy. She pointed me in the direction of Planned Parenthood.

I walked and sobbed. I could hear my dad's harsh, deep voice. "Keep your legs closed! Boys only want one thing from you!"

My parents meant well, but in my home, sex education was a combination of scare tactics, none of which taught me how to effectively and safely prepare for sex. I can't remember learning in school the importance of contraception or the implications of becoming pregnant or getting an STD. I do vaguely remember coming to school some days and someone would be missing. The hallways were filled with whispers that "she'd gotten knocked up and sent to the school for pregnant girls." In hindsight, how fucked up is that?

Abortions are expensive. I didn't have any money, and even though I knew my parents would probably help me, I was scared to tell them. They'd be so disappointed. Planned Parenthood sent me to see if I qualified for emergency Medicaid. I did. The office was bustling with people desperate to get financial assistance for themselves and their sick family members. The clerk was helpful but blunt. She couldn't be bothered with details, and why should she have to be?

I had to lie to my coaches. I couldn't tell them I'd had an abortion. What would they think of me? I kept it from all but one or two of my teammates. I felt a lot of shame about my decision. Not because I thought it was morally wrong but because I had to hide it from so many people in my life. The stigma around abortion meant that I had to lie to people because telling them opened me up to unnecessarily punitive judgment. The hardest part about having an abortion was the stigmatizing environment in which I was having it. I knew it was the only decision for me, and even though I didn't know a lot of women who'd had them, I knew they were ashamed—so I was ashamed too. We've created a culture in which we've attached a certain set of feelings to a specific set of circumstances. I was ashamed and grieving out of obligation when all I really felt was relief.

Ten years later, there is so much about my abortion story that's more fucked up than I could understand then. The shame that is associated with abortion and other difficult reproductive health decisions forces women to display an act of grieving whether they feel that way or not. The alternative meaning you're entirely morally bankrupt. The doctor's comment about my being articulate meant he had made some assumptions about me (and other women who sat straddling his head full of curls). What the implications of those assumptions are I didn't know, but it felt unnerving. Every day I work in reproductive justice trying to compel other people to be brave and share their stories. But it has taken me a decade to tell this story, and that's because even within the "movement," there is stigma.

I identify as a Black queer woman. My Blackness makes my story all the more problematic for some people. The assumptions made about Black women's reproductive decisions mean that I will receive less compassion and acceptance than my white counterparts for having had an abortion—especially because I'm not repentant about it. As organizers, we are not always aware of our implicit biases, but there are plenty of white people who, in an effort to make abortion safe and accessible, are reaffirming negative stereotypes about women of color. This happens through negligent storytelling that says there is a right and wrong way to have the need to access an abortion.

The narrative that abortion gives women and trans people an opportunity to live the rest of our lives, to become doctors or lawyers or whatever, isn't true for everyone. For some of us, abortion just provides one more day. One more day to live our lives exactly the way we want to. For some of us, the decision isn't political; it's essential. It is essential to taking care of the children we already have, to circumventing difficult medical experiences, or to just not be pregnant. There is nothing heroic about having an abortion. It is an essential part of reproductive healthcare.

Every year on the anniversary of my abortion, I take off of work. Not to grieve but to celebrate: because of my right to choose, I am living my best life. Making the decision to have an abortion didn't mean I had the rest of my life; it just meant that I had one more day to live exactly the way I wanted, and for that I'm grateful.

Originally published on the Crunk Feminist Collective *blog on January 22, 2015.*

"Commonsense Childbirth":
A Q&A with Midwife Jennie Joseph

Elizabeth Dawes Gay

Jennie Joseph's philosophy is simple: treat patients like the people they are. Originally from England, Joseph has found this goes a long way when it comes to her midwifery practice and the health of Black mothers and babies.

In the United States, Black women are disproportionately affected by poor maternal and infant health outcomes. Black women are more likely to experience maternal and infant death, pregnancy-related illness, premature birth, low birth weight, and stillbirth.[1] Beyond the data, personal accounts of Black women's birthing experiences detail discrimination, mistreatment, and violation of basic human rights.[2] Media like the 2016 film, *The American Dream*, share the maternity experiences of Black women in their own voices.[3]

A new generation of activists, advocates, and concerned medical professionals have mobilized across the country to improve Black maternal and infant health, including through the birth justice and reproductive justice movements.[4]

Joseph founded a nonprofit, Commonsense Childbirth, in 1998 to inspire change in maternity care to better serve people of color. As a licensed midwife, Joseph seeks to transform how care is provided in a clinical setting.

At her clinics, which are located in Central Florida, a welcoming smile and a conversation mark the start of each patient visit. Having a dialogue with patients about their unique needs, desires, and circumstances is a practice Joseph said has contributed to her patients having "chunky," healthy full-term babies. Dialogue and care that centers the patient cost nothing, Joseph told *Rewire.News* in an interview earlier this summer.

Joseph also offers training to midwives, doulas, community health workers, and other professionals in culturally competent, patient-centered care through her Commonsense Childbirth School of Midwifery, which launched in 2009. And in 2015, Joseph launched the National Perinatal Task Force, a network of perinatal healthcare and service providers who are committed to working in underserved communities in order to transform maternal health outcomes in the United States.

Rewire.News spoke with Joseph about her tireless work to improve maternal and perinatal health in the Black community.

Rewire: What motivates and drives you each day?

Jennie Joseph: I moved to the United States in 1989 [from the United Kingdom], and each year, it becomes more and more apparent that to address the issues I care deeply about, I have to put action behind all the talk.

I'm particularly concerned about maternal and infant morbidity and mortality that plague communities of color and specifically African Americans. Most people don't know that three to four times as many Black women die during pregnancy and childbirth in the United States than their white counterparts.

When I arrived in the United States, I had to start a home birth practice to be able to practice at all, and it was during that time that I realized very few people of color were accessing care that way. I learned about the disparities in maternal health around the same time, and I felt compelled to do something about it.

My motivation is based on the fact that what we do [at Commonsense Childbirth] works so well it's almost unconscionable not to continue doing it. I feel driven and personally responsible because I've figured out that there are some very simple things that anyone can do to make an impact. It's such a win-win. Everybody wins: patients, staff, communities, healthcare agencies.

There are only a few of us attacking this aggressively, with few resources and without support. I've experienced so much frustration, anger, and resignation about the situation because I feel like this is not something that people in the field don't know about. I know there have been some efforts but with little results. There are simple and cost-effective things that can be done. Even small interventions can make such a tremendous difference, and I don't understand why we can't have more support and more interest in moving the needle in a more effective way.

I give up sometimes. I get so frustrated. Emotions vie for time and energy, but those very same emotions force me to keep going. I feel a constant drive to be in action and to be practical in achieving and getting results.

Rewire: In your opinion, what are some barriers to progress on maternal health and how can they be overcome?

Joseph: The solutions that have been generated are the same, year in and year out, but are not really solutions. [Healthcare professionals and the industry] keep pushing money into a broken system without recognizing where there are gaps and barriers, and we keep doing the same thing.

One solution that has not worked is the approach of hiring practitioners without a thought to whether the practitioner is really a match for the community that they are looking to serve. Additionally, there is the fact that the practitioner alone is not going to be able to make much difference. There has to be a concerted effort to have the entire healthcare team be willing to support the work. If the front desk and access points are not in tune with why we need to address this issue in a specific way, what happens typically is that people do not necessarily feel welcomed or supported or respected.

The world's best practitioner could be sitting down the hall but never actually see the patient because the patient leaves before they get assistance or before they even get to make an appointment. People get tired of being looked down upon, shamed, ignored, or perhaps not treated well. And people know which hospitals and practitioners provide competent care and which practices are culturally safe.

I would like to convince people to try something different, for real. One of those things is an open-door triage at all ob-gyn facilities, similar to an emergency room, so that all patients seeking maternity care are seen for a first visit no matter what.

Another thing would be for practitioners to provide patient-centered care for all patients regardless of their ability to pay. You don't have to have cultural competency training; you just have to listen and believe what the patients are telling you—period.

Practitioners also have a role in dismantling the institutionalized racism that is causing such harm. You don't have to speak a specific language to be kind. You just have to think a little bit and put yourself in that person's shoes. You have to understand she might be in fear for her baby's health or her own health. You can smile. You can touch respectfully. You can make eye contact. You can find a real translator. You can do things if you choose to. Or you can stay in place in a system you know is broken, doing business as usual, and continue to feel bad doing the work you once loved.

Rewire: You emphasize patient-centered care. Why aren't other providers doing the same, and how can they be convinced to provide this type of care?

Joseph: I think that is the crux of the matter: the convincing part. One, it's a shame that I have to go around convincing anyone about the benefits of patient-centered care. And two, the typical response from medical staff is "Yeah, but the cost. It's expensive. The bureaucracy, the system . . ." There is no disagreement that this should be the gold standard of care, but providers say their setup doesn't allow for it or that it really wouldn't work. Keep in mind that patient-centered care also means equitable care—the kind of care we all want for ourselves and our families.

One of the things we do at my practice (and that providers have the most resistance to) is that we see everyone for that initial visit. We've created a triage entry point to medical care but also to social support, financial triage, actual emotional support, and recognition and understanding for the patient that yes, you have a problem, but we are here to work with you to solve it.

All of those things get to happen because we offer the first visit, regardless of their ability to pay. In the absence of that opportunity, the barrier to quality care itself is so detrimental: it's literally a matter of life and death.

Rewire: How do you cover the cost of the first visit if someone cannot pay?

Joseph: If we have a grant, we use those funds to help us pay our overhead. If we don't, we wait until we have the women on Medicaid and try to do back billing on those visits. If the patient doesn't have Medicaid, we use the funds we earn from delivering babies of mothers who do have insurance and can pay the full price.

Rewire: You've talked about ensuring that expecting mothers have accessible, patient-centered maternity care. How exactly are you working to achieve that?

Joseph: I want to empower community-based perinatal health workers (such as nurse practitioners) who are interested in providing care to communities in need and encourage them to become entrepreneurial. As long as people have the credentials or license to provide prenatal, postpartum, and women's healthcare and are interested in independent practice, then my vision is that they build a private practice for themselves. Based on the concept that to get real change in maternal health outcomes in the United States, women need access to specific kinds of healthcare—not just any old healthcare, but the kind that is humane, patient-centered, woman-centered, family-centered, and culturally safe and where providers believe that the patients matter. That kind of care will transform outcomes instantly.

I coined the phrase "easy access clinics" to describe retail women's health clinics, like a CVS MinuteClinic, that serve as a first entry point to care in a community rather than in a big healthcare system. At the Orlando Easy Access Clinic, women receive their first appointment regardless of their ability to pay. People find out about us via word of mouth; they know what we do before they get here.

We are at the point where even the local government agencies send patients to us. They know that even while someone's Medicaid application is in pending status, we will still see them and start their care, as well as help them access their Medicaid benefits as part of our commitment to their overall well-being.

Others are already replicating this model across the country, and we are doing research as we go along. We have created a system that becomes sustainable because of the trust and loyalty of the patients and their willingness to support us in supporting them.

Rewire: What are your thoughts on the decision in Florida not to expand Medicaid at this time?[5]

Joseph: I consider healthcare care a human right. That's what I know. That's how I was trained. That's what I lived all the years I was in Europe. And to be here and see this wanton disregard for health and humanity breaks my heart.

Not expanding Medicaid has such deep repercussions on patients and providers. We hold on by a very thin thread. We can't get our claims paid. We have all kinds of hoops and confusion. There is a lack of interest and accountability from insurance payers, and we are struggling so badly.

Healthcare is a human right: It can't be anything else.

Rewire: You launched the National Perinatal Task Force in 2015. What do you hope to accomplish through that effort?

Joseph: The main goal of the National Perinatal Task Force is to connect perinatal service providers, lift each other up, and establish community recognition of sites committed to a certain standard of care.

The facilities of task force members are identified as Perinatal Safe Spots. A Perinatal Safe Spot could be an educational or social site, a moms' group, a breastfeeding circle, a local doula practice, or a community center. It could be anywhere, but it has got to be in a community with what I call a "materno-toxic" area—an area where you know without any doubt that mothers are in jeopardy. It is an area where social determinants of health (such as housing, nutrition, and transportation) are affecting mom's and baby's chances of being strong and whole and hearty. Therein, we need to put a safe spot right in the heart of that materno-toxic area so that she has a better chance for survival.

The task force is a group of maternity service providers and concerned community members willing to be a safe spot for that area. Members also recognize each other across the nation; we support each other and learn from our best practices.

People who are working in their communities to improve maternal and infant health come forward all the time, as they are feeling alone, quietly doing the best they can for their community, with little or nothing. Don't be discouraged. You can get a lot done with pure willpower and determination.

Rewire: Do you have funding to run the National Perinatal Task Force?

Joseph: Not yet. We have got the task force up and running as best we can under my nonprofit Commonsense Childbirth. I have not asked for funding or donations because I wanted to see if I could get the task force off the ground first.

There are thirty Perinatal Safe Spots across the United States that are listed on the website currently. The current goal is to house and support the supporters, recognize those people working on the ground, and share information with the public. The next step will be to strengthen the task force and bring funding for stability and growth.

Rewire: You're featured in the new film *The American Dream*. How did that happen and what are you planning to do next?

Joseph: The Italian filmmaker Paolo Patruno got on a plane on his own dime and brought his cameras to Florida. We were planning to talk about Black midwifery. Once we started filming, women were sharing so authentically that we said this is about women's voices being heard. I would love to tease that dialogue forward, and I am planning to go to four or five cities where I can show the film and host a town hall gathering to capture what the community has to say about maternal health. I want to hear their voices. So far, the film has been screened publicly in Oakland and Kansas City, and the full documentary is already available on YouTube.

Rewire: The Black Mamas Matter Toolkit was published this past June by the Center for Reproductive Rights to support human rights–based policy advocacy on maternal health.[6] What about the toolkit or other resources do you find helpful for thinking about solutions to poor maternal health in the Black community?

Joseph: The toolkit is the most succinct and comprehensive thing I've seen since I've been doing this work. It felt like, "At last!"

One of the most exciting things for me is that the toolkit seems to have covered every angle of this problem. It tells the truth about what's happening for Black women and actually all women everywhere as far as maternity care is concerned.

There is a need for us to recognize how the system has taken agency and power away from women and placed it in the hands of large health systems where institutionalized racism is causing much harm. The toolkit, for the first time, in my opinion, really addresses all of these ills and posits some very clear thoughts and solutions around them. I think it is going to go a long way to begin the change we need to see in maternal and child health in the United States.

Rewire: What do you count as one of your success stories?

Joseph: One of my earlier patients was a single mom who had a lot going on and became pregnant by accident. She was very connected to us when she came to the clinic. She became so empowered and wanted a home birth. But she was anemic at the end of her pregnancy, and we recommended a hospital birth. She was empowered through the birth, breastfed her baby, and started a journey toward nursing. She is now about to get her master's degree in nursing, and she wants to come back to work with me. She's determined to come back and serve and give back. She's not the only one. It happens over and over again.

Notes

1. "Pregnancy Mortality Surveillance System," Division of Reproductive Health, National Center for Chronic Disease Prevention, Centers for Disease Control and Prevention, last modified August 7, 2018, https://www.cdc.gov/reproductivehealth/maternalinfanthealth/pregnancy-mortality-surveillance-system.htm; "Racial and Ethnic Disparities in Birth Outcomes," March of Dimes, accessed January 15, 2019, https://www.marchofdimes.org/materials/March-of-Dimes-Racial-and-Ethnic-Disparities_feb-27-2015.pdf; "Stillbirth: Data and Statistics," Centers for Disease Control and Prevention, last modified August 16, 2018, https://www.cdc.gov/ncbddd/stillbirth/data.html.

2. Elizabeth Dawes Gay, "Report: Racial Discrimination Severely Undermines Black Women's Health," *Rewire.News*, August 13, 2014, https://rewire.news/article/2014/08/13/report-racial-discrimination-severely-undermines-black-womens-health/.

3. Paolo Patruno, *The American Dream*, YouTube video, 48:46, November 26, 2015, https://www.youtube.com/watch?time_continue=1&v=_UCXCcTpS6c&feature=emb_logo.

4. Kanya D'Almeida, "Exploring Birth Justice: A Conversation with Julia Chinyere Oparah and Alicia Bonaparte," *Rewire.News*, February 24, 2016, https://rewire.news/article/2016/02/24/exploring-birth-justice-conversation-julia-chinyere-oparah-alicia-bonaparte/; "Black Mamas Matter," Center for Reproductive Justice, accessed January 15, 2019, https://www.reproductiverights.org/feature/black-mamas-matter.

5. Nina Liss-Schultz, "Florida's GOP-Controlled House Refuses Medicaid Expansion, Halts Legislative Session Early," *Rewire.News*, May 1, 2015, https://rewire.news/article/2015/05/01/floridas-gop-controlled-house-refuses-medicaid-expansion-halts-legislative-session-early/.

6. Center for Reproductive Justice, "Black Mamas Matter."

Originally published on Rewire.News *on July 26, 2016.*

Insurance Coverage of Doula Care Would Benefit Patients and Service Providers Alike

Elizabeth Dawes Gay

Despite spending more on pregnancy-related care than any other nation, the US healthcare system continues to fail mothers and babies, especially those of African descent.[1] Black women are three times more likely to die from pregnancy-related causes than white women (42.8 versus 12.5 per 100,000 live births).[2]

Furthermore, there has been little policy change that would support improved maternal health outcomes. For example, a 2013 Medicaid services rule revision allowed reimbursement of preventive services recommended by a physician or licensed provider, including those provided by nonlicensed service providers, such as doulas.[3] Only the states of Oregon and Minnesota have taken legislative action since then to provide doulas with Medicaid reimbursement for their services. Logistical challenges and a lack of clear guidance for implementation from the Centers for Medicare and Medicaid Services means states would have to invest in configuring new policies and procedures for doula reimbursement.

This is bad news for Black women and Black doulas alike.

Like so many other things about the US healthcare system, insurance coverage restrictions on doula care create unnecessary hurdles for women seeking assistance during childbirth and those who provide care.

The report *Overdue: Medicaid and Private Insurance Coverage of Doula Care to Strengthen Maternal and Infant Health* notes that doula care is associated with reductions in the likelihood of medical interventions during labor and delivery, such as epidurals and cesarean sections.[4] It is also associated with shorter labors, higher newborn health indicators, positive birth experiences, and increased breastfeeding initiation.[5] Black women—who suffer disproportionately from negative pregnancy-related outcomes—could benefit the most from insurance coverage of doula care.

Cost is a significant barrier to receiving doula support, and lack of insurance coverage makes it difficult for Black women to make a living from providing doula care.

Shantae Johnson is a nutrition policy specialist for racial and ethnic approaches to community health in Oregon and a doula trained by the National Association to Advance Black Birth, formerly the International Center for Traditional Childbearing. She says that she has had difficulty getting paid as a doula and instead volunteers her services for free.

"I had a hard time developing a business model. I've been paid once, and that was $100 to provide postpartum support," Johnson told *Rewire. News* in a phone interview.

Johnson, who has experience as a single mother in school trying to make ends meet, did not feel comfortable charging clients referred to her from social service programs. "I was using my own food stamps and resources to bring food for [clients] and make food for postpartum mothers. I would have to ask my family to babysit my kids. It became a burden in a way. [Because I wasn't being paid] my family didn't see value in my doula work, so I eventually lost the support I had to even do it."

Johnson is one of a few doulas who live in a state that has legislation regulating Medicaid coverage of doula care. Oregon and Minnesota Medicaid plans allow coverage for doula care but have experienced challenges with implementation, as the *Overdue* report notes. In Oregon, doulas must partner with a Medicaid-enrolled licensed practitioner who is only reimbursed seventy-five dollars for doula support during a single labor and delivery, although these licensed practitioners can choose to provide the doula more than seventy-five dollars for their services. Johnson volunteers with the Oregon Office of Equity and Inclusion's Traditional Health Worker Commission to help advocate for improved Medicaid reimbursement of doula care.

In the absence of a national policy on reimbursement for doula services in both public and private insurance, many mothers who choose to have the physical and emotional support and healthcare advocacy a doula offers must pay out of pocket. There are a small number of community-based programs that offer doula support at no or low cost to women who could not afford it otherwise. But grant funding for these programs is limited and inconsistent.

In an email to *Rewire.News*, Nan Strauss, director of policy and research at Choices in Childbirth, explained, "A number of programs have started but had to close their doors when the time period for their grant was finished, with repercussions for doulas, women, and communities. To make a difference for the population as a whole, funding for doula support needs to be woven into the fabric of the payment system."

The *Overdue* report recommends that states take advantage of the Medicaid rule allowing reimbursement of doula services or that they mandate both public and private insurance provide comprehensive coverage of doula care.

Funding for doula support could be covered through cost savings to the healthcare system. The *Overdue* report explains that doula care could prevent nearly one-third of cesarean sections, saving more than $2.3 billion annually.[6] Beyond these immediate savings related to labor and delivery, doula care could reduce long-term expenditures by minimizing complications during labor and resulting follow-up care and by increasing positive postpartum behaviors, such as breastfeeding, which is associated with a number of health benefits.[7]

While insurance coverage of doula services could save money and enhance the birth experience and outcomes of women who receive that care, it will not eliminate the racial disparities that persist in the United States.[8] True health equity requires new and numerous efforts to remove social, systemic, and institutionalized factors that preclude healthy pregnancies and safe labor and delivery for Black women. Insurance coverage of doula care is a solid step in the right direction that could particularly benefit Black mothers and service providers.

"Doula support will only be widely available when doulas get fairly paid for their work by both private and government payers," Strauss aptly stated. "Until then, we have an inequitable model where the ability to pay out of pocket or the generosity and donated or discounted labor of a doula determines whether or not a woman can have access to evidence-based practices."

Notes

1. Elisabeth Rosenthal, "American Way of Birth, Costliest in the World," *New York Times*, June 13, 2013, https://www.nytimes.com/2013/07/01/health/american-way-of-birth-costliest-in-the-world.html.
2. "Pregnancy Mortality Surveillance System," Division of Reproductive Health, National Center for Chronic Disease Prevention, Centers for

Disease Control and Prevention, last modified August 7, 2018, https://
www.cdc.gov/reproductivehealth/maternal-mortality/pregnancy-
morality-surveillance-system.htm.

3. "Medicaid and Children's Health Insurance Programs: Essential Health
    Benefits in Alternative Benefit Plans, Eligibility Notices, Fair Hearing
    and Appeal Processes, Premiums and Cost Sharing, Exchanges:
    Eligibility and Enrollment; Final Rule," Centers for Medicare and
    Medicaid Services, 78 Fed Reg 42160, July 15, 2013, https://www.
    govinfo.gov/content/pkg/FR-2013-07-15/html/2013-16271.htm.

4. *Overdue: Medicaid and Private Insurance Coverage of Doula Care to
    Strengthen Maternal and Infant Health*, Choices in Childbirth, January
    2016, https://www.nationalpartnership.org/our-work/resources/health-
    care/maternity/overdue-medicaid-and-private-insurance-coverage-of-
    doula-care-to-strengthen-maternal-and-infant-health-issue-brief.pdf.

5. Katy Backes Kozhimannil et al., "Doula Care, Birth Outcomes, and
    Costs Among Medicaid Beneficiaries," *American Journal of Public
    Health* 103, no. 4 (April 2013): 113–21; Katy Backes Kozhimannil et al.,
    "Doula Care Supports Near-Universal Breastfeeding Initiation among
    Diverse, Low-Income Women," *Journal of Midwifery & Women's Health*
    58, no. 4 (July 2013): 378–82, https://doi.org/10.1111/jmwh.12065.

6. "Doula Care in the US," Choices in Childbirth, accessed January 15,
    2019, https://choicesinchildbirth.org/wp-content/uploads/2014/08/
    National-Doula-Infographic_8.5x11.pdf.

7. Ruth Jeannoel, "Celebrate Mothers Who Breastfeed, Including Black
    Women Who Do So Publicly," *Rewire.News*, August 7, 2015, https://
    rewire.news/article/2015/08/07/celebrate-mothers-breastfeed-
    including-black-women-publicly/.

8. Elizabeth Dawes Gay, "Report: Racial Discrimination Severely
    Undermines Black Women's Health," *Rewire.News*, August 13, 2014,
    https://rewire.news/article/2014/08/13/report-racial-discrimination-
    severely-undermines-black-womens-health/.

Originally published on Rewire.News *on January 14, 2016.*

The Largely Forgotten History of Abortion Billboard Advertising— and What Pro-Choice Advocates Can Learn from It

Cynthia R. Greenlee

Across the United States, billboards are visible evidence of the contentious abortion debate. Enlarged images of fetuses, cherubic babies, distressed women, and Bible verses tower over highways and byways like antiabortion sentinels overseeing America's culture wars.

Notice I didn't mention images that show happy, pro-choice women, for it's a lopsided roadside debate.

Rarely do we see billboards promoting abortion rights or the broader ideals of reproductive justice. There are a few examples, like reproductive justice organization New Voices Cleveland's recent sponsorship of billboards that affirmed, in the wake of the police killing of twelve-year-old Tamir Rice in the city, that reproductive justice includes the right to parent and protect children. But abortion opponents have effectively cornered the market on this advertising medium and, to paraphrase a hackneyed phrase from *American Idol* judges, have made the billboard their own.

But the good news is that the billboard is just a tool (like video is a tool)—and tools can be harnessed for any movement. In fact, past abortion rights advocates used billboards to good effect—even before *Roe v. Wade*.

Ideological warfare about abortion via advertising has a long track record, though it's a past largely forgotten in history's fog and the present's relentless attacks on abortion rights. Today's reproductive rights and justice advocates can't afford to forget that past. They may need to "go back to the future" to resurrect this tool in an era where women face increasing restrictions on abortion, and providers face proposed laws that would curtail their ability to offer reproductive healthcare to women most in need.

So what is it that advocates need to remember or learn? For starters, many early billboards functioned as straightforward advertising for abortion—even when it wasn't widely legal. In 1971, a roadside sign popped up in McGrann, Pennsylvania, and pointed people to neighboring New York State, which had legalized abortion in 1970.

Similar billboards featuring phone numbers began sprouting like giant flowers on the American landscape. Referral services—some nonprofit and some that operated as for-profit entities—also took to street sides before *Roe* to tell women that they could find reproductive healthcare in the form of abortion and sterilization.

Distributing information about abortion through billboards or other advertisements was not without risk; those who did so could face arrest. In 1972, Charlottesville, Virginia, newspaper editor Jeffrey Bigelow was charged with running advertisements for a New York–based abortion referral service and convicted under a state law banning any public promotion of abortion services. The case eventually made its way to the US Supreme Court but took a back seat to the bigger challenges to abortion bans: the cases that would become *Roe* and Georgia's *Doe v. Bolton. Bigelow v. Virginia* was eventually decided in 1975, and Bigelow's conviction was overturned because there could be no limits on the advertising of a service that had become legal.

At the same time, the young antiabortion movement was also rolling out its own billboards, said historian Jennifer Donnally, a Hollins University visiting professor who researches abortion politics and the New Right. From the early days when antiabortion advocates were organizing against state-level abortion law reform, they made billboards a key part of their messaging.

"Antiabortion billboards began to appear on highways in New York, Massachusetts, Michigan, and Washington [State] prior to the 1973 *Roe v. Wade* decision as part of statewide campaigns against abortion repeal efforts," Donnally told *Rewire.News.*

Many of those billboards were tied to specific ballot measures or potential law changes. In 1970, when Washington State planned a referendum where voters could decide to allow abortion in some circumstances, opponents (and their billboards) came out in full force.[1] "Kill Referendum 20, Not Me," implored a billboard picturing a fake fetus cradled in an adult hand. Accused of using tasteless scare tactics, Voice of the Unborn (the group behind the billboards) replied through a representative, reported by the *New York Times* in October of that year:

"They show an exact medical school replica of a 4-month-old baby. If the billboards seem to be shocking, perhaps it's the idea of abortion that's shocking." (The referendum passed with 56 percent of the vote and allowed women and girls to have abortions if they requested them, with the consent of their husbands or guardians, and if the procedure was performed by a licensed physician.)

Donnally noted that antiabortion billboards have taken different forms and served many purposes over time. They have moved from makeshift messages in cornfields to slick public relations creations, and they mobilize supporters in different ways according to the movement's age and successes.

"The publicity billboards educated the public and recruited potential activists. Behind the scenes, efforts to place billboards trained antiabortion activists in fundraising and media relations while also [making] activists feel effective when the movement was in its early stages, following setbacks or celebrating victories. Sometimes, billboard campaigns were sophisticated. Other times, a farmer in a rural area who had a hard time connecting to antiabortion chapters concentrated in cities and towns took action into his or her own hands," added Donnally. "They made a plywood antiabortion sign and posted it on their land next to a heavily traveled highway."

After the *Bigelow* ruling, antiabortion advertising gained steam in the mid-1970s. A February 1976 *Village Voice* article called John C. Willke, then a practicing obstetrician and a future president of the National Right to Life Committee, the "visual aids guru of the pro-life movement." Willke's first visual aids were often slideshows that Willke and his wife presented in talks to high schoolers.

But, according to the article, Willke's "newest project [was] the creation of the three billboard posters. The least offensive reads 'Abortion: A woman's right to choose.'" "Choose" was crossed out and replaced with "kill." A second billboard depicted tiny feet and this text: "This baby won't keep his mother awake at night . . . at least not yet." Willke planned to erect a fetus billboard atop a building across from a Minnesota hospital that provided abortions, the article added.

Willke's focus on the fetus and abortion's supposedly negative and life-changing effects on the woman—now cornerstones of antiabortion rhetoric—was an experimental and emergent strategy then. Emphasizing abortion as an emotional harm and women as its simultaneous victims

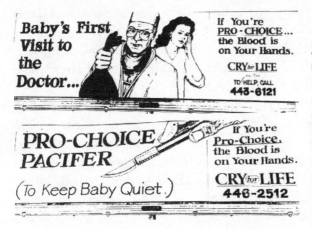

An early antichoice newsletter from a Mississippi group promoted this billboard design, which framed pregnant women as agents of violence against their own fetuses. Courtesy of the Schlesinger Library at Radcliffe.

and perpetrators, right-to-life groups were often explicit when telling their members how to best deploy billboards. An undated newsletter from the Jackson, Mississippi–based Christian Action Group provided hand-drawn illustrations of possible billboards, one showing "baby's first visit to the doctor," with a menacing-looking physician holding a Black sack and a frazzled woman hovering in the background. Also included was a sample billboard that showed a hand wielding a scalpel, labeled "a pro-choice pacifier."

The illustrations came with this advice on using billboards to the best advantage: "One form of 'advocacy advertising,' such as political advertising, is to convince people of the justification of your point of view. Another is to make people ashamed to be with your [opponents]. These billboards are the latter." Cultivating and multiplying shame was a tactic. As abortion opponents' philosophy went, Americans—even the most well-intentioned or those ignorant of the "real" story about abortion— needed to be confronted visually with their silent complicity.

When *Roe* came under significant legal challenge in the 1980s, billboards became even more overtly political. In 1988, the year before the US Supreme Court decision *Webster v. Reproductive Health Services* that allowed states to restrict abortion, a Planned Parenthood billboard showed six male (and mostly antiabortion) Supreme Court justices holding their own sign saying "Freedom of Choice," but with Chief Justice William Rehnquist slamming his gavel on the word "of" and Justices Harry Blackmun and Clarence Thomas holding a replacement sign with the word "from."[2] Also in 1988, antiabortion activists experimented with a new form of advertising by placing antiabortion placards in Atlanta taxis during the Democratic National Convention.

A year later, in 1989, Prolife Across America was up and running. It works as an antiabortion billboard mill, cranking out design after design (as well as radio spots and other advertising).

Therein lies the difference: billboards have been institutionalized in antiabortion media strategy and organizations, but they seem to have faded from the strategic agendas of reproductive rights organizations. In 2014, the Prolife Across America/Prolife Minnesota tax return reported that its designs were emblazoned on more than six thousand billboards, reaching Americans stuck in traffic or driving to work every day with its larger-than-life messages. The group often says those messages are hotlines for pregnant women, educational, and roadside ministry all wrapped into one. Other organizations provide templates or the actual printed vinyl panels that bear the messages and drape over the standard billboard frames for prices as cheap as $200 (not including the cost of billboard rental, which varies widely according to geography, company, and the estimated number of motorists and views at given locations).

As the billboard has become a consistent antiabortion platform, the messages billboards carry read like a conversation between abortion opponents and other social movements. Billboard makers have blatantly adapted the slogans of feminism and civil rights and even the images of Black political leaders, such as Frederick Douglass or Barack Obama— with varying degrees of deftness or tone-deafness.

By the 1990s, billboards in the Midwest had reworked a common feminist bumper sticker to read "Pro-life: The radical idea that fetuses are people." Later, billboards took an explicitly racial turn. In 2011, billboards proclaiming "Black & Beautiful" alongside pictures of Black infants appeared in Oakland, California. Sponsored by the antiabortion group Issues4Life, the billboards appropriated the language of the Black Panther movement, which had its most well-known and vocal chapter in the Bay Area city.

Images and messages on billboards that explicitly targeted Black communities—and paved the way for others aimed at Latinos and Asians— were not entirely new. As scholar Gillian Frank has pointed out, a 1972 Michigan referendum about changing that state's abortion law pushed antiabortion groups to begin developing brochures that pictured Black babies and compared abortion to slavery, now old-hat antiabortion fare.

More than twenty years later, diverse groups protested the encroach-
ment of racist billboards on their home communities. In Oakland in
2011, Strong Families and a coalition of multiracial groups joined forces
to persuade CBS Outdoor to take down controversial signage.[3] It was
similar to a campaign used a year before by the Atlanta-based SisterSong
Women of Color Reproductive Justice Collective when billboards also
owned by CBS and claiming that "black children are an endangered species" appeared in the Georgia capital. In 2015, the reproductive justice
group SisterReach successfully pushed for the removal of antiabortion
billboards in Tennessee.[4]

Yet the hand that giveth doth taketh away. Contemporary groups
fighting for abortion access find that many billboard and other advertising companies reserve the right to deny or take down controversial
content. And those contractual stipulations mean that some companies
will reject outright advertising that specifically references abortion or
simply points women to services—for fear that the other side will cause
a ruckus and demand its removal. Fears of the "A-word" have made it
into the online world, with Google determining that abortion ads were
"non-family safe" content and categorizing them with adult advertising
and entertainment.[5]

Whatever the advertising format, it's clear that this type of commer-
cial and political speech isn't going away. And few people know that
better than Jasmine Burnett, New Voices Cleveland's field organizer in
the Midwest. In 2010, she led the campaign to take down a SoHo, New
York, billboard that proclaimed the most dangerous place for a Black
person was the womb, and this year, Burnett was a driving force behind
the Cleveland billboard.[6]

Pro-choice billboards,
like this one erected
in Cleveland, OH,
are countering the
narratives of the
antiabortion billboards
that exhort people
to "save babies."
Courtesy of New
Voices Cleveland.

Burnett said that it's not enough to mount defensive campaigns that respond to the propagandistic billboards that increasingly dot urban and mostly Black neighborhoods. What's necessary is billboard activism that moves beyond reproductive rights' preoccupation with abortion and, in keeping with a reproductive justice lens, addresses the racism that's an American bedrock.

"Anti-abortion billboards are an affront and an attack. [In doing the billboards, New Voices Cleveland] wanted to provide other spaces for creative thought, affirmation, and liberation," said Burnett. "We work for the full health and well-being of Black women and people. For us, full health means having a different image of ourselves, being able to control and discuss our reproduction, and thinking about how we navigate self-determination in the midst of white supremacy.

"There are not many [billboards or other advertising] that talk about Black people's lives," Burnett added. "And we wanted our billboards to say, 'We support your decision and right to parent or not parent. And we care about your life.'"

Notes

1. "Heated Campaign Fought in Washington State over Abortions," *New York Times*, October 25, 1970, accessed June 6, 2019, https://www.nytimes.com/1970/10/25/archives/heated-campaign-fought-in-washington-state-over-abortions.html?searchResultPosition=1.
2. Richard A. Harris and Daniel J. Tichenor, eds., *A History of the US Political System: Ideas, Interests, and Institutions* (Santa Barbara, CA: ABC-CLIO, 2010), 462.
3. Eveline Shen, "The Triumph over Racist Billboards in Oakland: We Did It Together," *Rewire.News*, July 14, 2011, https://rewire.news/article/2011/07/14/triumph-racist-billboards-oakland-together/.
4. Cherisse Scott, "Exploiting the Black Family: A Divisive Campaign of the Anti-Woman, Pro-Life Movement," *Rewire.News*, May 15, 2015, https://rewire.news/article/2015/05/15/exploiting-black-family-divisive-campaign-anti-woman-pro-life-movement/.
5. Nina Liss-Schultz, "Google and Hulu: Abortion Ads Are Like Sex Toys, Porn, Gambling Sites," *Rewire.News*, May 8, 2015, https://rewire.news/article/2015/05/08/google-hulu-abortion-ads-like-sex-toys-porn-gambling-sites/.

6.   Jasmine Burnett, "Advancing Reproductive Justice for Black Women and Women of Color in Cleveland," *Rewire.News*, November 18, 2014, https://rewire.news/article/2014/11/18/advancing-reproductive-justice-black-women-women-color-cleveland/.

Originally published on Rewire.News *on July 30, 2015.*

Want to Win on Abortion? Talk about It as an Issue of Love, Compassion

Yamani Hernandez

The abortion "war" is waged on multiple fronts: in clinics, in courthouses, on TV shows where people mull over ending unintended pregnancies, and in how we frame what's at stake. For many years, reproductive rights messages about abortion have talked about privacy, protecting women's health and rights, and the toll that restricting abortion takes on those who have them. In March 2017, Echoing Ida publishing partner Rewire.News *published a commentary that argued that nonemotional, economics-based claims about abortion—for example, that its costs disadvantage poorer people—don't strike a chord with Americans and are at the heart of why the abortion rights movement has lost ground. Echoing Ida's Yamani Hernandez, executive director of the National Network of Abortion Funds, had this to say.*

Eleven years ago, I joined the fight for abortion access after a fourteen-year-old parent, made pregnant again by an adult, told me it was cheaper to pay friends ten dollars each to beat her up and force a miscarriage than it was to afford an abortion. She said she would lose her housing if she was pregnant again and that it would be easier to explain getting beat up to her family than wanting an abortion.

This young woman's journey opened my eyes to the myriad ways abortion access affects our survival.

Abortion invokes many emotions and feelings, especially for those of us who have had them. It is undeniable, however, that the economics of accessing abortion exacerbates an already challenging situation for those seeking the service. This is why economic injustice must be central to the conversation.

In "Want to Lose on Abortion? Talk about It as an Economic Issue," Anat Shenker-Osorio and Sharon Rose Goldtzvik argue that talking about abortion in economic terms is a losing issue and, as a "double fail-ure," does nothing to advance economic justice issues.[1] Citing the failed messaging around tax fairness and marriage equality, as well as the cost of the death penalty to taxpayers, the authors argue that monetizing the issue is what loses the debate.

It's true, we should never monetize someone's existence, and money shouldn't determine the importance of an issue. But abortion—and pregnancy writ large—is an issue in which how much money someone has in their pocket determines what kind of care and what kind of life they have access to, if at all.

Talking about abortion through an economic lens is not about "mon-etizing abortion" and it is not a "losing strategy." It's not about "hiding," "deflecting," or "obscuring" anything, as Shenker-Osorio and Goldtzvik suggest. It's quite the opposite. Many people have never thought about abortion beyond morality and legality and thus do not know that people with lower incomes and in rural communities are treated differently than people of means when accessing abortion.

Are the authors unaware of this fact, or do they believe it's not worth mentioning?

More than 50 percent of participants in a 2015 survey said they did not have $1,000 saved and 25 percent did not have $100 saved.[2] Shenker-Osorio and Goldtzvik wrote, "People do not principally *think* about abortion; we *feel* about it." However, for people who have no money, money is an especially important thing. It's always front of mind, includ-ing in abortion decisions, perhaps even before they can "feel" about the pregnancy or abortion, as the authors also suggest.

Dispensing with the "obvious," such as childcare, transportation, lodging, and the cost of the care itself, is insensitive to the reality that for many, the self-determination the authors speak of is not currently possible in today's society without access to resources and, yes, money. Additionally, for many, those related costs are not that obviously asso-ciated with seeking abortion care.

The National Network of Abortion Funds (NNAF) builds power with individual members and seventy grassroots member organizations in thirty-eight states to help remove financial and logistical barriers to abortion access. NNAF members center people who have abortions and organize at the intersections of racial, economic, and reproductive jus-tice, talking with people every day who feel a range of emotions, not the least of which is stress about the expense of their abortions.[3] We hope as a result of our work to provide relief when the financial burden at least is taken off their list of concerns. Further, we strive to help people know that their inability to pay is not their fault but a systemic injustice that must end. (Antichoice politicians made it that way by design.) We message by way of truth telling, storytelling, and intersectional values. We want much more than to "win" at polling; we want to address the deeper systemic issues while centering the voices of people who have abortions.

Abortion funds field more than 100,000 calls per year from people who cannot afford their abortions due to unjust and discriminatory policies that punish people for having lower incomes by making it harder to access care. When we provide funding for abortions, we echo back emotion and empathy for the most vulnerable among us—funding an abortion requires engaging at an emotional level. Not to talk about abortion as an economic issue, in particular an economic justice issue, is denying the experiences of people who have abortions and the work of our twenty-four-year-old organization, as well as local organizations and churches in our network that have been doing this work for even longer.

Talking about economic injustice helps us paint a picture beyond the legality and morality of abortion itself. It helps us address those deeper systemic issues that must be resolved alongside abortion access.

I am left wondering if the authors fully researched the current messaging around economic justice being employed by coalitions like All* Above All and its allied organizations that focus on the economics involved in abortion access by using innovative messaging informed by public opinion. While the piece references the reproductive justice framework in problematizing "choice" as a message, it also seems to have disregarded the women of color leadership within the reproductive justice movement to repeal the Hyde Amendment by suggesting that talking about abortion through an economic frame is a losing strategy. (Reproductive justice is a human rights framework and social movement created by Black women in 1994. It advocates for the freedoms to terminate pregnancies, to continue pregnancies, and to raise children in safe environments where all have the ability to thrive. To see the movement framework, visit SisterSong's website.)[4] Instead of modeling the complexity that it calls for in talking about abortion, the piece collapses "an economic frame" into a shallow losing container without nuance and with no racial analysis of the linkages between race and who experiences the most economic barriers.

The authors are concerned about the troubles of the Democratic Party's brand. To deny that economic, racial, and reproductive justice are indelibly linked would do more harm than good for the Democratic Party, which already has a serious race problem[4] and is opening its arms to antichoice candidates while ignoring the risks that poses to real people seeking abortions.[5] To suggest that by neglecting economics in its messaging, the abortion access movement would somehow contribute to the Democratic Party's return to glory is a fantasy and a demand of the worst kind: the authors demand that we lie by omission.

One-size-fits-all messages that we all repeat won't be enough to inspire empathy, no matter how many times they are polled. What if we reframed the conversation to include economics but with more personal narratives to create the kind of intimacy between people that is actually needed for empathy to happen?

If we knew what we could say to win the fight for abortion access, we would already be living in the world we seek. No one person has all the answers, so we would do well not to condemn each other wholesale and to instead encourage truth telling and empathy together, side by side. It is important to have conversations about messaging, and I agree that to talk about abortion *only* as an economic issue would be dismissive of other parts of people's lived experiences, including their emotions. However, I can never agree with guidance that tells us "just because something is true doesn't make it persuasive." This is a dangerous directive that tells people their personal truth and the truths of their communities do not matter—especially in a time and a history that has told Black, Brown, and poor people that they and their stories are not enough.

Public opinion research can inform how we shape messages, but it cannot be the beginning and end of every story, especially if it silences the realities we face when we need care. There are truths we *must* speak: *It is immoral to punish the poor. It is immoral to discriminate based on race, income, and zip code. And the economic realities many pregnant people have to navigate matter. Everyone loves someone who has had an abortion. Let's ensure that we can all afford the care we need without shame and hardship.*

Activist Assata Shakur told us, "We must love each other and support each other. We have nothing to lose but our chains." And we will never lose when we tell the truth about the intersecting oppressions in our lives.

Talking about abortion through an economic frame is not about removing feelings from abortion but about highlighting the many chains that bind our decision making and oppression.

Notes

1. Anat Shenker-Osorio and Sharon Rose Goldtzvik, "Want to Lose on Abortion? Talk about It as an Economic Issue," *Rewire.News*, May 31, 2017, https://rewire.news/article/2017/05/31/want-lose-abortion-talk-economic-issue/.

2. Jack Holmes, "More Than Half of Americans Reportedly Have Less Than $1,000 to Their Name," *Esquire*, January 12, 2016, https://www.esquire.com/news-politics/news/a41147/half-of-americans-less-than-1000/.

3. National Network of Abortion Funds, *Tiller Fund Report: Five Years of Abortion Funding Data Released*, February 21, 2017, https://abortionfunds.org/tiller-fund-2017/.

4. Graham Vyse, "Minutes: The Democratic Party Has a Race Problem," *New Republic*, February 5, 2017, https://newrepublic.com/minutes/140419/democratic-party-race-problem.

5. Jodi Jacobson, "Setting the Record Straight: What the Election of Heath Mello Tells Us about the Democratic Party," *Rewire.News*, April 26, 2017, https://rewire.news/article/2017/04/26/setting-record-straight-elevation-heath-mello-tells-us-democratic-party/.

Originally published on Rewire.News *on June 7, 2017.*

FAMILY MATTERS

Introduction

Kemi Alabi

Family: Our support system. Our "we." The ones who hold us down.

See also that other thing: the tribe to whom we're told we belong.

Blood and law have long defined family ties, but our bonds form beyond these shallow markers. The relationships that best sustain us take so many shapes. We create family beyond children and romantic partnerships. Beyond normative genders and sexualities. Beyond biology and borders. But that's far from accepted fact.

The word *family* conjures up a too-specific scene: a straight, cis man married to a straight, cis woman; their biological children; the private property and private love they share. Our culture views it as deviant or undesirable to coexist outside this supposed norm—although most of us do.

This concept of family is a critical beam propping up the house white supremacy, patriarchy, and capitalism built. If you dare live and love outside this specific family system, you're seen as undeserving of resources, safety, and survival. And this ideal has been strategically weaponized by the state against Black and queer folks, casting us to the margins as damaged misfits unworthy or incapable of care.

Issa lie! The damage and carelessness belong to those oppressive systems, not our families. Yes, we struggle—not everything ends as sweetly as an episode of *Family Matters*—but there's power in telling the truth about who we are and how we care for each other. Jasmine Burnett, Bianca Campbell, and Raquel Willis redefine family, charting radical bonds from our homes to our movements. Gloria Malone and Cynthia R. Greenlee reveal unsung sides of Black mamahood in all its grief and glory. Brittany Brathwaite and Malone hold up pop culture's few but mighty mirrors of our family lives while Samantha Daley and I point to America's cruel distortions of them. This work shares a simple truth: there are many routes to belonging. Join us and reimagine what our families can be.

A (Midwestern) Black Lesbian's Reflections on 20 Years of Being "Family"

Jasmine Burnett

It started with a phone call to my mother one hazy June afternoon in Indiana. I called my mother every day, multiple times a day, but this day was different. This time, I was going to tell my mother that I was a lesbian.

Before I could even get the words out, I started bawling. I was so fearful of what our relationship would be like on the other side of my declaration. My tears were warranted because after I told her, she told me, "You know I don't believe in that lifestyle, and the Bible says you're going to burn in hell."

Having gone to worship with my mother for most of my life, I knew that hearing this from her was consistent with what our church believed. But I thought her unconditional love for me would be an expression of God's grace. I tried to explain that I wasn't "choosing" to be gay, that I was just trying to live my life. She grew more unbothered. I explained that I wasn't trying to upset her or anger God. Yet through my hysterical crying, she told me that she didn't want to talk to me "until I was straight again and remembered how I was raised."

I would test her will by calling her after that, but the conversation would invariably go like this:

Me: Mom, I was just calling to hear your voice.

Her: Are you dating a man yet?

Me: No.

And she would promptly hang up the phone.

This distancing from my family started with my mother and went on to include my aunts, who told my younger brother and cousins not to talk to me. Needless to say, I was devastated, lonely, and lost. What did this mean? I had done all of the things that respectability dictates are a product of good parenting. I never got into trouble at school, always made good grades, and was involved in band all of middle and high school. I went to a college that my mother wanted me to attend so that I could be close enough to home, and she could have bragging rights. I mean, damn. I thought all of the things I did in my life to be a "good girl" would cancel out this one big thing. Sadly, it didn't. And the result was being emotionally depleted and physically abandoned by my family.

Eventually, in order for my mother to speak to me again, I claimed that I was in a bisexual exploratory phase and that it would pass. But the next year, when I was twenty years old, I just said, "Mom, I'm a full-blown lesbian. I'm not exploring bisexuality, and even if I am ever with a man again, I'm certain that I will have a long-term relationship with a woman." (In 1998, marriage equality seemed so far away.)

"I hope you can support me," I pleaded. "I tried to do what you wanted, and it didn't work for me." Needless to say, she again resorted to her harshest tactic and told me I could not come home, nor would she speak to me. In fact, because of "my lifestyle," my mother didn't speak to me with any level of kindness or respect for three long years. She didn't even call me to wish me a happy twenty-first birthday. That was beyond painful and such a low blow.

Eventually, my aunts talked to me again, but at the same time, they also talked *about me* behind my back. They said they didn't want my "gayness" to rub off on my younger cousins, especially because my mother's frame of reference was that I chose to be gay. I did have one family member, my cousin Bubbles, who supported me and was truly the only person who could get my family together when they were talking stuff about me. I appreciate her to this day for that.

But even with Bubbles's consolation, I needed something to fill my mother's absence in my life. I was still living in Indiana and attending school on a pretty conservative campus. I needed an outlet, and, more importantly, I needed community.

I found that community outside of campus, starting with my hairstylist Denzell. He was styling my hair one day, and, of course, we talked about dating because hairstylists actually double as therapists. I was being evasive about who I was seeing because I didn't gender the person I talked about.

He asked, "Darling, are you family?" I had not heard that expression before, but he then explained that gay folks identify each other by asking if you're "family" rather than, "Are you gay?" He also shared that we call each other family because so many of us are blacklisted by our own families, so we find our kin in the LGBTQ community. My mind was blown; my heart broke open, and I found my people.

Soon I was sneaking into clubs, flirting with women, having sex, and getting involved in the LGBTQ movement. I participated in this Black lesbian social group in Indianapolis called "Indy SoulSistahs," where a Black lesbian couple hosted biweekly Sunday brunches that would go into early Monday morning. I was one of the founders of Indiana Black Pride, a Black LGBTQ organization.

I became socially and civically engaged with my community and eventually was "gay for pay" when I worked as a development manager at the Damien Center, an AIDS service organization in Indianapolis, and later at the Black AIDS Institute in Los Angeles.

Once I was part of this big, amazing extended "family," I felt protected and held again. To clarify, I call the family that raised me my "blood family" and the family that embraced me my "queer family." I share blood with both—one with direct DNA lineage, the other more symbolic.

Yes, there is just as much violence attached to being Black as there is to being a woman and a lesbian, yet within my queer family, I felt that someone cared about me as I am, not as they wanted me to be. My queerness is a reflection of my deep desire to live free for as long as I am gifted breath.

My mother passed away on February 7, 2018, which was a Wednesday. The Sunday before her death, we had a conversation about her acceptance of my sexuality, which was as close as she would ever get to understanding how the lack of her full acceptance of me impacted my life. She told me, "I accept that this is your lifestyle, and I love you unconditionally." Though she never met my current partner, who I've been with for three years, she did offer to meet her in that conversation—but we ran out of time.

Since I came out, my blood family has grown in queerness: My younger brother is a Black gay man, and my sister is a biracial lesbian. I have a cousin who recently came out as a lesbian and another cousin who is a Black transgender woman. This new wave of acceptance in my family was not granted by my sacrifice alone. My maternal grandmother's sister, Aunt Betty, was a closeted lesbian who held an after-hours spot in her basement in Dayton, Ohio, from the mid-1950s to the early 1980s and was with her life partner, my Aunt Annie, for thirty-five years.

My great-grandmother never embraced Aunt Betty, and I suppose her behavior toward Aunt Betty was the blueprint for my mother's behavior toward me. The intergenerational cycle of homophobic trauma in Black families has to end. It is literally wounding and killing us, leaving our relationships with one another one-sided and incomplete.

The community of queer people of color has also evolved for me in these twenty years. I had the opportunity to be in Washington, DC, for DC Black Pride this year, where I attended a party with my beloved friends and Echoing Ida writers Amber J. Phillips and Jazmine Walker. They took me to a queer people of color party at the Howard Theatre, a historic site that has housed generations of Black talent and excellence. We took a shortcut through a back alley to get to the entrance. As we inched closer, I saw a light in a doorway and a guy who looked like he was security. I assumed this was the entrance because of my muscle memory from the Ten, the gay club I would sneak into twenty years ago in Indianapolis; it was in a back alley too. It was in that moment that I realized that I was stepping into my righteous inheritance—from the ability to endure my blood family's silence and still be here and thriving, to my entering into my sanctuary (a.k.a. "the club") via a well-lit building with a front entrance facing a busy street.

Of course, I've been to many clubs that had front-door entrances in the course of my twenty years being out, but this time it felt different. This time, I was entering with intention and perspective as a Black lesbian, a Black dyke, a Black bulldagger powerfully moving through my life.

Through this process of reflection, I realize it has taken me being a caretaker of my mother for seven years and losing her this year for me to have the time, space, energy, and capacity to even think about what being out for this long has meant for my life. In Toni Cade Bambara's *The Salt Eaters* she says, "[G]ot to give it all up, the pain, the hurt, the anger and make room for lovely things to rush in and fill you full."

I am ready for wholeness. I am ready to live daily in my healing. I am ready to belong to myself and to clear the way for what I need to be loved without sacrificing for others' comfort. After twenty years with both of my families, I am ready.

Originally published on The Root *on June 28, 2018.*

Stigma around "Nontraditional" Families Won't End with Assisted Reproductive Technology

Bianca Campbell

What mamas do you see on Mother's Day cards? Who's missing and why? Mamas Day, an annual Forward Together project, creates radical cards that pull our mamas from the margins to the center. Echoing Ida writers participate with stories that help us fully see and celebrate our families. This piece, written alongside a Mamas Day card by artist Mojuicy, reveals the beauty and struggle of queer routes to parenthood.

A 2015 study predicted the use of skin cells and stem cells to create biological children for same-sex couples, single parents, and heterosexual couples with difficulty conceiving.[1] As a queer full-spectrum doula of color considering mamahood in the near future, I want as many parenting options as possible. But I wonder if this assisted reproductive technology will be truly accessible to me and my community and if it reinforces a nuclear family ideal that further stigmatizes our choices.

Queer and trans folks have been making babies for a long time, and it's rarely ever easy. Even when we create biological children, we have to fight to be recognized as their parents. In 2014, a Texas same-sex couple fought for custody of their two biological newborns.[2] (They used a surrogate, so they are each the father of one of the two boys.) The parents' names weren't even allowed on the birth certificates of their respective biological children. Without addressing the legalized discrimination against our families, the new technology won't be enough to shield our reproductive choices from attack. Respectability[3] through biological reproduction (and government-sanctioned marriage, might I add) will not save us.

"There's a lot of weight that's put on biology and often that's too much," said student-midwife Courtney Hooks, who has helped several queer and trans families give birth in Oakland, California.

2015 Mamas Day card by artist Mojuicy.

The biological emphasis in family planning creates an ableist culture at infertility clinics that focuses on "correcting" our bodies instead of celebrating our sexual lives and family choices. Many queer and trans folks, Hooks said, are fertile. "We just haven't been having that kind of sex." Instead, the language and framework at many clinics, not to mention the language in state and federal policies, see our bodies, transitions, and sexualities as a problem, and this new technology should be acknowledged with that in mind.

If it weren't for the high cost, social stigma, and legal barriers, many of us could have children with the support of our communities, coparents, and partners using the variety of methods already available. It's not only necessary to make skin cell and stem cell technology accessible but also to make sure all the ways we form families are affirmed.

Barriers to Having the Families We Want

For most people, access to health insurance is essential to comfortably and safely sustaining and growing families. In 2014, however, 25 percent of LGBTQ adults could not afford medical care, compared to 17 percent of non-LGBTQ people.[4] The poll reported that people identifying as bisexual and lesbian were the most likely of all groups categorized by sexuality to forgo care due to cost and the least likely to have developed a relationship with a medical provider. Further, a different survey found that trans people are disproportionately affected by a lack of insurance, affirming providers, and access to essential medical care.[5]

Insurance isn't the only barrier to having the families we want. In Atlanta, Jhavia Etheridge, a wellness counselor, and her partner plan on starting a family, preferably aligned with when the technology becomes available. Etheridge is excited about the possibility of using stem cells to have biological children with her partner. However, even with insurance, she fears that the technology, like others in the past, will be financially out of reach. A single in vitro fertilization treatment costs an average of $12,000 (basic treatment cost of $12,000 does not include fertility drugs, specialized testing, or a hospital delivery),[6] and pregnancy is not guaranteed on the first treatment. Some families then incur the additional expense of surrogacy.

"More power to folks who can afford it, but I definitely cannot," Etheridge said. She intends to stick with her plan to adopt, which can have its own financial hurdles. (The cost of US domestic infant adoptions average from $20,000 to $40,000. Domestic foster adoptions average from $0 to $3,500.)[7]

Right now, many of us are still trying to find and afford insurance. Once we get it, we seek a network of doctors who will give unbiased care.

Reproductive justice activist Amir Jones focuses primarily on improving healthcare access for queer and trans people in Atlanta, Georgia. When asked about the top health issues he hears when out in the community, Jones said, "People want to look at holistic health and wellness. They want to build relationships with affirming providers."

We're already less likely to seek medical care due to the transphobia and homophobia in the medical industry that we experience or anticipate. Fifty percent of the respondents to a survey on transgender health reported having to teach their medical providers about transgender care, and 28 percent said that they had been refused care.[8] It's not very surprising, then, that 28 percent of the respondents said they had postponed or avoided medical treatment when they were sick or injured, and 33 percent delayed or did not try to get preventive healthcare. It is not as easy for our community to enter a fertility clinic as it might be for other groups. We want to connect with a provider we can trust with our major decision to parent.

Many of us also face legal barriers to creating and sustaining the families we want. In some states, for example, if the sperm or egg donor is a "known donor" and not an anonymous donor from a clinic, they have the right to contest custody of the child.[9] There are less expensive, more intimate options to create families outside of clinics, but families are at risk of entering taxing legal battles with sperm or egg donors.[10]

Resiliently, we have dealt with these stigmas and barriers by creating loving, dynamic, nonnuclear families.

The Families We Already Have

Many of us either grew up in or descended from a family that did not look exactly like the white, American, heteronormative, patriarchal suburbanites we've been told to aspire toward. My grandmother never gave birth, but she raised five children, including me. (We referred to her as grandmother, even though she wasn't our biological grandmother, out of respect.) People of color, queer people, and trans people buck against those societal expectations all the time and have for decades.[11]

Play cousins, neighbors dubbed auntie or tia, stepparents, and coparents: not being able to create biological children is not the same as not being able to create a family.

Media maven Raquel Willis, who affirms the experiences of queer and trans people through her writing and her role at the Transgender Law Center, said the potential for biological children is positive, but it's a path toward a family she is no longer pursuing.

"Even as a kid, I thought about having children. I used to cry because I thought I couldn't have kids," she said.

"A lot of my worry was that my family wouldn't accept my adopted children as much as my [siblings'] biological children." Willis said it's a worry she still occasionally has.

"But then, I realized good parenting goes beyond the biological." Willis said she will adopt queer and trans youth specifically, a group facing disproportionate rates of homelessness. (LGBT youth make up no more than 10 percent of that population segment, yet total 40 percent of homeless youth.) She said she hopes to use her lived experience to support her children as best she can.

We need to uplift the beautiful, multiple ways we already create families and demand the access to sustain these families. Our society, from the way we celebrate national holidays to the way we roll out new reproductive technologies, should do more to remind us that we are enough: our partners and our families are praiseworthy regardless of marriage and biological connection.

Notes

1. "2-Father Babies a Possibility 'in Two Years,' Research Suggests," RT, February 23, 2015, https://rt.com/news/234723-two-father-babies-cells/.
2. Michelangelo Signorile, "Jason Hanna and Joe Riggs, Texas Gay Fathers, Denied Legal Parenthood of Twin Sons," *HuffPost*, June 18, 2014, https://www.huffingtonpost.com/2014/06/18/jason-hanna-and-joe-riggs_n_5506720.html.
3. "Respectability" is a concept that suggests that oppressed peoples are at fault for their issues because they do not conform to societal expectations. For example, Don Lemon thought the answer to the mass murder of unarmed Black people by our militarized police state was to ensure that our pants are always pulled up. See Fredrick C. Harris, "The Rise of Respectability Politics," *Dissent*, Winter 2014, https://www.dissentmagazine.org/article/the-rise-of-respectability-politics.
4. Gary J. Gates, "In U.S., LGBT More Likely Than Non-LGBT to be Uninsured," Gallup, August 26, 2014, https://news.gallup.com/poll/175445/lgbt-likely-non-lgbt-uninsured.aspx; Kellan Baker and Laura E. Durso, "Why Repealing the Affordable Care Act Is Bad Medicine for LGBT Communities," Center for American Progress, March 27, 2017, https://www.americanprogress.org/issues/lgbt/news/2017/03/22/428970/.repealing-affordable-care-act-bad-medicine-lgbt-communities/.
5. Lindsey Dawson, Jennifer Kates, and Anthony Damico, "The Affordable Care Act and Insurance Coverage Changes by Sexual Orientation," Kaiser Family Foundation, January 18, 2018, https://www.kff.org/disparities-policy/issue-brief/the-affordable-care-act-and-insurance-coverage-changes-by-sexual-orientation/.
6. Nina Bahadur, "The Cost of Infertility: This Is How Real People Pay for IVF," *Self*, January 8, 2018, https://www.self.com/story/the-cost-of-infertility.

7. Editorial Team, "Can We Afford? The Cost of Assisted Reproduction and Adoption," *Adoptive Families*, March 1, 2014, https://www. adoptivefamilies.com/how-to-adopt/adoption-costs-surrogacy-costs/.

8. "New Report Reveals Rampant Discrimination against Transgender People by Health Providers, High HIV Rates and Widespread Lack of Access to Necessary Care," National LGBTQ Task Force, n.d., http://www.thetaskforce.org/new-report-reveals-rampant-discrimination-against-transgender-people-by-health-providers-high-hiv-rates-and-widespread-lack-of-access-to-necessary-care-2/.

9. "The Legal Considerations of Using a Third Party Sperm or Egg Donor," Center of Reproductive Medicine, October 7, 2016, https://www.infertilitytexas.com/blog/the-legal-considerations-of-using-a-third-party-sperm-or-egg-donor.

10. Douglas T. Carrell and C. Matthew Peterson, eds., *Reproductive Endocrinology and Infertility: Integrating Modern Clinical and Laboratory Practice* (New York: Springer-Verlag, 2010), 20.

11. Sharon J. Lettman-Hicks, "The State of Black LGBT People and Their Families," *HuffPost*, last modified May 13, 2014, https://www.huffingtonpost.com/sharon-j-lettmanhicks/the-state-of-black-lgbt-p_b_4949992.html.

Originally published on Rewire.News *on May 5, 2015.*

Trans Women Are Women. This Isn't a Debate.

Raquel Willis

Sometimes we need to have a family conversation—not blood fam to blood fam but sister to cister. Black women are not a monolith, but the struggle against white supremacist patriarchy requires some common ground. In this viral ~~clapback~~ intervention, Raquel Willis clarifies a nonnegotiable fact for her cisgender siblings in the struggle.

I first encountered the words of Nigerian writer and feminist Chimamanda Ngozi Adichie through her "We Should All Be Feminists" speech in 2013. It was just a few months shy of Beyoncé's surprise release of her iconic anthem "***Flawless," which heavily sampled Adichie's stripped-down thesis on her understanding of feminism.

I had just finished undergrad at the University of Georgia with a BA in journalism and a minor in women's studies, so I was still reeling from the ways my eyes were opened to how systems of oppression, particularly the patriarchy, touched every aspect of my life. Most of my classes, including one titled Black Feminist Theory, were awash in whiteness, which had made my social justice awakening quite isolating. And prior to that class, I was mostly aware of just the white contributions. It was inspiring to witness another Black woman so unapologetically claim the feminist label and so willing to discuss it publicly. However, I erred by expecting Adichie to be trans inclusive simply because she understood being marginalized for her Blackness. Yes, her analysis of womanhood excludes transgender women, and she's not alone. Plenty of other mainstream feminists, including Germaine Greer, have shared their own transmisogynistic (anti-trans) views with a conflation of gender, sex, and socialization in their core beliefs about equality.

Adichie's stake in the Trans-Exclusionary Radical Feminist Movement bubbled to the surface of popular discourse after the release of a Channel 4 News interview in March 2017. In it, presenter Cathy Newman asks her an already flawed question: "Does it matter how you've arrived to being a woman? For example, if you're a trans woman—who grew up identifying as a man, who grew up enjoying the privileges of being a man—does that take away from becoming a woman? Are you any less of a real woman?" In her response, Adichie proceeds to gaslight trans women by attempting to champion inclusion and understanding of our experiences while claiming those that they didn't equate to true womanhood. "My feeling is trans women are trans women," she says. By refusing to simply say, "Trans women are women," Adichie rhetorically categorizes trans women as an "Other" from womanhood. Trans women are a type of woman, just as women of color, disabled women, and Christian women are types of women. Just as a person would be bigoted to deny these women their womanhood, so would they be bigoted to deny trans women theirs.

Then Adichie vaguely invalidates trans women for not having a certain set of experiences. "I think if you've lived in the world as a man (with the privileges that the world accords to men) and then sort of change or switch gender, it's difficult for me to accept that then we can equate your experience with the experience of a woman who has lived from the beginning in the world as a woman and who has not been accorded those privileges that men are," she says. "I don't think it's a good thing to conflate everything into one."

When cisgender women assert limited criteria for womanhood, it's reminiscent of how white women in the United States benefited from initially being viewed as a more valid type of woman than Black women. In her iconic 1851 "Ain't I a Woman" speech, abolitionist Sojourner Truth spelled out how inaccurate and privileged it is for us to use these limitations in public discourse. "That man over there says that women need to be helped into carriages and lifted over ditches, and to have the best place everywhere," she said. "Nobody ever helps me into carriages, or over mud-puddles, or gives me any best place! And ain't I a woman?"[1] Truth and other Black women of her time were combating the existence of chattel slavery and the centuries-old idea that they were less human and by proxy less women. Similarly, trans women are combating restrictions powered by the gender binary and the idea, also centuries old, that people who have more complex relationships to their gender or sexual identity are less valid. Just as it is bigoted for womanhood to be narrowly defined within the hegemonic white woman's experience, so too is it wrong for womanhood to be defined as the hegemonic cisgender woman's experience. Cis women, like white women, may be the majority, but that hardly means their experiences are the only valid ones.

Adichie's next major point that womanhood is "about the way the world treats us" is problematic and uninformed as well. Defining womanhood purely by how we're oppressed strips us of our agency and self-determination and empowers the patriarchy. I am a woman regardless of my experiences of sexual harassment and being invalidated by men at various points in my life. Further, these are experiences that she either thinks trans women can't undergo or it matters less when these things happen to us. But that is far from the truth of trans women's experiences. If we play by the Oppression Olympics view of who has it worse, many could easily make the case that trans women do.

In the 2011 survey "Injustice at Every Turn," trans people were reported to be twice as likely to be unemployed and four times as likely to make less than $10,000 a year. Then, in a 2013 report by the National Coalition of Anti-Violence Programs, trans women were found to be 1.8 times more likely to experience sexual violence than other survivors. Within the LGBTQ+ community, trans women account for 72 percent of homicides, far surpassing percentages for cis women who identify within the initialism. It gets worse: from 2016 to 2018, each year garnered the title of the deadliest year on record for transgender women in the United States, and it's not just a domestic issue. The numbers for our trans sisters in Brazil have consistently been the highest in the world for each of those years as well.

I am not interested in a three-fifths compromise on my womanhood. It is true that many trans women are not perceived as women for at least a portion of our lives. This, however, does not mean that we are afforded the experience of men. Does this mean that we can get back our "100 percent woman" distinction once we're out as trans for more than the time we were perceived as a different gender? Does this mean that the growing group of young trans girls who transition at a single-digit age will never be respected in their womanhood? This is a slippery slope, and if you define the experiences of trans women in this way, then you're defining the experiences of cis women who may not be able to live up to those expectations too.

Despite my disappointment in Adichie's assessment of trans women and our experiences, I am not interested in throwing out my sister. Prominent Black women who misspeak or misstep or further marginalize a group are disposed of in ways that our white counterparts are not. If you stand on a pedestal and denounce Adichie, you should do the same to white women like Lena Dunham and Amy Schumer who consistently feed into anti-Blackness. And while you're at it, understand that liking posts on Facebook and retweeting Twitter threads isn't the only way to confront transmisogyny. Trans women should be offered opportunities to share our own thoughts and experiences on our own terms, and we should be compensated for that labor whenever possible.

Holding people accountable requires a mixture of patience and empathy. When I hold my Black cis sisters accountable, as a Black trans woman, I acknowledge societal positionality in a nuanced way. Black women, in general, are overlooked, spoken over, and ignored in mainstream conversations on women's issues. Understanding this allows me to approach the conversation with a certain sensitivity to our common struggle. Now, I'm not interested in coddling cis people, but I believe that if we show more care than not, our conversations will be all the more fruitful. I urge Black cis women to do the same and also realize that not all Black trans women are interested in or owe you this dialogue.

If your feminism does not respect trans women in their full womanhood, it's not truly intersectional. If you don't advocate for the liberation of trans people, you aren't truly invested in equality. And if you don't advocate on behalf of Black trans women, then you aren't truly invested in Black liberation.

Notes

1. "Modern History Sourcebook: Sojourner Truth: 'Ain't I a Woman?', December 1851," Fordham University, https://sourcebooks.fordham. edu/mod/sojtruth-woman.asp.

Originally published on The Root *on March 13, 2017.*

On Being a Proud Teen Mom: I Don't Hate Myself as Much as You Wish I Did

Gloria Malone

A fearless champion of young parents, Gloria Malone's work busts shame and stigma to smithereens. Her 2016 contribution to Mamas Day didn't mince words, turning the magnifying glass away from teen moms and back toward the reader.

The problem with being a teen mom is that I don't hate myself nearly as much as you wish I did.

My humble pride and my happy life upset you because I do not embody the self-hate and stereotypes you want me to.

My existence challenges everything that you've been told to believe about me, which makes you uncomfortable. And instead of getting to know me, you cast hate and anger at me. Hoping that your negativity will tell me to quit, hoping that I will amount to the nothing you desperately want me to be, and hoping that your negativity will give you a voice for a moment.

I am a proud teen mom. My family is happy. I graduated high school on time and with honors. I am a college student, and I am looking for a master's degree program. I've been published in the *New York Times* and other major news publications expressing my views. My daughter is intelligent, healthy, and happy. I'm on my way, and I won't let you get in the way.

When you do choose to hear my accomplishments, you seek to belittle and change them so that they make you feel comfortable: "You're an exception, not the rule," "So what? You think you deserve a medal or something?", "Big deal. You did what you were supposed to do," or, "That only happened because you're a statistic and need to be the proof that ___ is diversified."

What you fail to realize is that your negativity and hate comes from within. The anger you feel comes from you beginning to realize that, instead of thinking for yourself, you've been trained to think—that is what upsets you.

Fortunately for me, your projected self-hate is something that I have encountered since I became pregnant at fifteen. I've worked too hard to let your projected self-hate determine whether or not I will graduate or continue to be the best parent to my child.

In fact, your negativity reminds me to speak louder, to encourage others to speak, and to do what you do not want us to achieve—our own greatness.

The problem with being a teen mom is that I don't have as much of a problem with my existence as you want me to. The problem is you.

Originally published on Forward Together's Strong Families *blog on May 11, 2013.*

For My Mother: A Day without Cancer

Cynthia R. Greenlee

How do we hold space for grief and uncertainty on days marked for cele-
bration? Our mamas need so much more than flowers and chocolates—
this 2013 Mamas Day contribution shares a daughter's true Mother's
Day wish.

When I found a lump in my breast several years ago, I couldn't bear
to tell my mother. She was already walking in the shadow of cancer—
not because she had it herself, but because she had become a cancer
caregiver.

My family tree is blighted with cancer. My paternal grandmother had
a radical mastectomy in rural North Carolina in the 1940s, a procedure
that left her with an open, weeping wound where her breasts had been.
Family legend says that she couldn't find a white doctor (there was no
Black doctor for miles) to take her as a patient. She went instead to the
local veterinarian, who referred her to a white doctor who didn't let race
get in the way of his oath "to do no harm." On that same side of the family, a great-grandfather shot himself to death after a cancer diagnosis, an
act of deadly pragmatism to avoid his cells' painful betrayal.

My mother and cancer taught me much of what I know about caring and caregiving. When I was a child, relatives often recovered from
cancer-related procedures at our house. My aunt Johannah lived in the
North Carolina mountains and needed life-extending treatment only
available five hours away but closer to our house. My mother worked
nights as a nurse but was up in the morning to drive Johannah, her sister-
in-law, to her doctor's appointments an hour away. Sister-in-law number
two recovered from her biopsy in my sister's bedroom. When another of
my father's sisters was diagnosed, my mother drove over immediately

Baby Cynthia and her mother.

and then took over the kitchen (because we're Black and southern, and we believe that food, even the food that will clog your arteries, can temporarily beat back a crisis). And my mother did it all with a gentle smile and genuine graciousness. I inherited the smile but can only imitate the graciousness.

In late 2008, my mother's older sister, Mary, didn't make it to our family Christmas gathering a few miles from her house in Lake City, South Carolina. We knew something was terribly wrong. She'd been suffering from some leg problems that her primary care doctor assured her were "just arthritis." "Just arthritis" was soft-tissue sarcoma, an exceedingly rare cancer.

We found a sarcoma expert four hours away at Duke University, near my home; though considered an expert, he had only seen seventeen of these tumors in his career. He was excited to see one so large. As offensive as that may sound, we were grateful that her case piqued his interest. Even if he saw her as little more than a mass of cells gone awry, maybe he could save her life.

This began my mother's all-out crusade to save her sister. Fresh from retirement, my mother relocated to my sister's apartment near the hospital and took care of Aunt Mary while we waited for the diagnosis and endured the cycle of boomerang hospitalization. Mom juggled all the appointments, the ambulance rides, the insurance claims, and the calls from relatives, some of whom were mad that she had "taken Mary so far away." She and my sisters did the literally heavy lifting of turning Aunt Mary in the bed, getting her to the bathroom, and attending to her comfort. I brought food, especially the soft-serve ice cream she loved; held her hand; and tried to talk in an overly bright voice about everyday things.

All this while, the doctors were saying that they might be able to save Aunt Mary if they could amputate her leg from the hip down. We

When my aunt Mary Daniels Beckett died, I broke open a lockbox in search of her will. Inside among her cherished belongings was this picture of prekindergarten, snaggle-toothed me on a family trip she and my mother organized to Myrtle Beach, South Carolina, where we pretended to swim, harvested sand dollars, and went pottery shopping.

were willing to relinquish that piece of her—and accompany her through rehabilitation, finding a handicapped-accessible home—to keep her among us.

Aunt Mary had no biological children, but she was my mother too. Not merely "like my mother." I am grateful that Aunt Mary didn't believe in that wrong-headed adage that "children should be seen and not heard." Aunt Mary managed to laugh at my inane knock-knock jokes when they numbered in the thousands and must have driven her batty. As a schoolteacher, she bought me books, helped me grow seahorses in the summer, and tutored me in the fine art of elementary school oratory, urging all her pupils to "say it with feeling this time." Every trip with her was an adventure. When I was six, she bought me my own coat of many colors—a hideous fur cloak that shed all over the school bus seats but made me feel like a miniature Foxy Brown. As an adult, I would often talk to her on Sundays after she'd taught Sunday school—as she had for decades. When she died, I found this picture of me in her lockbox, where she kept the most important documents of her life.

Aunt Mary's illness and death reordered our family's universe. My ninety-year-old grandmother, once under Aunt Mary's wing, was now my mother's ward. And then their younger sisters were both diagnosed with cancer.

My mother's days are once again packed with appointments, as she manages an elderly mother and one sister's continuing battle with breast cancer. Her mornings are consumed with making breakfast, checking medications, and getting everyone ready for a day of chemotherapy or radiation. The cancer treatment center is forty-five minutes away.

We're now all part of a weird "sandwich generation." My mother is stuck between caring for her mother and sister, as well as my senior father, who lives in our family home in another state. Cancer, in its tyranny, demands that she be elsewhere. My sisters and I shuttle between our elderly father, the demands of our lives as young professionals and students, and caring for our mother, who has become everyone's caregiver.

We can't totally shoulder her burden, but I keep my phone on all night to take her early morning calls. Sometimes, she needs to talk at 5:45 a.m. because that's the only time when everybody else is asleep. I send her weekly shipments of her favorite artisanal bread that she can't get in the small town that has become her primary home. Whatever we do, it's not enough—enough of us to handle the workload, enough minutes in the day, enough rest, enough money for all those little expenses, enough ways to tell other relatives they have to wait. This is not the life I want for my mother.

I grew up in a family that said never to say the word "hate." You didn't hate anybody or anything, though we all really did.

But for the record: I hate cancer with a violence that surprises me. I hate that Black women are struck with more virulent types of breast cancer, and I hate the health disparities that mean we get less and later treatment.

That said, I can't stand that breast cancer tends to be all people think about when they think about women and cancer. I detest that rare cancers aren't common enough or lucrative enough for more research into their causes and cures.

I'm angry that I can't see my mother as much as I used to because she's doing the work of keeping other loved ones alive, often to the detriment of her own health. Then I feel ugly and selfish for those thoughts or the moments where I insist that I have to do my own work and live my own life. I hate that cancer has left gaping holes in my family tree and that it will likely one day invade my body. So far, I've been lucky: that lump was nothing more than the patently unglamorous lumpy-breast syndrome.

More than anything, I hate that my mother, who is in her seventies, is spending her twilight years tethered in place by cancer. And I hate that people who do nothing to help salute her and say that "she's strong." I know, from experience, that cancer kills strong Black women. I know that what doesn't kill you—caregiving, for instance—can make you sick.

Aunt Mary died. We couldn't work that outcome away—couldn't will it not to happen.

For some time after her death, butterflies would land on me, kiss my face, flutter on my shoulders. I thought it was a sign. *Slow down, enjoy the moment, look at the beauty in the world. I'm still here.*

For some time after her sister's death, my mother had to get used to not being the one physically caring for everyone. It took her some time to get the full night's sleep I wished for her because her body had retrained itself to sleep lightly, to wake up easily, to hear the sounds of discomfort, to obey the schedules and mandates of other people's bodies.

I don't want to think about how many years it has been since Aunt Mary died. Time is no universal healer. It just reminds me of the distance between this world and whatever realm follows this existence, the absence of her humor and vitality, how I wished I'd kept voicemails so I could hear the South Carolina coast in the way she spoke my name.

And on Mother's Day, I don't want my mother to think about it either. But that's asking too much of her to abandon the family memories, the toll of cancer, and her Herculean labors of love and obligation.

I want her to know that she's not a de facto nurse for other people. She has moved to a new place—bought the first house she's lived in alone and without children pulling on her leg. My father has dementia, but he's in a facility a few miles away. We, her children, had to fight her so she wouldn't insist she could care for him at home.

I want her to have a day without having to think about cancer or dementia. Or of other people at all. On this day, I hope she can browse an antique store as long as she wants, run out to lunch without notice, ignore the ringing phone, tell her adult children she's going to her painting class, so she can't chat now. I wish her a day when she doesn't have to be strong. I wish her a day when she can just be.

Originally published on Forward Together's Strong Families *blog on May 12, 2013.*

I'll Always Love Big Poppa: How Biggie Smalls Helped Me Understand My Parents' Deaths

Brittany Brathwaite

On March 9, 1997, rapper Biggie Smalls, born Christopher Wallace, had his life taken way too early. He was twenty-four years old. He was gunned down after leaving an industry party in Los Angeles, six months after the death of rapper Tupac Shakur. Being from Bedford-Stuyvesant, Brooklyn, and seeing how this entire New York City community came together to mourn—by pouring into the streets and openly grieving—helped me learn how to understand death and loss in a way that I didn't get at home.

I was one month shy of my second birthday when my biological mother died. I don't remember anything about my mother's death, her funeral, or what happened immediately after. I have no memory of my mother. I don't know what she smelled like. I cannot recall what her voice sounded like, how she laughed, or how she walked. All I had was a photo album of pictures of her with her friends, ex-lovers, and middle school class.

Two years later, my father would lose his battle to Hodgkin's lymphoma. I remember some things about my father. How tall he was and how white his teeth seemed to be. I have memories of a trip to the zoo, of him purchasing me a life-size Barney, and giving me a puppy we named Matrix. While I didn't remember much about either of my parents, one thing was true: they were both gone before my first day of kindergarten.

Although I was far too young to process my parents' deaths, when I was seven, I was clear that Biggie Smalls had died, that he wasn't coming back, and that many people whom I knew and loved were really upset—a phenomenon I would later learn was called grief.

I remember returning to school the week after Biggie's death. I attended a small Christian school in Bed-Stuy—I jokingly say I attended a "historically Black elementary school." Murder, violence, drugs, territory, beef—none of that was fictitious to us. Many of us knew and loved someone who had been a victim of gun violence. We tried to keep our whispering down; we weren't even supposed to talk about rap music—it was the "devil's music," according to the school administrators.

Even though we were in first grade, my classmates and I knew all the words to "Big Poppa," "Juicy," and "One More Chance." While our understanding of the world was still being crafted, we connected with the realities in B.I.G.'s songs—because for Black kids growing up in Bed-Stuy, those were some of our realities too.

Biggie's life meant a lot to us, but his death meant more to me.

I always knew that I wasn't like the other children. I would listen to adults in my family stumble over questions from school administrators about my parents. Where were they? How did they die? What was I feeling? They would hush a rowdy uncle when he would start reminiscing about good times with Strike (my father) or quickly change the conversation when the topic of how fashionable Delores (my mother) was came up.

I can only hope that they were trying to shield me from hurt, but when it came to discussing my parents' deaths, I always felt alone. I had so many questions about death and dying. Where did they go when they died? How did they split their time between the cemetery and heaven? If they were in heaven, why do we keep bringing flowers to this cemetery in New Jersey? My family made frequent visits to my parents' graves (holidays, birthdays, anniversaries of their deaths, all the days). That's how they grieved. I preferred to grieve differently, but at age five, I had no platform to voice my concerns. I had no one to talk to.

I spent too much time feeling angry that I didn't have my own memories of my parents. And the memories that other people had, they seemed to hold on to tightly, rarely sharing them with me. Because I didn't know everything about my parents, I felt as if I couldn't love them like everyone else did. B.I.G.'s death showed me how diverse groups of people had birthed him, recorded music with him and mentored him, and some (like me) just listened to his music. We all had different relationships with him—but all loved him. I could create my own memories of my parents and love them for that, always.

I remember the day when people came back to the block after standing on Fulton Street watching the procession of Biggie's hearse through the streets. I was home because I was seven, but I remember people saying, "I can't believe he's gone." I felt the sadness and heaviness of my community's loss in particular, as if I had lost someone. The air was heavy, and people were mad at "the West Coast," where I had never been.

I remember watching the news footage of people in the street when they started playing "Hypnotize" to the crowd. I knew that it was okay to celebrate life and what people had given you while they were on earth. I wanted to know what my parents left behind—where I could find the joy in their existence, as people found in Biggie's songs when his mother, Voletta Wallace, returned home to Bed-Stuy.

I was never told that crying, or feeling angry and upset, was okay— that these were normal and just reactions to death. People pouring into the streets, crying publicly at award shows and TV interviews, showed me that I didn't need to cry in the closet or the bathroom. There was nothing to be ashamed of. My pain was valid, and all people feel that as a part of life. I was not alone. B.I.G.'s death normalized grief for me.

More than that day, I remember the songs and videos that came out following his death—"I'll Be Missing You" and "We'll Always Love Big Poppa"—especially because they have children in them. Every time these videos came on, I would stand directly in front of the TV, mesmerized, and sing along with Diddy (then Puff Daddy), Faith Evans, and 112. I remember Diddy rapping, "In the future, can't wait to see if you'll open up the gates for me," and children dressed in all white running into what looked like forever, one of them Biggie's daughter, T'yanna.

Years after Biggie's death, I would think about his children. They were rich, but would they be like me? Orphans? T'yanna was three years old and Christopher Jr. was only four months old at the time of their father's death. Would they remember their father? Have someone to talk to about his death? Did they secretly cry in the bathroom or the closet when they missed him? Learn the word "grief" before they were in high school?

Less than a month after Biggie's death, *Life After Death* was released. To me, this was B.I.G. living beyond the grave. It allowed me to move past the memories of my father's funeral and what those tiny red roses that we placed on his coffin smelled like.

I loved the Notorious B.I.G. who made music about surviving and thriving despite the odds. That's what I had to do as a Black girl who lost both of her parents while growing up in Bed-Stuy in the 1990s. This would change a little bit after a few women's studies courses and a deep dive into Joan Morgan's *When Chickenheads Come Home to Roost: My Life as a Hip-Hop Feminist.* Nevertheless, Biggie still has a place on my altar and in my heart today because his death and how the world reacted to it helped me do what I now know was grieve.

My father, my mother, and even B.I.G. had more living to do after the funeral services were over. Every time I heard a song from *Life After Death*, I believed that more and more. My parents did not leave me an album to be released posthumously, but they created me. I am my parents' legacy—I get to be that. I am a living manifestation of their hopes and dreams and the continuance of their lives here on earth. I don't believe that they are just resting but, rather, that they are here resisting, creating joy, and building Black futures alongside me and inside me every day.

Originally published on The Root *on October 28, 2017.*

The Backlash to Beyoncé's Pregnancy Is an Example of the Attack on Black Motherhood

Gloria Malone

Whether you're a card-carrying stan or certified hater, a time will come to defend the Queen. Her every move brings a chorus of praise (or hype if you're a hater) that barely covers misogynoir's blare. Fame and fortune will never be enough to shield Beyoncé from the shit hurled at Black women—it littered the internet in steaming piles after her 2017 pregnancy announcement and the viral hate got personal for Black mamas like Gloria Malone.

Beyoncé announced her pregnancy via Instagram on the first day of Black History Month to—almost—everyone's delight. But just as quickly as the joy, excitement, and celebration circulated across social media platforms, so too did the judgment, anger, and hate. One publication called her announcement "tacky," while others argued that people who cared about Bey's pregnancy should focus on "more important" topics, like politics or the state of the Black family, as if it's impossible to discuss more than one thing at a time. While Yoncé seems to evoke a strong negative reaction in many, her experience is not unique. Black mothers, whether they're famous or not, always seem to be under attack.

Beyoncé has been on the receiving end of disrespect and hate since she came on the scene, but jabs seemed to intensify after she became a mother. From people alleging she faked her pregnancy with Blue and the Change.org petition calling for someone to "comb Blue's hair," to the recent backlash over her beautiful maternity photos, Beyoncé can't seem to catch a break. But she's not alone.

Another famous Black mama at the center of unfounded hate for Black motherhood is Ciara. The singer received so much criticism and disrespect for calling off her engagement to rapper Future, who is also the father of her son, that she sued him for defamation of character.[1]

Although she later dropped the lawsuit, Ciara continues to be subjected to name-calling and irrational hate for finding happiness in her relationship with her husband Russell Wilson. Despite Black women deserving real love too, as a writer argued in *Ebony* last year,[2] when it comes to Black mothers, many people don't agree.

The truth of the matter is that public ridicule is not reserved for Black mothers who are celebrities. We see especially visceral reactions of hate and judgment for Black mothers who have lost their children to state-sanctioned violence and/or extrajudicial murders by law enforcement officers.

Not only did Lesley McSpadden have to deal with the untimely extrajudicial killing of her son Mike Brown by police officer Darren Wilson—who was not held accountable for his actions—she also received a lot of backlash for "not raising her son right." The unfounded argument was that her assumed lack of parenting was the reason her son had been killed in the first place.

However, the opposite is true.

In her book, *Tell the Truth & Shame the Devil: The Life, Legacy, and Love of My Son Michael Brown*, McSpadden speaks to being a young mother who, despite experiencing various forms of violence, created a way to raise Mike in a community of love and joy. Years later, when Mike felt the world did not value his life and finishing high school wasn't worth it, McSpadden used the same love, joy, and community to motivate her son to graduate a few short months before he was killed.

Similar acts of diminishing Black motherhood were used against Tamir Rice's mother, Samaria Rice. Tamir playing in a park across the street from his home where he was killed was somehow a topic for ridicule and an example of "poor judgment" on his mother's behalf. However when non-Black parents who exercise "free-range parenting" allow their children to do the same, it is not a topic of national scorn; it's considered another parenting option.

Gender presentation and sexual orientation complicate the hate Black mothers receive even more. Recently popular YouTuber Domo found herself at the center of hate for being a Black pregnant lesbian who some would describe as "masculine." An Instagram post showing off her pregnant belly received many hateful comments, some even calling her "too masculine to be pregnant" or arguing that she "must be a confused stud." Domo shut down the hate by posting a beautiful photo of herself, smiling and showing off her belly, with the caption, "I am a woman. I am a woman who has always wanted a child. I am a woman who likes to dress how she pleases and doesn't give two sh-ts about your stereotypes. Who cares if I like to wear snap backs and joggers? Who cares that I'm not the 'normal' look of a pregnant woman?"

The disdain for Black mothers is not reserved for a specific "type" of Black mother. However, things like lower financial means, age, marital status, number of children, gender presentation, and sexual orientation can intensify the hate their families receive. Despite all of this, Black mothers continue to thrive, love, and raise families that are creative, joyous, and innovative. It's time that we realize #BlackGirlMagic comes from #BlackMamaLove and celebrate both.

Notes

1. Nedra Rhone, "Ciara Sues Ex-Fiancé Future for Slander and $15 Million," *Atlanta Journal-Constitution*, February 9, 2016, https://www.ajc.com/blog/talk-town/ciara-sues-fiance-future-for-slander-and-million/Ues60knO3Oz00JOyPnrf3I/.
2. LaSha, "Black Women Deserve Real Love, Too," *Ebony*, October 27, 2016, https://www.ebony.com/news/ciara-pregnant/.

Originally published on Ebony *on February 6, 2017.*

The Criminal Justice System Is Failing Black Families

Samantha Daley

Narratives about incarcerated people keep them atomized and othered— as though they aren't our sisters, mothers, cousins. To fully address the harm of our punishment system, we must name the damage done to our families.

In 2014, Marissa Alexander, a Florida mother of three, faced a retrial and possibly sixty years in prison for firing a warning shot into the air to ward off her abusive and estranged husband.[1] Though the bullet didn't hurt anyone, Alexander was initially given a guilty verdict and would have served a twenty-year sentence if the ruling had not been overturned following her first trial. She is Black and a woman, and that's all those who prosecuted her cared to know.

Cyntoia Brown was a teen and a sex trafficking victim who killed the john who purchased her. She was sixteen. Cyntoia was sentenced to a minimum of fifty-one years before being eligible for parole. She served fifteen years and was granted clemency in January 2019 after years of grassroots organizing. Her ability to be a teenager and raise a family was almost taken from her.

Cyntoia's imprisonment, and the historical injustices suffered by so many Black and Brown people, have led to major uproar and deeper conversations about the criminalization of Black women and its significant effects on the Black family structure. The criminalization of the Black community is breaking up the Black family, and by doing so, it is perpetuating the cycles of poverty and oppression in our society, especially when Black children are being put in foster care at a greater rate than other children.

Now that I've shared some of Alexander's and Brown's history, here is a snapshot of mine.

It's 3:00 a.m. I am awakened by bright lights and men with big attitudes. Police officers have entered my mother's home without warrants, guns at the ready, pointed at my eighteen-year-old brother. I have never felt more in danger than I do at this point, surrounded by individuals whom I'm supposed to trust to protect me. Instantly, I realize that my little brother, whom they assume is my big brother—the person they are really after for missing a court date—is a threat simply because of his Black maleness.

My big brother is not home that night, but the police find him at a friend's house a few weeks later. I recall seeing the scars on my brother's arms and shoulders from that day. The wounds were left by the dogs that the police unleashed on him; the dogs bit into him to the muscle, and the scars, visible and invisible, never fully healed. He was handcuffed and hauled away, and I was left behind—writing to him while he was in jail, then prison.

He was a criminal, and he was Black; that's all the police cared to know when they treated him in that violent manner.

Even before the moment the police stormed my home, my life had been greatly affected by the systematic expansion of the prison system and excessive criminalization of my community. At a time when lines are drawn on the value of Black lives,[2] we must unearth and fight how the unjust system most harms those who are already suffering. In Florida, the private prison industry is a booming business, and the GEO Group, a Florida company, is the largest prison and detention center contractor in the world. Based in Boca Raton, its site states it's leading in providing evidenced-based rehabilitation programs, but for Black people in Florida, they are leading in capitalizing off of Black bodies—in essence, modern-day slavery. By global comparison, Florida has higher numbers of incarcerated folks than that of every country worldwide.[3]

While the specifics of Alexander's trial and defense are unique, she is not alone. Thirty percent of African American women have experienced domestic abuse, which puts their lives in constant danger.[4] This has been seen time and time again and is currently a mainstream issue because of a video that surfaced of Ray Rice, former NFL player with the Baltimore Ravens, abusing his now wife in an elevator. Although the Ray Rice/

NFL scandal has received international attention and criticism, so many more women experience this violence every day and will be forgotten when the next big story hits. There is a clear link between intimate partner violence and a person's ability to maintain bodily autonomy and care for their children—two crucial tenets of reproductive justice. She may have successfully shooed away her abuser, but instead of supporting her in finding safety and protecting her children, the state has relinquished Alexander's freedom and her ability to bond with her youngest child.

Another way the justice system affects the Black family can be seen in how incarceration disproportionately affects people of color.[5] Black people in this country are imprisoned at more than five times the rate of whites; one in ten Black children has a parent behind bars, compared with about one in sixty white kids, according to the Stanford Center on Poverty and Inequality.[6] Keeping a family structure intact is nearly impossible with the incarceration of a parent. Separated children are often put into foster care, even though studies show that children raised in the foster care system are more likely to end up in the criminal justice system in the future.[7]

Dr. Dorothy Roberts, a scholar and social justice activist who has spent most of her career highlighting the intersections between gender, race, and class, is right: Incarceration of women "inflicts incalculable damage to communities . . . [transferring] racial disadvantage to the next generation."[8]

Roberts has also clearly laid out the intersections of the foster care and prison systems and their disproportionate impact on Black women.[9] She writes that the fact that one-third of foster care children are Black and landed there after being removed from Black women's care "is evidence of a form of punitive governance that perpetuates social inequality." Nearly 80 percent of women behind bars are mothers serving time for offenses largely related to domestic violence, sexual abuse, drug addiction, other health problems, and homelessness.[10] In fact, over three-quarters of the women sitting in prisons have histories of severe violence by an intimate partner as adults, and 82 percent have suffered physical or sexual abuse as children.[11] This is another example of how the justice system fails women who are actually in need of counseling programs, support groups, and treatment programs so that they can live and raise their families in a productive and healthy way.

Instead, from 1986 to 1991, the incarceration rate of Black women drug offenders increased 828 percent.[12] In 2010, Black women were put in jail at nearly three times the rate of white women. And the majority of jailed women lived with their minor children before their arrest.[13] These trends do not seem to be slowing. According to the National Association for the Advancement of Colored People, Black women are incarcerated at twice the rate of their white counterparts.[14]

The criminalization of Black women makes it nearly impossible for Black women to care for our families. When we do try to protect our families, we're punished, as in the case of Marissa Alexander, and even when we're not punished, our children are harassed and harmed. This injustice toward Black mothers cannot continue!

Far from rehabilitating in the ways our communities need, this system is attempting to break us.

There was never a mention of drug rehab programs or rehabilitation programs to help my brother rejoin and be productive in society.

The disproportionate and constant surveillance, harassment, threats, arrests, and family separation experienced by my older brother, and many Black men and women in my community, illustrate how our justice system fails people of color and hurts the communities that need justice most.

Amid this dire situation, if there's one thing I know about my folks, it is that we are resilient: we will find a way to survive, fight back, and keep on. Organizations and individuals are seeing this attack on families of color and taking a stand to protect our families and communities. SisterSong, an Atlanta-based reproductive justice organization that fights to ensure people can raise their families in healthy environments, and the Free Marissa Now campaign, which worked to help Marissa fight her conviction legally and get her story out across the country, joined together over the summer to host "Standing Our Ground"—an event to discuss the intersections of the (in)justice system and reproductive justice in the case of Marissa Alexander and others, and to shed light on attacks of this kind on communities of color throughout the nation. Having attended the conference, I was struck by all the organizations and beautiful women of color who showed up—bringing their expertise and experiences to the table. I knew I was not alone. My story and our suffering are connected. That power and the determination to win the battle for our rights and the rights of our families are carrying me through the events in Ferguson, Missouri, where a senseless killing and the outrage that followed showed us that our basic right to live is being challenged.

Conversations like these are lifting the veil that has obscured the connections between domestic violence, reproductive justice, and the criminalization our communities experience for simply being. Things will only improve when Black women and mothers are seen as human—when our lives are treated as though they matter as much as anyone else's; when our bodies and privacy cannot be violated, and if they are, the incidents are met with public outrage; and when communities join together to fight laws that turn those suffering from violence into criminals.

It's become clear that in order for our people to survive and thrive, we must call out this unjust criminal system and take a stand for ourselves. The "American dream" sold to us never included Black people and doesn't enable us to raise our families in safe environments. We as women of color—often the foundation and heads of our households— need to start trusting ourselves and making our own seats at the table. No longer should officers be able to push us around in our own homes and take away our right to protect our families.

We are the experts on our communities, while those in power are just outsiders looking in with no real connections to our day-to-day lives and lived experiences. We're told that prisons are supposed to protect our families from danger, but in reality, the policing of our communities and families presents a danger so grave, I question whether we can survive it. We must stop living in fear and call out those in positions of power and the policies they create that are out to harm and hinder our communities. We must join together and stop being our toughest critics because now more than ever our communities are under attack. We have come to a time in history, again, where simply being able to walk outside and live our lives is being threatened. We are resilient as a community, and our resilience is being challenged. It's no longer time to be on the defensive; it's time we stand because it's clear that our justice system isn't looking out for us.

Notes

1.   Steven Nelson, "Marissa Alexander Now Faces 60 Years for 'Warning Shot' at Husband," *US News & World Report*, March 3, 2014, https://www.usnews.com/news/articles/2014/03/03/marissa-alexander-now-faces-60-years-for-warning-shot-at-abusive-husband.

2. Katie McDonough, "Ferguson's Massive Problem: What Mike Brown's Death Means for Black Families," *Salon*, August 14, 2014, https://www.salon.com/2014/08/14/fergusons_overlooked_victims_what_mike_browns_death_means_for_black_families/.
3. Jerry Iannelli, "Florida's Incarceration Rate Is Higher Than That of Every Country on Earth, Report Notes," *Miami New Times*, June 6, 2018.
4. Feminista Jones, "Why Black Women Struggle More with Domestic Violence," *Time*, September 10, 2014, http://time.com/3313343/ray-rice-black-women-domestic-violence/.
5. Sophia Kerby, "The Top 10 Most Startling Facts about People of Color and Criminal Justice in the United States," Center for American Progress, March 13, 2012, https://www.americanprogress.org/issues/race/news/2012/03/13/11351/the-top-10-most-startling-facts-about-people-of-color-and-criminal-justice-in-the-united-states/.
6. Eli Hager, "A Mass Incarceration Mystery," The Marshall Project, December 15, 2017, https://www.themarshallproject.org/2017/12/15/a-mass-incarceration-mystery.
7. Melissa Jonson-Reid and Richard P. Barth, "From Placement to Prison: The Path to Adolescent Incarceration from Child Welfare Supervised Foster or Group Care," *Children and Youth Services Review* 22, no. 7 (July 2000): 493–516, https://www.sciencedirect.com/science/article/pii/S0190740900001006; "Incarcerated Women and Girls," The Sentencing Project, June 6, 2019, https://www.sentencingproject.org/publications/incarcerated-women-and-girls/.
8. Dorothy E. Roberts, "Prison, Foster Care, and the Systemic Punishment of Black Mothers," *UCLA Law Review* 59, University of Penn Law School, Public Law Research Paper no. 12–45 (August 2012): 1474, https://papers.ssrn.com/sol3/papers.cfm?abstract_id=2184329.
9. Roberts, "Prison, Foster Care."
10. "How the Criminal Justice System Is Anti-Women," Political Research Associates, last modified May 2005, http://www.publiceye.org/defendingjustice/pdfs/factsheets/14-Fact%20Sheet%20-%20System%20as%20Anti-Women.pdf.
11. "From Protection to Punishment: Post-Conviction Barriers to Justice for Domestic Violence Survivor-Defendants in New York State," Avon Global Center for Women and Justice at Cornell Law School and Women in Prison Project of the Correctional Association of New York, 3, https://static1.squarespace.com/static/5b2c07e2a9e02851fb387477/t/5c4f6b398985830b349383c1/1548708669444/2011+Post+Conviction+Barriers+for+DV+Survivors.pdf.

12. Martin A. Geer, "Human Rights and Wrongs in Our Own Backyard:
     Incorporating International Human Rights Protections Under Domestic
     Civil Rights Law—A Case Study of Women in the United States
     Prisons," *Scholarly Works* 388 (2000): 1–70, https://scholars.law.unlv.
     edu/facpub/388/.
13. The Sentencing Project, "Incarcerated Women and Girls."
14. "Criminal Justice Fact Sheet," NAACP, accessed August 14, 2020,
     https://www.naacp.org/criminal-justice-fact-sheet/.

Originally published on Rewire.News *on September 19, 2014.*

The Names of Things

Kemi Alabi

Some folks can call flowers by name. Dragonsbreathladysucklehibiscus. Dandiorchard Tigerpoppyleaf.

Dirt. Seed. Stem. That's as far as I get.

Georgia Burt didn't have a garden—she had eight kids, the corner store, and a reverend husband slumped into a puddle of hooch. She had the Lord and his three names and always Newports—none of that CamelMarlboroughVirginiaSlims shit.

Oops, she'd say. *Your mama don't want me to curse 'round you kids. I'm sorry.*

There's promise born into the names of things. Can't ask for shit if you don't know the word.

*

Little brother texts me for the first time in months.

My name is Brantley now.

I tell him I like Hakeem better.

No. Brantley or Corbett.

He's last of three, but the only one awarded a proper Nigerian naming ceremony. The only one to ever get a party at our house. I dressed the part of princess, shuffling around in stiff, shimmery fabric Mom wrapped four times tight around my little hips, balancing a matching head wrap tied pretty well for an American wife, for a girl from Milwaukee with a surgically corrected lazy eye.

Your uncle told me when I grew up, I'd have a little girl ugly as me.

But I prayed and prayed and prayed to God, Please let my daughter be pretty, *and look at you! Girl, you better praise Him!*

The neighbors seemed to arrive at the same time in the same white people clothes with the same white people names, and though my parents still live in the same white people place, this was the last time they invited the neighbors inside. Dad showed everyone around the new Jacuzzi and the new sauna and the new deck. He wore all five components of the king's outfit, and, as required, older brother dressed the part of the prince, my partner child doll in matching scratchy print.

He has Dad's name, a full-mouthed thing with one too many vowels, so he sometimes just goes by TJ.

When girls called the house for this TJ, Mom would tell them they had the wrong number and hang up.

But the ceremony: Dr. Olu had the honor of naming the now year-old boy. Doctor of what, I don't know—these are the titles Nigerian men use in lands that refused them kingdoms. Years later, he told me I'd be a doctor or a lawyer or nothing at all. Even at his funeral, no one heard his wife call him by his first name.

Hakeem Yekini Alabi, Dr. Olu proclaimed as the water cup blessed his tiny, squirming head. *Yekini* after the grandfather who'd died in Lagos before we'd ever met. *Hakeem*, as in *the dream*, where the Lord spoke to Mom and told her to have one last child. She didn't want to, but who was she to deny the voice of God? How could the boy He demanded have any other name?

It's Brantley now. Or Corbett.

*

In English, my middle name is inevitably mispronounced. Asia, after my grandmother. But no, say, *Ashaya*. This is how I spell it now. Asia Alabi's first and only visit to America was in January of the worst Wisconsin blizzard of my life. She only spoke Yoruba, so we watched Dad talk to her, sharing stories as though he'd always told stories, just never here, with us.

O tutu! O tutu!

Alabi, what does that mean? I've never heard Mom call Dad by his first name.

He threw his head back and laughed. *It's cold! It's cold!*

Mom bought a book and a series of tapes, but whenever Dad overheard her attempts to speak his language, he'd laugh hard from his throat until he nearly choked.

*

In college, I met the first American Africans who'd actually lived in the land of their names.

What's your full name?

Just Kemi.

I know an Oluwakemi, a Folakemi, but not a just Kemi.

Older brother got Dad's one-too-many-voweled name. Mom is just Kerry, American as sweet potato pie. Kemi is a compromise, a third world and second class pummeled into something that could maybe stand a chance.

You must get Kimmy a lot.

Yeah. And Cammy. I respond to both.

*

Years later, after she died, we learned Asia was a nickname. Grandmother's full name was Asiata. No one had known.

*

A-L-A-B-I? And you say it how? I know a few Alabis. They don't say it like that.

Every part of my name shivers like it might die refugeed in this empire's mouth, mispronouncing itself. I throw my head back. I laugh until I choke.

*

Dad has never called me just Kemi, always *Kemi, my lovely daughter.* After the stroke, his words became a carousel of phlegm spinning around two languages, tilted on a half-junked brain. Six voicemails this week, all the same: *Kemi, my lovely daughter, this is your dad, Taofiki Alabi.* A reintroduction. A reminder. An affirmation.

*

Hollowed father, these are your children: TJ, Kimmy, Brantley.

*

Dirt, seed, stem; *shit. I'm sorry.*

*

Faithful mother, this is your God: trust me. When you pray for them, I know who you mean.

*

Lord, let our children be pretty. Let them bloom gorgeous in this empire's mouth, and if there's promise born into the name of things, let them be Georgia, Yekini, Asiata. Kerry. Taofiki.

May they know how to pronounce their own names. May they claim the language that spoke them into this world. May they own the land upon which they tend their gardens. May they know the words for every color, fragrance, and bud.

Let them bury us beneath the roots and call us Amaryllis. Calla Lily. Wild Bergamot. May they know every way to ask for Sun and Water. May they forgive us for the impossible soil below.

Originally published on The Toast *on June 4, 2015.*

NAKED POWER

Introduction

Janna A. Zinzi

Josephine. Eartha. Pam. (Lil') Kim. Cardi.

Black sexuality is unabashed, sultry, and raw. Our curves and our confidence inspire many but threaten others. We have been worshipped and vilified for being naked and fierce. And God/dess forbid, we have something intelligent to say! We have been simultaneously desired and shamed for our innate sex appeal by a dominant, colonized gaze. The entire country was built by the subjugation of Black bodies and especially the rape of Black women to build wealth. Our body parts have been literally put on display in cages and museums for white supremacist consumption. We've been intentionally branded "jezebels" with insatiable sexual appetites to justify white violence against us. White supremacy survives by making us forget our innate power and replacing it with shame.

But through it all, Black folks have been booty shaking, shimmying, and twerking our way to freedom because our DNA remembers, and our ancestors remind us of who we are. We are reclaiming our bodies for ourselves. Nothing is juicier than centering our pleasure and claiming it as our birthright.

Together as Idas over the years, we've twerked naked in an ocean together, had outings to support our local Black strip club, and rehearsed burlesque and erotic poetry for one another. We have celebrated our collective Black bodies as a force for inspiration, change, and joy!

The iconic celebrities noted earlier model freedom in their bodies and inspire fantastic, if not extravagant and exaggerated, versions of liberation. They broke down barriers for us to fearlessly celebrate our bodies, our nudity, and our sexual expression. But more importantly, we learn from each other: the people in our community. Our homies, sistren, and even aunties can be reminders to express our desires courageously and joyfully.

Being naked isn't just about physical sex and body parts, it's also about vulnerability and honesty. We are sharing our truths with another . . . or sometimes just loving up on ourselves. Being naked feels powerful when it is on our own terms, free of shame and objectification. Sex can be healing and delicious connecting with a partner (or several) through caressing, kissing, stroking, or fisting. Sometimes it's just mind sex. No matter what, sexual freedom comes from acknowledging our fantasies and our needs; we tryna get OURS!

Yet we know as Black women and nonbinary folks that we've internalized deeply entrenched messages about what our bodies mean, and we have experienced how they are politicized. Ancestral experiences of sex shape how we show up today. But respectability will not keep us safe or satisfied! We are part of an era where we can throw away the "rules" our families needed to survive. Together, we are rejecting these constructs and fucking who we want, how we want it. We are discarding and rejecting the antiquated frameworks pushed on us by well-meaning family members, ignorant healthcare providers, politicians on all sides, and even myopic tech bros. No más! We are claiming our orgasms while rejecting binaries and boxes that limit our sexual expression. It's your business how you get off (*wink*).

The pieces in this section are here to decolonize our thoughts and our communities by reminding us to ask for what we want and to reject anything less. In the same way that healthcare, affordable housing, economic security, and reproductive justice are civil rights, pleasure is our birthright.

We have seen our bodies commodified by capitalism, culturally appropriated, and chopped up, disembodying our humanity. We have also reclaimed our autonomy. We resist simply by owning our sexuality, our curves, our divots and dimples, and our desires. As technology advances and social media connects geographies and generations, we have more outlets to celebrate all the ways our bodies look, how we move, and how goddamn fine we are. What is more powerful than a naked and free Black body reclaiming its divinity?

Auntie Conversations: Black Women Talk Sex, Self-Care, and Illness

Charmaine Lang

"You're just being nosy," one of my aunts said after I asked her if she enjoyed having sex with her husband. I assured her this was all part of a research project on the intimate lives of Black women. She relented a bit but still gave me the side-eye.

I've been engaged in archival research for the last year. While the personal letters of Black women writer-activists[1] and the newspapers of the Third World Women's Alliance[2] are remarkable and informative, they provide little insight into the intimate lives and sexual desires of Black women. After all, sex improves our mood and alleviates stress: that immediate gratification of pleasure and release is a way to practice self-care.

So on a recent trip home to Los Angeles, I asked my aunties to share their stories with me at a little gathering they threw in my honor.

And they did.

I asked them, "What's your sex life like?" "Do you want to have sex?" "Are you and your husband intimate?" "You know . . . does he kiss you and hold your hand?" And I learned that, contrary to tropes that present us as either asexual mammies or hypersexual jezebels,[3] the Black women in my life are vulnerable and want love and loving partners, at all stages of life.

Between 1952 and 1969, my maternal grandmother had six daughters and one son. All of them grew up in South Central Los Angeles, witnessing white flight, the Watts Riots of 1965, and the crack epidemic. At the same time, the women have kept the family intact. They are the ones who always plan big dinners for the holidays and organize food drives for their churches. And they arranged care of their mother toward the end of her life. I've always wondered how they were able to prioritize family and their own desires for intimacy.

So I asked.

My fifty-seven-year-old aunt who is a retired customer service representative living in Pomona, California, told me, "My lifetime of sex consisted of first starting off with getting to know the person, communicating, establishing companionship. Once that was done, the sex and intimacy followed. When you're younger, you have no frets. You experiment all the time."

I wanted to know more.

"You're not just trying to get in our business? You're actually going to write something, right?" was my mother's response.

When asked about the state of her sex life, my fifty-nine-year-old aunt, a social worker, said, "I am a married woman without a physical sex life with my husband. His illness has a lot to do with this, along with the aging process."

My Pomona aunt went into more detail about how as we get older our ability and desire change.

"You try to keep pace with pleasing your partner, and he tries to please you. But it is hard when you are a full-time worker, wife, and mother, and you commute to work. You're tired. Hear me: *you're* tired; they are not. You grow older, gain weight, and get sicker. You start to take medicine, and all that affects your ability and desire to perform."

"For me, in a nutshell, [sexual activity] feels like work: I don't feel excited. When it happens, it happens," she said.

I learned that the combination of energy spent on wage work, domestic labor, and mothering is draining, dissipating the mood for sex or intimacy. A husband who does not have the same domestic responsibilities has more energy for sex. The unbalanced load equates to differences in desire.

I wondered: Did my aunts talk to their partners about this?

Illnesses, such as diabetes and cancer, can cause anxiety, depression, and fatigue, which interrupt lovemaking. Talking to a partner can help to create a new normal in the relationship.

However, as my social worker aunt made clear, "It takes two to talk openly and honestly, which I find very difficult most of the time."

"To be vulnerable is hard because I do not want to get hurt emotionally, so I protect my heart from harm," she explained. "[My husband and I] can be harsh and curt to each other at times, which leads to me shutting down and not expressing my true feelings. My husband can be prideful and unwilling to admit there are issues within the relationship."

Aunt April, a forty-seven-year-old Los Angeles teacher, had some things to share too. "My love life is complicated. After suffering an overwhelming and devastating loss in 2011 of my husband and mate of nearly twenty years, I'm very hesitant to fully try again."

She hasn't dated since 1991. After much counseling, grieving, and encouragement from her twelve-year-old daughter, she decided to give it a try.

"I have been seeing someone, but I have a lot of fear that if I relinquish my heart to him, he will die. So, I think about sabotaging the relationship so that I don't have to get to know him and start worrying about his well-being and wondering if he feels the same way I do. In my mind, it's easier to be casual and not give too much of my heart," she said.

Intimacy, then, is also about being vulnerable in communicating how one feels—and open to all possibilities, even hurt.

As a thirty-four-year-old queer Black woman figuring out my dating life, my aunt's words about communication struck me. At times, I can be guarded, too, fearful of letting someone get close. I started to ask myself, "What's my sex life like?" And, "What role does intimacy play in my life as I juggle a job and doctoral studies?"

These auntie conversations were just as much about me as they were about my aunts and mama. I really want to know what to expect, what to anticipate, and, perhaps, even what *not* to do as I age and grow in relationships so that I, too, can have a fulfilling and healthy partnership.

"I enjoy sex more now than I did before," my mama, Jackie, said. Now fifty-five, she remarried in 2013. She lives in Gilbert, Arizona, and works in the accounting and human resource field. "My husband loves me unconditionally; with him, I'm more comfortable. It's more relaxing."

My mama expressed her ability to enjoy herself with her husband because of the work she put into loving herself and prioritizing her needs.

I always talk to my mama about my dating life: heartbreaks and goals. She always says, "Learn to love yourself first." It really isn't what I want to hear, but it's the truth. Self-love is important and central to the success of any relationship, especially the one we have with ourselves. My social worker aunt often takes trips to the spa and movies, and my aunt April is an avid concertgoer. They have found ways to have intimacy in their lives that is not informed by their relationship status.

The journey to self-love can be arduous at times as we discover parts of ourselves that we don't like and want to transform. But with much compassion and patience, we can learn to be generous with the deepest parts of ourselves and each other. And isn't that a necessary part of intimacy and sex?

The stories shared by my womenfolk reveal a side of Black women not often seen in pop culture. That is, Black women older than forty-five learning how to date after the loss of a partner and finding love and being intimate after fifty. Neither mammies nor jezebels, these Black women, much like the Black women activists of the 1960s and 1970s I study, desire full lives, tenderness, and love. My aunts' stories reassure me that Black women activists from decades past and present have intimate relationships, even if not explicit in the body of literature about them.

Notes

1. Kimberly Springer, *Living for the Revolution: Black Feminist Organizations, 1968–1980* (Durham, NC: Duke University Press, 2005).
2. For the newspapers of the Third World Women's Alliance, fifteen periodicals can be found in Special Collections at the University of Wisconsin-Milwaukee Libraries.
3. Numerous Black women historians and intellectuals concerned with controlling images have criticized the mammy and jezebel archetypes. The mammy, according to Barbara Christian's *Black Feminist Criticism*, is the "most prominent black female figure in southern white literature, is in direct contrast to the ideal white woman. . . . Mammy is black in color, fat, nurturing, religious, kind, above all strong, and [. . .] enduring." Like the mammy archetype, the jezebel is also a controlling image, which, according to Patricia Hill Collins, reflects the "dominant group's interest in maintaining Black women's subordination." The hypersexualized jezebel, "whore, or hoochie" is a representation of Black women's supposedly deviant sexuality. See Barbara Christian, *Black Feminist Criticism: Perspectives on Black Women Writers* (New York: Pergamon Press, 1985), 2; and Patricia Hill Collins, *Black Feminist Thought: Knowledge, Consciousness, and the Politics of Empowerment* (New York: Routledge, 2000), 72, 81.

Originally published on Rewire.News *on July 12, 2016.*

Shaming Women about Having Sex Doesn't Stop Us from Having Sex

Emma Akpan

I ask about one hundred people, either by phone or by knocking on doors, the same question each week as an organizer at a reproductive health nonprofit.

"Are you a supporter of women's health services, such as breast cancer screenings and birth control?" I say. Typically, people will tell me "sure," say they aren't interested in taking my survey, or tell me that they are already strong supporters of the movement and will fill out whatever I have for them that day.

One particular morning while out canvassing, I knocked on a door and a woman answered. After running through my usual spiel, I was taken aback by her answer. "No, I practice abstinent sex and depend on the Lord for my health services," she told me.

I smirked to myself as I tried to interpret "abstinent sex," which I assumed meant that she is celibate now to strengthen her spirituality.

But then I sounded a lot like that nearly a decade ago.

When I was fourteen, I decided to wait until marriage to have sex. I was so proud of this revelation that I wore it like a badge of honor as part of my identity as a teen. Sometimes I would try to determine who the virgins in my school classes were and the nonvirgins—of course, the latter were, in my mind, the bad kids.

I held the moral high ground as a "good girl." The premise was simple: Good girls were girls who did well in school and did not pay attention to boys. Good girls were those who waited for love and marriage; we took the time in our youth to develop other interests in academia and community service (in our churches, usually). It was as if as soon as a young woman had sex, she would become disinterested in school, church, and volunteer activities.

I was playing by the rules of my Christian upbringing. I learned in church that sex was bad, unless I was married, because the Bible said so. Preachers referred to Scripture, such as 1 Corinthians 6:19 ("or do you not know that your body is a temple of the Holy Spirit that is within you, whom you have from God?") and Galatians 5:19 ("now the works of the flesh are evident: sexual immorality, impurity, sensuality"), to support their claims that sex outside of marriage is sinful in the eyes of God and makes one dirty.

And yet, as a minister now, I realize that these Scriptures do not speak directly to sex inside of modern marriage as we know it, and "sexual immorality" could mean many things. For example, many biblical scholars agree that *porneia*, from which the word "fornication" is loosely translated, does not necessarily mean premarital sex. It can refer to many sexual sins. As scholar Boykin Sanders explains in *True to Our Native Land: An African American New Testament Commentary*, in 1 Corinthians 6:9 *porneia* refers to men being sexually involved with their father's wives and other forms of adultery.

But for many churchgoing young people, the pressures to abstain from sex, based on inaccurate interpretations of Scripture by preachers and other church leaders, are compelling. For me at least, abstinence meant that I could stay spiritually and physically pure and able to focus on things that were important to me, such as school, deciding on a career, and loving myself outside of a relationship. These are positive teachings from church, but it is also important for young people to understand that having sex doesn't necessarily mean that we lose those parts of ourselves just by doing it.

I've frequently heard in church the idea that our bodies are "temples" to discourage individuals from having sex. But, I wonder, how does having sex dishonor our temples? This question made more sense to me when I learned in divinity school about Western philosophy and the idea that our bodies and souls are separate and that, in order to be a good Christian, we fulfill the desires of our spirits by denying the desires of the body.

Not only does that philosophy encourage women to be abstinent, it encourages people to pray about illness instead of seeking treatment, encourages Christians to ignore mental health issues, and doesn't allow Christians to grieve in their own unique ways. Growing up, I frequently heard sermons for people who were in real pain, where they were told to pray, and God would give them strength. Indeed, prayer can give us strength, but prayer as a quick fix without acknowledging pain and grief can invalidate legitimate feelings.

Over the years, I've also come to understand that abstinence is a spiritual practice, and while it is a fine one, all of us do not have to adopt such a practice in order to achieve spiritual enlightenment. It's actually impracticable to seek to attain the exact spiritual practice of others since we all walk different paths in life. A starving person, for example, would not be able to fast, nor would someone with diabetes or another medical condition that affects their diet. They would need to adopt other methods to practice their religion. Many people who choose not to abstain from sex adopt other spiritual practices to fulfill their religious experience as well.

Abstinence would not help me in my advocacy work fighting back against poverty, inequality, racism, and the patriarchy. Yes, I could hold the badge of honor that I was celibate, but if that was the only thing I did to practice my religion, I would be doing it wrong.

Ultimately, shaming me from having sex did not improve my spiritual journey; it just made me feel guilty about my own natural urges.

The first time I had sex, I thought it was going to be life changing—and it wasn't. We did it and held each other after, and the next morning, as I usually do as a young minister on Sunday mornings, I went to church.

I always thought I would feel differently, that it would change me, or that I would feel an incredible loss. Or worse, that I would be forever attached to the person (I'm not). It was an important milestone in my life, and I was careful about choosing the person with whom I experienced it. But it didn't change who I was as a person.

As much as I was discouraged by faith leaders from having sex before marriage, I still did it, like many spiritual women who have come before me. In fact, a 2011 study from the National Campaign to Prevent Teen and Unplanned Pregnancy revealed that 80 percent of young people who self-identified as evangelical Christians are having sex.[1] Additionally, an overwhelming majority of African American regular church attendees support access to contraception and abortion.[2] Why? Because we are having sex and understand that contraceptives and abortion are essential parts of our healthcare.

Many people in both religious and political leadership believe women should be punished for having sex. They believe pregnancy is a consequence of acting irresponsibly, so women must endure it whether they want to or not. Instead of saying they don't agree, they depict sex as a traumatic experience and stigmatize reproductive healthcare, painting abortion as a sinful and regrettable act.[3] They believe women who have had sex should be deemed ineligible for dating and future relationships. Some faith leaders believe women should be punished by experiencing spiritual turmoil and feeling separated from God. But we don't have to—and shouldn't—feel shame. I don't feel bad about living out my humanity in this way.

I'm not going to apologize or feel guilty about being a sexually active Christian, especially based on ambiguous theology, which intends to crucify our humanity. We are made in the image of God; God made us human, and I will experience every part of that creation.

Notes

1. Tanya Somander. "Study: Majority of Young Evangelicals Have Pre-marital Sex, Exposing Flaws with Right-Wing Attacks on Sex Ed," *ThinkProgress*, September 29, 2011, https://thinkprogress.org/study-majority-of-young-evangelicals-have-pre-marital-sex-exposing-flaws-with-right-wing-attacks-on-3d270802ed04/.
2. Belden Russonello Strategists LLC, "African American Attitudes on Abortion, Contraception, and Teen Sexual Health," February 2013, http://www.bwwla.org/wp-content/uploads/2012/02/memo-final-2.8.pdf.
3. Anna Merlan, "Study: 'Overwhelming Majority' of Women Don't Regret Their Abortions," *Jezebel*, July 13, 2015, https://jezebel.com/study-overwhelming-majority-of-women-dont-regret-their-1717542325.

Originally published on Rewire.News *on October 9, 2015.*

A New "Pum Pum Palitix": Carnival and the Sex Education the Caribbean Needs

Bianca Campbell and Samantha Daley

Seeing Rihanna on Instagram in her sparkly bejeweled bikini and feather wings brought Caribbean Carnival tradition to mainstream pop culture. But besides Carnival being an annual excuse to wear scandalous glittery outfits and party in the streets all night, most Americans, including African Americans, don't know much about its rich traditions and history. (We just know about people getting wasted and flashing their titties at Mardi Gras!) As of 2017, 4.4 million Caribbean immigrants lived in the United States, but representations of Blackness in America often neglect or silo our family from throughout the diaspora.

In this piece, Bianca Campbell and Samantha Daley, two Caribbean American Idas from the South, share what Carnival symbolizes about sexual expression and the politics that try to regulate pleasure after da party done.

Bright colors, glorious headpieces, glitter. Steel drums and xylophones. As people with Caribbean roots, we feel our chests swell with pride and our hips begin to sway immediately when we think of Carnival and the ancestral rhythms of island cultures from Trinidad to Jamaica.

The costumes are sexy, sassy, and everything we aspired to be as Caribbean American preteens. We fawned over Carnival outfits like many tweens do for their future prom gowns. The feathers, the strings, and the beads became our markers of someone no longer a child but a grown individual who could finally do grown things: show off your body, stay up late, drink, wine[1] the night away, and, of course, have sex. Without a doubt, Carnival is about ownership of our bodies, about an annual recommitment to our sexuality and broader sense of liberation. Through dance, we tell and retell a true, old-timey story of freedom fighting and of pleasure for pleasure's sake. When we rush the DJ stage to party front and center at the show, when we jump in the parade "playing mas," we re-create together the movements of our ancestors who rushed gates, barricades, and slave owners for their freedom. ("Playing mas" in the modern day refers to being a part of the annual Carnival parade.) It is a reminder that movement is part of movement work and part of social justice.

It is impossible for us and, we suspect, many other Caribbean-descendant women and femmes to separate this sacred time of year from reproductive justice in all of its fullness. We know sex happens during Carnival. For some, that's kind of the point. So why aren't we talking about everything else that comes along with it?

Carnival's freedom of expression doesn't always extend to other parts of island culture, especially music with contradictory messages about sexuality. Trinidadian musician Lady Gypsy sings the hilarious "Old Time Wine," which is a hypocritical and classic example of the impossible pressure to be both reserved and unrestrained sexually. We are simultaneously told to "put on your bodysuit" and cover up and to "move your pumsy as you please." She criticizes women for leaving "nothing for men to wonder" while also letting you know that "old women who look like me" can still be amazing, provocative dancers who are incredible in the bedroom.

It's like not knowing when to jump in a game of Double Dutch. Are we supposed to have sex or not? Bold sexuality is squeezed into the confines of Carnival, a bacchanal, or Junkanoo.[2] But conversations about sex, reproduction, and abortion are left for another day that never comes.

Though every country is different, the Caribbean's powerful figures—from legislators to pastors and teachers—have pushed us all to lean into oppressive patriarchy since the end of slavery and the uptick of globalization. We must be palatable to foreign cultures, tourists, and the growing conservative majority, except during Carnival and other times of approved public sexuality. The end result: Caribbean women and femmes face a restrictive double standard.

In Marlene Henry's *Pum-Pum Palitix: The Blessing and the Curse* (her PhD dissertation at the University of the West Indies), the rumored 2006 dancehall queen in Jamaica and Japan discusses the gendered suffocation she and many have experienced.[3] She was revered for mastering a sensual, athletic, and technical style of dance, executing all the moves that make pastors blush. Yet she had to navigate a complicated culture that yearns to be both conservative and liberated.

In her iconic dissertation, Henry combines being a theorist and practitioner who shows us the multiple ways the body is a terrain for freedom struggles. She writes that individuals are lambasted and limited by genitalia ("pum" means vagina) and cisnormativity in Caribbean cultures, but that our oppressed bodies could also be a site where renegotiation of freedoms and power dynamics can occur.

"We have to think (about) the symbolism and prominence of the genitals in micro level socio-sexual relations," and the ways these relations are encouraged on macrolevels, Henry writes.

So now that mas is done, the paint, mud, and glitter washed off, we must continue to ask ourselves, What does it mean to be free within our bodies, our desires, and our sexualities all of the time?

Are we truly evoking the spirit of mas and of our ancestors when several Caribbean countries haven't mandated sex education for young people? Or when we have oppressive antiabortion laws and high rates of maternal and infant mortality, despite being some of the most literate and well-educated groups of people in the world?[4] We know exactly what could improve the quality of life for us.

Currently, Jamaica and other countries don't mandate comprehensive sex education in schools, despite knowing that many Jamaicans report having sex as early as age fifteen.[5]

And just mid-February 2017, days before Carnival, Trinidad and Tobago Minister of Education Anthony Garcia acknowledged that students in both primary and secondary schools are engaging in sexual activity, but said he would never allow the distribution of condoms.[6]

"We will always resist that," he said.

Trinidad and Tobago's then-recently-elected Unified Teachers Association president Lynsley Doodhai said he wasn't aware that there is a set standard sex education course in the country, but that it could be beneficial. The hurdle: getting teachers and parents on board.

"I know that teachers have expressed to me that they would have felt uncomfortable in teaching or educating students about sex education," he said to local media outlets. This sentiment is echoed in a 2011 UNICEF documentary about teachers from several islands as well.[7]

Trailblazers Sonia Folkes, president of the Jamaica Family Planning Association, and Denise Chevannes-Vogel, executive director of the

National Family Planning Board in Jamaica, are demanding that we not only have comprehensive sex education in schools but also start early.

Folkes argues that even primary school children must learn about their bodies and what consensual touch is and know that they are in control of themselves. And as former Caribbean tweens, we know how important that would have been for us and how the old saying "books before boys because boys bring babies" didn't go quite far enough to prepare us for adulthood.

Similarly, Chevannes-Vogel echoes the need for starting young. She also advocates for gender-specific conversations to disrupt dangerous societal norms around gender compliance and heteronormativity.

"For boys, you have to have 'nuff gyal inna bundle [a bundle of girls].'[8] You cannot be thought to be gay," she explained in the *Jamaica Observer.*

"For girls, the notion [is] that you need a man to validate who you are; the notion [is] that if you haven't had a child by the time you are a certain age, you are a mule. . . . All of these are the cultural attitudes that we also have to empower our young people against," she said.

In his 2016 address to the Family Planning Association, US ambassador to Trinidad and Tobago John L. Estrada had this to say about his home country and what could be possible for reproductive health and sexual liberation for all Caribbean people through bold, open conversations about sex:

"My wish is for effective, evidence-based formal sex education to further improve and reach all the children growing up in the United States and Trinidad and Tobago. . . . A girl needs to know that her body is her own," he said.

He continued, "Adolescents who struggle with their sexual identity should know that they are not alone, and they have nothing to be ashamed of. Teenagers need to know that love doesn't have to hurt. And that there is no tolerance for domestic violence. A young couple dealing with an unintended pregnancy should know the resources and options available to them in addition to marriage."

We envision and fight for a Caribbean where the ability to obtain holistic counseling, contraceptives, abortions, safe birth, and hormones is met with dignity and affirmation. Where LGBTQ young people can love boldly without fear of violence and with pride. Where a country's leadership doesn't outlaw medical care affecting the health and well-being of more than half the country just because the laws aren't aligned with their oppressive "ethics." Abortion, for example, is outright illegal in seven countries in Latin America and the Caribbean, and it is only permitted to save a woman's life in eight others, including Jamaica.[9] A 2008 study in St. Martin, St. Maarten, Anguilla, Antigua, and St. Kitts showed that abortions were being performed against the law and that the practice was the sole way women were able to obtain abortion services on those islands.[10]

We envision a world where Carnival is celebrated, where sex positivity and pleasure are the norm. We must resist the pressure to conform. Instead, we bask in the culture that has been carved by the women of color who wined before us. We have nothing to be ashamed of, but we have so much to lose. If we do not take a stand, our identities, femme sparkle, and entire cultures are at risk. Comprehensive sex education is a start.

Notes

1. "Wine" is an iconic dance style from the Caribbean. There are variations particular to the music genres of calypso, dance hall, reggae, soca, zouk, kompa, and others.

2. A "bacchanal" is a noun referring to misbehaving, although that is the very anti-sexuality framing this article hopes to debunk. Bacchanal refers to the freedom to be sexual, to be unhinged, although also sometimes literally unruly. Sexuality in this case is unfortunately linked to other types of behavior. Junkanoo is a celebration similar to Carnival in origin and importance. In Jamaica and Barbados, it is celebrated in the winter, close to December 26, and the outfits on those holidays pull more from the influence of West African ancestors to this day, whereas the outfits of Carnival have varied more over the centuries.

3. The full dissertation has been hard to find; there are and only clips floating around the internet (mainly on Tumblr), which bring many to believe it doesn't exist. However, there's still no denying the brilliance in the bits we do have whomever the author is and regardless of it being connected to a PhD dissertation.

4. In 2015, the *Jamaica Observer* referenced approximately sixteen women die every day in the Caribbean and Latin America from complications of pregnancy or childbirth, while 250 babies die each day before having reached twenty-eight days of age. A 2013 article by the same source references a study revealing an estimated fifteen per one thousand live births in Latin America and the Caribbean

died within the first twenty-eight days postpartum. UNESCO reports Jamaica's literacy rate across gender to be 88.7 percent. The United States, the United Kingdom, Germany, and many other similar countries do not submit literacy reports to UNESCO. "Maternal Mortality Continues to Be Unacceptably High," *Jamaica Observer*, April 18, 2015, http://www.jamaicaobserver.com/news/ Maternal-mortality-continues-to-be-unacceptably-high_18766170.

5. Tanesha Mundle, "Another Call for the Teaching of 'Sex Ed' in Schools," *Jamaica Observer*, July 18, 2012, http://www.jamaicaobserver. com/news/Seven-is-the-age-of-reason_11943466.

6. "Garcia: No Condoms in Schools," Loop News, February 17, 2017, http://www.looptt.com/content/garcia-no-condoms-schools.

7. http://www.open.uwi.edu/hflecaribbean/content/unicef-teaching-sex-education-schools-caribbean (site discontinued).

8. "You need to be with many girls." This is an English translation of a popular song by Jamaican artist Beenie Man entitled "Nuff Gal." The song also explicitly asks youth to take after his example by demanding women brush his teeth and wash his feet, among other things.

9. "Unintended Pregnancy and Abortion Worldwide," Guttmacher Institute, July 2020, https://www.guttmacher.org/fact-sheet/ abortion-latin-america-and-caribbean.

10. Gail Pheterson and Yamila Azize, "Abortion within and around the Law in the Caribbean," *Puerto Rico Health Sciences Journal* 27, no. 1 (2008): 93–99, https://www.ncbi.nlm.nih.gov/pubmed/18450240.

Originally published on Rewire.News *on March 1, 2017.*

Exam Rooms and Bedrooms:
Navigating Queer Sexual Health

Taja Lindley

I've been giving praises for Obamacare because for the first time in two years, I have health insurance. I celebrated on January 2 with a long-overdue Pap smear and sexually transmitted infection (STI) roundup. Everything was going well, until the awkward moment I told my doctor that I'm queer.

Yes, I have sex with women.

It wasn't awkward for me to share that information. It was awkward to have to repeatedly ask the same questions over and over again because my healthcare provider wouldn't acknowledge my questions with direct answers.

In the exam room, I asked the nurse practitioner about STI risk and transmission. I had specific concerns about herpes and human papillomavirus (HPV). I kept emphasizing that I have sex with women, and she kept not answering my questions, dodging them, and responding without directly taking on what I asked her. She went into a spiel about shame and stigma, telling me not to worry about potentially contracting herpes or HPV because they're prevalent infections and the hardest part of dealing with those infections would be the shame and stigma, not the infection itself. While I appreciated a conversation about reducing shame and stigma, that didn't answer my questions. I was asking about the science, the transmission.

What does HPV transmission and risk look like for women who have sex with women? How risky is my sexual activity? How reliable is the herpes test? Can I get the lay of the land, the overview of STI transmission, and risk for women who have sex with women? What should I be concerned about? How do I navigate safe sex? I didn't want to ask Google, WebMD, or the Centers for Disease Control and Prevention (CDC); I wanted to get the nitty-gritty in that room. Having waited two hours to get that fifteen-minute exam, I planned to leave with all of my questions answered.

After a lot of back and forth, the nurse practitioner finally admitted that she did not know much about the subject as it relates to women who have sex with women and directed me to another staff member who could answer my questions. Thankfully, the next healthcare provider I spoke with gave me all of the information I was looking for.

But my frustration lingered as I questioned why I had to go through all of that to get some answers. I wondered why she took so long to admit that she did not feel equipped to answer my questions. Did her need to be the expert get in the way? I also thought about her other patients who may not be as persistent and demanding as I was; how would they get the information they need? Perhaps the most disturbing aspect of all this was that it occurred in a progressive, gay-friendly health clinic where I assumed everyone would have answers to my questions and referrals for such basic inquiries would not be necessary. Surely I'm not the only woman who has sex with women who has sought their care.

Queer sexuality is not a specialty in reproductive healthcare. And as a 2014 case of woman-to-woman transmission of HIV confirmed by the CDC reveals, healthcare providers need to tell their patients about the risks associated with all sex.[1]

Indeed, people are having all kinds of sex, regardless of how they identify their gender and sexual orientation. We need a healthcare system that is prepared to address everyone's questions, issues, and concerns about sex, sexuality, and sexual and reproductive health. Unfortunately, sex education and sexual health services remain within a heteronormative context. This must change.

With the rollout of Obamacare, thousands of previously uninsured LGBTQ folks who haven't seen a healthcare provider in years are navigating plans, finding providers, and likely going through the same trial and error that I did to find someone who gets them. Thankfully, there are resource guides to aid in this journey, and yet the exam room isn't the only place where the conversation is awkward and where their questions will be sometimes avoided.[2]

When I used to identify as straight and had sex with cisgender men, life seemed so much simpler. No condom? No sex. My mother, a registered nurse who gave birth to me at age nineteen and raised me on her own, had the birds and the bees talk with me when I was in the second grade. We covered anatomy, intercourse, and the process of pregnancy and birth. And while I thank her for the early crash course in sex education, its focus on pregnancy left out a whole lot of other information—like STI risk through sexual activity beyond intercourse. She probably focused on pregnancy because she was concerned about me becoming a young mom too, but good intentions aside, there was a gap in my sex ed that was not filled by the public education system in metro Atlanta.

As I navigated the waters of sexual health as a straight woman, information was relatively easy to find, and healthcare providers were ready with answers to my questions. Public materials and ads about safe sex were everywhere—for straight people. I saw a few about men who have sex with men but absolutely nothing about women who have sex with other women. So in 2010, when I had my first sexual experience with a woman, I was ill-equipped to have conversations around safe sex and put that into practice. My sex ed didn't prepare me for this part of my sexual expression, and my mother didn't anticipate her daughter being queer. (I'll save my coming out story for another article.) So what's a queer girl to do?

I tried to figure it out on my own. As a queer woman, I had been having the most unprotected sex I had ever had in my life. With pregnancy off the table and HIV reportedly being low risk, I rarely used finger cots and dental dams. If conversations about sexual health and history happened at all, it'd be a conversation after we'd already had sex. I became less diligent about testing and annual Pap exams, and not too long after "coming out," I lost my health insurance.

Late last year, I started dating a woman who is really passionate about LGBTQ sexual and reproductive health. During one of our late-night sexy calls, she interrupted to ask me about my sexual health and history and to share hers. This was the first time in my queer life that another woman initiated this conversation with me.

She was diligent about her own testing and wanted to make sure I got tested before getting intimate. We ended up becoming intimate before we shared our results, and we chose to have protected sex, using dental dams and finger cots, until my results came in. My conversation with her and the open enrollment of Obamacare gave me a sense of urgency for applying for health insurance and making my doctor appointments. Although we are no longer dating, I appreciated that we had open, clear, and consistent communication about our sexual health and history before and during our time of intimacy. It was not an experience I was used to as a queer woman. But it's worth getting used to.

In fact, I am inspired to have more frank and candid conversations with my partners about our sexual health, history, and practices, like I did when I was sleeping with men. I'm also feeling inspired to have these conversations with my queer girlfriends, sharing what I learned in my last gynecological visit, swapping stories and information, and making sure we're all having safe and pleasurable sex. And yet it's not all on us. As more of us get healthcare, we must demand that our providers are meeting our needs, in every context.

These frank conversations, in both exam rooms and bedrooms, will ensure that folks ain't out here groping in the dark.

Notes

1. Martha Kempner, "CDC Confirms Rare Case of Woman-to-Woman HIV Transmission," *Rewire.News*, March 14, 2014, https://rewire.news/article/2014/03/14/cdc-confirms-rare-case-woman-woman-hiv-transmission/.
2. "Strong Families Network," *Forward Together* (blog), accessed May 28, 2019. https://forwardtogether.org/programs/strong-families-network/.

Originally published on Rewire.News *on March 18, 2014.*

Why Doesn't the Trans Community Have a Legit Dating App Yet?

Raquel Willis

Tinder, the famed mobile dating application, has brought about the dawn of the "Dating Apocalypse," declared the headline on a *Vanity Fair* article in September 2015. The piece, which used interviews with members of the ever-maligned millennial generation to conclude that—surprise!—it's easier than ever to hook up in the smartphone age, was just one in an endless stream of think pieces declaring dating apps the harbinger of the end of human romance.

For many cisgender people, it truly is easier to date, hook up, and otherwise couple than ever. But for those who are trans or gender non-conforming, dating online is much trickier.

Navigating popular dating apps while trans can often feel like diving into shark-infested waters. In June 2015, reports emerged that transgender Tinder users were being "reported" to the service as gender nonconforming and banned.[1] In June, nearly a year later, Tinder CEO Sean Rad announced the app will unveil a better experience for gender nonconforming users within the next few months, albeit with scant details as to exactly what they have in store.

On Grindr, one of the world's most widely used gay dating apps, trans users report near-daily harassment;[2] Trans Men on Grindr, a Tumblr that chronicles the bald-faced discrimination trans users face there (and on other gay dating apps like Scruff), makes brutally clear that even on supposedly progressive queer dating platforms, trans users are subject to bigotry and intolerance.

"We take the experience and the safety of all our users seriously, both in and out of app," a Grindr spokesperson wrote in an email to *VICE*. "While we can't make people behave better overnight, we in no way support any form of discrimination." They went on to elaborate that Grindr bans profiles containing hateful content, as stated in the app's terms of service, and vets user reports of such activity daily.

A market void exists in online dating for safe, supportive, gender-inclusive platforms. And while one might think that cash-flush Silicon Valley would be working doubly hard to reach trans users, new options that emerged to fulfill the need—including Teadate, GENDR, and Thurst—are either unproven, yet to launch, or lackluster at best.

"I don't believe the majority of our society has seen trans lives as human up until recently," user experience designer Robyn Kanner told *VICE*. The advocate for gender inclusivity and diversity in tech says she's experienced easily avoidable discrimination via some popular start-ups. "In a way, it's no wonder why the tech community is just now starting to scratch the surface on what the trans community actually needs."

Among established players, OkCupid has emerged as one of the most queer- and trans-affirming platforms in the industry. In November 2014, the site released what should have been a game-changing number of gender and sexuality options: twenty new gender identifiers and ten new orientation options.

"When we launched our expanded gender and orientation options, 20 percent of the OkCupid team identified as LGBTQ+," OkCupid CEO Elie Seidman told *VICE*. "Inclusivity is a genuine part of our team's DNA and something we're always thinking about. [The expansion] created user experience problems to solve within our site and apps, but these challenges were worth it, because we understood and believed in the need; for many other apps and sites, this complexity could be a deterrent."

Seidman notes that initially, many within OkCupid's user base expressed confusion as to the meaning of these new options—but rather than define those terms themselves, they turned to those who identified with them to create a crowdsourced dictionary they call *Identity*.

Among the smattering of apps that try to address the gender-inclusivity market gap, most come up short or are too new to success-fully judge. Teadate, founded by trans-attracted entrepreneur Michael Osofsky and transgender model Pêche Di in summer 2015, aims to pro-vide an affirming environment for trans folks and those interested in dating them to meet. However, in this reporter's experience, the site is buggy and often stalls.

Two new apps—GENDR, which launched in July 2016, and Thurst, which will launch in beta in September 2016—are setting out to redefine how queer, trans, and gender nonconforming folks interact and connect with like-minded (and like-experienced) individuals.

On GENDR, the brainchild of event producer Barry Brandon and experiential marketing consultant Christine Courtney, dating and sex take a backseat to loftier goals: establishing a safe community for transgender people where sharing one's story is part and parcel of the user experience.

"There are dating apps for both the straight and gay community, but my intention wasn't to date or hook up—it was to just start conversation," Brandon told *VICE*. "It felt as if there was a need for a safe space where people can present their authentic selves without the pressure of romantic or sexual interaction."

With three hundred users so far, user profiles on the app focus beyond the physical, emphasizing instead common interests, like music, gaming, activism, and more. The app's creators say GENDR's subscription-based membership model, at five dollars per month or thirty per year, will support live events and subscriber workshops while deterring trolls.

GENDR already features posts on a range of topics, from coming out to traveling while queer to advertisements for events hosted by the app creators. Users of almost every gender or sexual identity imaginable are represented. In the app's infancy, the small user base has shown a high amount of engagement with the platform—but people of color may find the app lacking, as most users are white.

That's where Thurst comes in. Developed by self-taught genderqueer coder Morgen Bromell, who uses gender-neutral pronouns, the platform grew from their own experience navigating online dating. Bromell is still crowdsourcing funds to provide a fiscal cushion ahead of the launch of what "could be the first truly inclusive dating app," as the *Daily Dot* wrote last February.[3]

"I really hated existing apps like Tinder, OkCupid, and others," Bromell told *VICE*. "It's so much easier for cis men, especially cis white men, to date on those platforms. For people of color and any other gender or orientation, it's difficult."

Bromell thinks that the entire app creation process needs to evolve in response, which inspired them to launch Thurst.

"These apps are based on white male sexual desire. There's something that needs to change in the building process—the consideration of how we interact and connect with people," they said.

Designed with simplicity at its core, Thurst's beta will focus on inter-actions most people are accustomed to: matching, messaging, reporting, and blocking. Bromell hopes to expand the user experience in future iterations. In fact, their only worry is finding funding, which has been grueling to come by.

While both GENDR and Thurst can't promise perfect experiences and long-lasting love, it at least matters that trans and gender noncon-forming folks and queer people of color are finding their voices and the tools to make a reality of the lives they desire.

Notes

1. Madison Malone Kircher, "Transgender People Are Reportedly Being Banned from Tinder," *Business Insider*, June 3, 2015, http://www.businessinsider.com/transgender-tinder-users-reported-and-banned-2015-6.
2. David Levesley, "Grindr's Trans Dating Problem," *Daily Beast*, April 14, 2017, http://www.thedailybeast.com/articles/2015/01/09/grindr-s-trans-dating-problem.html.
3. Molly Stier, "5 Great Dating Apps That Aren't Tinder," *Daily Dot*, February 29, 2020, https://www.dailydot.com/debug/best-dating-apps/.

Originally published on VICE *on August 11, 2016.*

Sexy MF: Celebrating Prince, New Orleans Baby Dolls, and Not Giving a F*ck

Janna A. Zinzi

"I'm not a woman. I'm not a man. I am something that you'll never understand." The timeless lyrics of "I Would Die 4 U" reverberated down Claiborne Street. Somebody's auntie dressed head to toe in purple spandex peddled past me on her bike carrying a massive speaker. I smiled real big watching her weave through the crowd waving at folks. In New Orleans's historic Tremé neighborhood, I was part of a sea of "rainbow children" adorned in purple wigs, sequins, and an array of Prince paraphernalia. People of all ages, races, gender expressions, and backgrounds followed the buoyant brass band horns and booty-shaking drumbeats of the second-line parade commemorating Prince a few days after his death. We clapped, shouted, and sang to the heavens because the Crescent City knows how to party. There was no better place to have been, or that seemed more appropriate, to celebrate and mourn our beloved Purple Majesty.

I, like so many other people there, grew up with Prince. I remember seeing the "Little Red Corvette" and "When Doves Cry" videos as a toddler and becoming obsessed. I saw myself in him, this magical being playing the guitar in skin-tight pants and heels while ladies with spiked hair played the keyboards behind him. Prince made me feel like it was normal to dance around half naked, that it was okay to be all the way extra. As a young biracial Black girl who loved cheesy eighties metal as much as Michael Jackson, his musical fusion of rock, funk, and soul showed me Black music was beyond boxes and that we can do everything. I couldn't really understand his early lyrics because I was so young, but I knew it was taboo and provocative, and I was mesmerized.

Back on Claiborne, Mardi Gras Indians with brightly colored, ornately feathered, and beaded suits strutted along the I-10 overpass embodying the ties between African slaves and Native Americans.

Numerous "social aid and pleasure clubs," community organizations that were set up by Black communities in the Jim Crow era, marched through the streets; their brass bands creating a cacophony of Prince cuts. This is the spirit of Tremé, the New Orleans neighborhood that was the birthplace to numerous aspects of African American musical culture, especially jazz. Prince is part of this legacy. All four of his grandparents were from Louisiana, and music is in his DNA; his mother was a jazz singer, while his dad was a pianist and songwriter. He was also unapologetically Black, just like New Orleans, Louisiana (NOLA).

I stopped on the sidewalk to soak up the energy, people-watch, and take video when I ended up next to a couple of "Baby Dolls," members of a group started by African American sex workers in 1912. Vanessa, a petite, fiery woman, perhaps in her fifties, was sashaying in a purple satin baby doll dress with white ruffles and waving her white parasol. Her energy was infectious and joyous. She was joined by another woman sporting a purple sequined fedora, the daughter of legendary Baby Doll Queen Mercy. NOLA royalty. I shimmied with them, chanting "Purple Rain," and we strolled down the block. They both stopped to hump a motorcycle with a (Black) policeman still sitting on it while I fell back and watched them with disbelief and utter joy at their audacity. Everyone was cracking up, and the crowd that gathered cheered them on. This was totally on brand for the Baby Dolls.

As I watched Vanessa and her dance partner in ribaldry, I realized that Prince and the Baby Dolls came from the same spirit of free sexual expression that is particularly taboo for Black people in America. Us Black girls with a Christian upbringing (strict or not) are expected to be prudish, proper ladies who keep our legs closed . . . at least outwardly. You don't want to be known as a "fast" girl. It's the pressured appearance of chastity that feeds respectability politics and internalizes shame. That never felt right to me, even as a youngster, so Prince's videos normalized sexual expression for me.

The release of "Diamonds and Pearls" coincided with my onset of puberty. Although I didn't have sex until much later, I imagined it sounded like his guitar riffs, soulful grooves, and electronic synth beats. They even looked like orgies and celebrating pleasure. He expanded my imagination of what a free Black body can look like. In a legendary performance of "Gett Off" at MTV's 1991 Video Music Awards, he showed out in an ornate lace-like yellow suit with the ass cut out. He shocked the

Ida Janna A. Zinzi (right) smiles for a selfie with two of the Legendary Baby Doll Ladies at the second line honoring Prince in New Orleans on April 2016. Photo by Janna A. Zinzi.

audience by gyrating his booty and singing the lyrics, "Now move ya big ass round this way." I had never seen a Black man's butt on full display on TV, let alone with pride and on his terms. In a world (and entertainment industry) that capitalizes and exploits women's bodies, Prince used his own nudity to challenge ideas of masculinity . . . and to tantalize.

Similarly, the Baby Dolls used costume, performance art, and their bodies to disrupt. According to Kim Vaz, historian and author of *The "Baby Dolls": Breaking the Race and Gender Barriers of the New Orleans Mardi Gras Tradition*, the African American women of Storyville (the segregated red-light district at the time) wanted to "mask" for Mardi Gras like their white counterparts—and competitors. They decided to dress in short skirts and bonnets like little girls to make fun of imposed gender constructs. They adopted other stereotypical male behaviors like "smoking cigars and flinging money at the men" to assert their independence. The early Baby Dolls even sang songs criticizing the men who judged them. Like Prince, they highlighted and challenged how race and culture intersect with these gendered expectations. Just like the Baby Dolls, Prince gave Black folks permission to be sensual, bawdy, and entrepreneurial. Remember that time he changed his name to a symbol no one could pronounce to protest his record label's control over his music? They all rejected ownership and asserted their autonomy.

Seeing Prince as a youth and then learning about the Baby Dolls as a woman connected me to my soul family. I felt less alone and even as if I'm carrying a torch. They paved the way for burlesque dancers like me to use nudity for social commentary and to remember to center my pleasure. I admire how they use unabashed sexuality to make people uncomfortable. By asking others to confront their own repression, they taught me that I have to release my own. They became my Black history icons and models of decolonizing my mind, body, and spirit.

Along the party route, I stood by a column holding up I-10 with "Big Up the Black Woman" spray-painted in purple on it. I smiled because Prince would have appreciated that. He mentored so many dope Black women musicians and used his influence to give us a voice in a misogynist industry. Around the corner, an adorable young queer being in a black G-string and devil horns twerked for partygoers using a gold-painted wooden cross to keep their balance. I'm here for satirizing patriarchal Christian imagery because my personal Jesus wants me to enjoy sex and orgasms, okay? Womxn and bois showered the dancer with great appreciation and dollars. Their outfit was clearly a nod to Prince's provocative album cover for *Dirty Mind*: black panties and a leather jacket. It was like watching someone "catch the spirit" in a church of freaks. We were a multiracial, gender-variant, intergenerational congregation worshipping the spiritual dimension of raw sexuality.

Being able to celebrate the life and artistry of Prince in New Orleans was truly a divine gift. His death felt like a personal loss, a major hit to the Black community, and the end of a musical era. Since I had come to town for the epic annual jazz fest, I got to see artists like Janelle Monáe, J. Cole, and Kermit Ruffins and Cajun local bands like Los Po-Boy-Citos pay tribute to him all weekend long. Jazzfest was a catharsis while the second line was a fucking party! It is forever etched in my heart. Seeing a truly diverse crowd of thousands in fellowship singing, dancing, and communing together reminds me of the power of art to connect and heal people. Our authentic, literal, and figuratively naked selves are how we can model freedom to others. I'm committed to carrying on that legacy.

Originally published on The Root *on June 7, 2016.*

This Is What Naked Power Looks Like

Taja Lindley

The lights go down. Sultry music fills the theater as a performer struts onto the stage, adorned with sequins, feathers, and tassels—the embodiment of decadence. She confidently removes her costume, piece by piece, until she reveals her nearly naked body. This is the time-honored tradition of burlesque, and it is unexpectedly on the front lines of resistance against racism, objectification, and gender injustice.

Burlesque is an art form with a rich history. *Ecdysiasts* is the formal name for striptease performers like Josephine Baker. Famed for her provocative banana skirt performance in 1920s Paris, Baker was also an activist. She refused to perform for segregated audiences and spied against Axis powers during World War II. Many burlesque artists of color carry on the practice of performance art as advocacy today.

As an artist-activist, I have had the pleasure of learning from ecdysiasts who know their craft, celebrate its history, and continue its legacy. I spoke with three leading performers, exploring the political side of this traditionally bawdy art form: Miss AuroraBoobRealis, a mother, cofounder of Brown Girls Burlesque, and cofounder of brASS: Brown RadicalAss Burlesque; Chicava Honeychild, the creative producer of Brown Girls Burlesque, performer, historian, and documentary filmmaker of Black burlesque; and Perle Noire, an award-winning artist with accolades from critically acclaimed burlesque festivals.

Taja Lindley: What stories do you create with your body onstage? How is that similar to or different from the stories others have placed on your body and life?

Perle: Growing up, I survived a lifetime of ridicule and verbal abuse. I was told that I was ugly on a daily basis. I was taught that my skin tone was too dark to be beautiful and loved. I was taught that a woman's place in this world is nothing more than [as] a man's fantasy, with or without her consent. All of the lies skewed my perception of beauty, glamour, and myself. Through the art of burlesque, I found the power in my own voice and, most importantly, my sacred body. It's not about nudity when I bare my soul to the audience. It's deeper than that. I'm reclaiming my body, voice, love, and power with each reveal.

Aurora: Central to my existence in this world is the fact that, as a person, I cannot and will not separate myself from my art, my race, and my political beliefs. I use my body to tell stories, sometimes clothed, sometimes not. And it is with this understanding that I felt called to make *Still Happening* to Cassandra Wilson's haunting cover of "Strange Fruit," expressing with pain, frustration, and rage that this song was still relevant in 2015. My bare skin is all at once a canvas and a reminder of our collective humanity. After one performance of it, a young woman came up to me and expressed how powerful it was to see my confidence in my body, a body that has given birth, isn't perfectly toned, and has wobbly bits, because that isn't something that she sees regularly. With *Din Daa Daa*, a piece to the classic eighties

Burlesque pioneer and brASS cofounder Miss AuroraBoobRealis. Photo by David L. Byrd.

Burlesque performer, historian, and teacher Chicava Honeychild onstage in New York City.

song by George Kranz, I am celebrating my passion for rhythm and play, and the biggest reveal isn't my breasts but the discarding of my heels so that I can truly get down. I am not a distant beauty one puts on a pedestal but an embodied wild woman who sweats and smiles and radiates joy.

Taja: While you're teaching burlesque, what barriers do students often face in authentically expressing their sexuality?

Aurora: We are so programmed in this society to think that sexuality is a bad thing, especially expressing it publicly outside of the nar-rowly defined heteronormative structure. These prescribed norms are insidious and get into our psyche no matter how vigilant we are. When I teach, I come from a place of transparency, sharing my own struggles with authentically expressing my sexuality. It isn't about being perfect [or] doing a set of moves that reads as empowered and sexy onstage but rather being embodied and present in the moment. Through exercises, I help participants explore, define, and celebrate their own brand of sexy.

Chicava: Ladies are so quick to see themselves as not doing anything right. Women will exhaust themselves looking after others and feel like they should have done better. We don't have a culture of self-care.

Perle Noire, the Black Pearl. Photo by Susan Wolf.

It might be that the highest expressions of self-care are the things no one can see but that emanate off of a woman for having done them.

I want how I share burlesque with women to be a part of a culture shift that encourages women to accept, appreciate, and love themselves exactly as they are. The next layer of challenge is battling against every image of "this is sexy" that they have ever been confronted with in media and life. It causes comparison, which is a joy thief.

Tajay: Why and how is performance art—burlesque in particular—integral to our social movements?

Perle: Art has always been the catalyst for gender equality and social awareness, and burlesque is no different from any other art form. Along with the neo-burlesque revival, burlesque has adopted a new face. It's not just women who are being booked worldwide to celebrate the art of the striptease. So many powerful men are dominating festivals and corporate events. This is truly inspiring because the men are masculine, feminine, and transgender. That is the power of art and the power of burlesque.

Chicava: Burlesque as theater, meaning before it became dominated by striptease, was one of the first opportunities onstage that Black people had to create from their own point of view. The glorification of the Black girl began on the burlesque stage in the 1890s with ladies like Dora Dean, Stella Wiley, and Aida Overton Walker, creating the first works that situated Black people off the plantation and in city environments. Their work took on Jim Crow, Orientalism, and, on the lighter side, the topical and funny skits and bits we associate with burlesque and vaudeville.

Taja: How can people who do not identify as artists, or are nervous about performing burlesque on a stage, learn from and use this art form—personally and politically?

Aurora: Being naked in public is a huge fear in our society. Overcoming that fear, and actually moving beyond it to revel in the feeling of being naked in public, can give someone so much more confidence in their daily life. In creating a burlesque piece, you must distill what you want to say to this essential thing that fits in a three-to-six-minute song. The skill it takes to successfully do that teaches you clarity and efficiency in communication, and communication is key for one's personal and political presence in this world.

Originally published in YES! *magazine on July 5, 2016.*

Black, Queer, and Dating in the Buckle of the Bible Belt

Jordan Scruggs

For the longest time, I was afraid to date. During middle school, high school, and two and a half years of college, I dreaded the courtship games that supposedly make the years of youth exciting and anxious at the same time.

My anxiety went deeper into overwhelming exhaustion and isolation territory. It was like being caught in an everlasting *Groundhog Day*–like loop of regret and doubt.

Now add dating to that. And add queer dating as a Black southerner living in Chattanooga, Tennessee, once voted to be the most "Bible-minded" city in the country.

I went to mostly white Christian schools from fifth grade until I graduated high school. It wasn't that people were often condemned or judged publicly. But when it did happen, it was always related to "inappropriate" relationships or behavior. Liking girls was definitely inappropriate, and I remembered hearing television stories about Matthew Shephard's death when I was eight. I didn't want what happened to him to happen to me.

I was legitimately afraid of what would happen if my five-foot, five-inch Black uterus-having body told the girl across the hall she was cute. I tried to literally shut down any and every "inappropriate" part of me. So there were no slumber-party nights of giggling with friends over whom we liked in the class. Instead, I closed my eyes under the covers and repeatedly mumbled, "I'll get over this and be normal."

Yet this was my normal. My normal was hiding and not dealing with my depression to protect my queerness. I had to protect it even from those closest to me. I wish that there had been just one moment of seeing myself—some queer, nonbinary Black person—in media, history, my family, or my friendship circle. Younger me didn't know that there were people in my social network who were just as anxious as I was about being outed.

Hindsight being twenty-twenty, it's not surprising that I literally don't know how to date. At age twenty-eight, it's no longer weird that my friends are getting married or that I show up in a tux. Some friends have popped out kid number three.

Meanwhile, I feel as though I'm playing catch-up, trying to have a third date.

It's not that I'm unready. It's more than I'm uneasy. I feel ashamed, ears burning, just to say that because I'm twenty-eight, and I don't have this shit figured out. Ask me what kind of qualities I want in a date or partner, and I have ideas of what I want—ideally. But they're just ideas of ideals because I don't have enough relationship experience to base it on anything concrete.

Neither do I have an answer to the worst unanswerable question I commonly get: "Why aren't you dating anyone?"

On the one hand, it's a simple answer. I don't go out to a lot of places. It's hard to meet new people at your own house. When I've tried online dating, people start conversations and then stop replying. I know that's par for the course, but it knocks my confidence down a few pegs every time it happens.

And I do have standards. A potential date is holding a gun in their profile picture. Nope. They only said, "Sup?" in the first message they sent me—not a promising beginning.

I also really only want to date other people of color, which adds another level of complexity to my dating struggle. Whiteness and white family members refusing to let go of their privilege is a hell of a ride I don't want to take. I can't deal with the potential of educating a relative at every single Easter Sunday on why "heritage, not hatred" is a stupid and racist thing to believe. Isn't it exhausting enough having to navigate white supremacy at work, at the store, on vacation, and at sporting events?

Also, I'm allergic to cats and dogs and am not fond of rodents. Which rules out at least 80 percent of my options before I even open up a dating app.

So, no, I don't date. But I want to. I have goals: to go across the room and tell someone I find them attractive. Or I want to be able to actually swipe right, read a profile I like, and follow it up with an invitation to conversation. One day, I will be comfortable admitting I want sex and want to feel sexy. There's nothing wrong with desiring another adult when you are also an adult.

My brain finds it hard to take a first step—saying hi to that girl at the concert—and to believe that a second step is possible. I second-guess sending a "good morning!" text and stress over the true meaning of emojis and overuse of exclamation marks. I am a Watson in a Sherlock Holmes dating situation.

I am working on it. The most important thing I've realized is that everyone is working on something. Just because I feel like I'm playing catch-up doesn't mean I am. I'm just experiencing this part of my life and myself at a different time than others, and I don't have to beat myself up over things I've missed.

In one way, I'm ahead of the curve. Because I love my kind of awkwardness. I'm comfortable not knowing what to say or being uncomfortable with other people my age.

Just like I embraced being awkward, I'm trying to trust the journey. I'm happy to be dating while queer, anxious, and Black in the buckle of the Bible Belt. I'm learning to be happy that I'm dating. To be happy about being giddy over crushes. I get to stress over whether my butt looks cute in these pants. I can declare and believe that I'm dating someone if I'm dating someone. I'm happy to have wing women, hype men, and givers of supportive you-can-do-this-dating-thing challenges.

I used to tell my friends, acquaintances, and dating tutors that "I was single and too awkward to mingle" whenever they asked about my social life.

I'm revising that motto. I'm single and ready to mingle. Maybe. But rat lovers still need not apply.

Radically Truthful Dating Profiles

Various

Ever write an online dating profile? If you're playing the game to maxi-
mize your matches and find more potential dates, it can be a vexing pro-
cess of choosing the right picture, avoiding the appearance of desperation
or alienating smartness, and sharing too many opinions to be convention-
ally "likable." It's a minefield and a mindfuck where details matter and
(ironically) depth often doesn't. But it's also the way millions of Amer-
icans find companionship. No pressure there at all. Online dating can
be doubly fraught for Black women and nonbinary people, who navigate
racial and gender bias in a social "meet market" that privileges whiteness,
canned beauty, and norms. But when Ida Yamani Hernandez was writing
a dating profile, she decided to do something radical: Tell the truth, her
truth—about her body, her family, her tender spots, and her trauma. A
number of other Idas joined her in the exercise at our 2018 retreat.

Yamani Hernandez

"I'm not gonna sit around and waste my precious divine energy trying to
explain and being ashamed of things you think are wrong with me."
                                   —"Precious" by Esperanza Spalding

Black, messy, hairy, divorced, pansexual, switchy, Buddhist, artistic,
Capricorn, intersectional feminist. Manages depression, anxiety, trauma,
and a national organization. Deeply committed to healing, justice, and
(mostly) amicable coparenting of two extraordinary younglings ages
twelve and seventeen (one with an intrusive obsession that his mom is
contaminated). Heavily tattooed. Has stretch marks and cellulite like
most humans. Any perceived lacking in ass is amply accounted for in
thighs, belly, and mom bosom. Pastimes include frequent urination,

avoiding domestic tasks, IG scrolling, truth telling, sketching, writing, amateur photography, hiking, sporadic running, yoga, testing fate as a nonswimming kayaker, and other adventures. Olivia Pope + Wednesday Adams + Lisa Bonet. Very loving but will never again ignore intuition. An anomaly you won't ever forget.

Cynthia R. Greenlee

Bibliophile with four eyes (all the better for seeing bullshit). Pit bull person who loves dogs more than most people. Tender headed and big-hearted. Won't ever change my southern accent. Prone to extended fits of sarcasm. Skin the color of cornbread done just right. Resists through overachievement. Born writer and brunch enthusiast. Likes men the way I like my bourbon: dark, strong with a hint of sweetness, and goes down easy. My passport has many pages. Recovering holder of Olympic-size grudges and admitted grammar snob. I always capitalize Black (as in "Black people"). Behind-the-scenes puller of strings, would love to be a farmer but way too lazy. Expects to be worshipped but will return the favor. Leo ego tempered by Cancer sensitivity. Craves summer tomatoes and reciprocity. #TeamSapiosexual but can be briefly impressed by the superficial (six-packs much appreciated). Underdogs are my jam. Extroverted introvert. Tar Heels basketball fan known to bellow Dick Vitale–style during UNC-Duke hoops games. Doesn't believe in guilty pleasures (why feel guilt if it doesn't hurt anybody?). Tell me I do "white things," and you'll be banished. Can sleep anywhere, but I'm always awake.

Charmaine Lang

Queer Black feminist, in theory and continued practice (not perfection). Dedicated to freeing Black people, starting with self. Maker of products that remove callouses around the heel and heart. Aries sun, Libra moon, Aquarius rising. Seafood lover who avoids water activities for fear of being touched by curious fish. Coupled with a loving, playful, methodical bisexual engineer. Together, we make space for growth, five dollar Tuesday movie nights and male lovers. Heartbreaks include the soul-crushing reality of pursuing a PhD, wildlife that didn't make it to the other side of the road, and scorched scrambled eggs. Hobbies include receiving bald-head massages, daydreaming about being a beast of a Chicago-style stepper, gazing into the future, digging in the archival crates of Black women thought leaders and writers from the 1970s. At night, can be found devising escape routes from Milwaukee to warmer climates.

Taja Lindley

Taja like Taj Mahal.

Bald-headed Black queer femme feminist woman committed to living an adventurous, miraculous, intentional, and unreasonable life.

Femme as in worship and expression of the divine feminine.

Femme as in beat face, bold lips, and bright nail polish.

Femme as in self-possessed Goddess.

Artist-entrepreneur actively liberating my mind and body with daily acts of love and courage. I stay moisturized and hydrated. Prioritize eight hours of sleep. Low-key emo Cancer sun and Pisces moon who fantasizes about making love to nineties R&B slow jams.

Attracted to smart people with smart mouths who are into crystals, oceans, money magic, moon cycles, and making our own rules. Turn-ons include direct and consistent communication, integrity, and walking (y)our paths with passion and purpose.

Jordan Scruggs

Proud to be a Black Queer af southerner.

Will 100 percent sort you into a Hogwarts house whether you like it or not. Will tell you your pet pics are super cute, but if they have four furry legs, reptilian skin, or aren't in a fish bowl, I probably won't care about them beyond the pics. #SorryNotSorry

Don't @ me if you voted for an orange bigoted 45. I don't care about both sides. You either fucks with me and #BlackLivesMatter, or you literally don't fucks with me at all.

"As" by Stevie Wonder is the greatest love song of all time, and Whitney Houston is the greatest voice of all time. Don't @ me.

I'm awkward and comfortable in it. Probably hungry, probably watching cartoons, and/or napping.

Will ignore you unapologetically if there's a baby in the room.

I'm cocky about being funny and witty because I know I am.

If you don't bake your mac and cheese, we won't work.

PS. White people don't hit up these DMs. I'm not trying to be with anybody who makes me argue with their racist no-lip-having-ass uncle at Thanksgiving for free.

Be blessed.

Janna A. Zinzi

Tinkerbell meets Mad Max. A lover and a fighter. Glitter rules everything around me. Bicoastal bae building bridges between New Yawk and LA manifesting my fellow globe-trotting international homieloverfriend and partner. Unabashed booty shaker and tassel twirler. Aquarius sun shining, Leo rising and roaring, Libra moon illuminating my divine femininity. Often spotted with my headphones on or car speakers turned up dancing toward my destination. NYC subway platforms, LA traffic, and TSA precheck lines are some of my favorite stages. Finding connections to the spirit world in the mundane is what's usually taking up brain space, and I like making animal friends even tho I'm allergic to lots of them. Beaches and mountains are my sanctuary. Nature restores my faith and sense of wonder. DMSR (dance, music, sex, romance) is my eternal mood, and I wanna dance with somebody who loves me. You must have an appreciation of exuberant cursing and various permutations of the word "fuck." Pastimes include public nudity, subverting white supremacy and patriarchy, tequila and mezcal, and long walks that spark conversation, verbal elation, stimulation. Best tamed by booty rubs. Working on sitting still long enough to finish books and watch movies. I Django, never sambo. Love is my heritage.

BEAUTY BREAKS

Introduction

Cynthia R. Greenlee

"U-G-L-Y. You ain't got no alibi. You ugly! Hey, hey, you ugly!" So ugly that we Ebonically dropped the verb.

This was a favorite cheer at my 99.5 percent Black high school in the South. In the stands, we knew it was "ugly"—not nice—to do this chant. But in the tradition of playing the dozens, we relished the insult. Actually, we thought little about calling each other ugly and doing so publicly. White schools were never on the receiving end of this chant.

We've spent our lives countering ugly claims. Flipping scripts written on our flesh.

Dark skin (amazing in how it absorbs all the light. Black is made of all colors, after all).

Wide nose: all the better to breathe.

Full lips: all the better to kiss, to eat, and to tell the truth.

Full hips, ample thighs: our bodies have carried many a burden and much joy.

Nappy hair: it's aerodynamic and architectural, our curls resistant to the straightening comb and the lye that have made appearances in so many of our lives (and will in this section).

Beauty goes beyond these persistent anti-Black judgments. There's beauty in sculpting a body to express gender identity, refusing to give in to the brow-grooming industrial complex, and coming to peace with your body, boob sweat and all. There's beauty in the process of wrestling with an aesthetic playbook that was not FUBU: for us, by us.

Why I Debated Getting My Breasts Augmented— and Why I Finally Did

Raquel Willis

One summer day, during an annual family trip to Jacksonville Beach, Florida, I stood alone, my feet in the sand, the chilly air hitting my hairless, androgynous chest. I was eleven years old. I felt so exposed with just my swim trunks on, sensing that I needed to cover up—even though there was nothing there. I wondered why I didn't feel comfortable like my brother and my dad being shirtless in the sun. Seagulls circled ominously above us, foreshadowing the struggle I would continue to have with my body throughout what I would later call my "first" puberty.

A decade later, in the summer of 2012, I took my first estrogen injection as a part of my gender transition. Within a few weeks, the sensitivity and soreness of the new buds forming under my skin gave me hope. Soon, though, I felt a new sort of shame—this time from an external source. My friends and partner at the time quickly urged me to get my first sports bra. Even though I was excited about my changing body, that excitement was charged with an undercurrent of annoyance. Why were my barely protruding nipples already becoming politicized, a piece of public property to be controlled and critiqued?

By summer 2015, I was mostly satisfied with my body. My face had softened considerably, my skin was smoother, and I had some semblance of breasts. But whenever I was naked, any confidence in my womanhood would quickly deflate. Those now medium-sized buds, though larger, were still a source of discomfort for me. I started considering the possibility of getting my breasts augmented.

I stewed over the decision for months before asking others for advice. Most of the time, I was met with static. My mother would respond with well-intentioned platitudes, like, "You're beautiful the way you are." Everyone else in my life had similar opinions: "You shouldn't get them done," some would say. "Natural is always better." "A handful is enough."

This flood of comments made me wonder whether it mattered how I felt about my breasts if everyone else in my life insisted that they were fine the way they were.

Throughout my transition, my chest wasn't the only thing that made me feel vulnerable. There was also my Adam's apple, which would be sore for days on end from my attempts to push it in so much. I had it surgically shaved down early in my transition, after which I half-heartedly vowed that I wouldn't have any more cosmetic surgery done. I wanted to be able to more easily say, "I'm all natural." It gave me a sense of superiority—especially because I wanted to be the kind of feminist who not only speaks out against cisnormative and patriarchal beauty standards but eschews them in her own daily life.

Around September of last year, my discomfort with my breasts began to supersede my desire to adhere to an unwritten feminist standard. I thought that if this was something I wanted—if it would truly improve my life—why not go for it. But I was worried about what the choice would mean when it came to my relationship with feminism.

As the cliché goes, any time you're unhappy with something in your life, change it. That's the accepted mindset when it comes to losing weight, getting a new job, or doing something new with your hair—but when cosmetic surgery is invoked, it's almost never supported with such flippant positivity.

Prior to my breast augmentation, I made my fair share of jokes about celebrities and their augmented bodies, à la Michael Jackson, Lil' Kim, and Kylie Jenner. There was a self-righteousness that accompanied shaming folks who have had cosmetic work done. I found myself far more vocally supportive of good, subtle surgeries than botched or drastic ones. I was also just as harsh as the rest of the world on folks who elect plastic surgery outside of what's deemed medically necessary.

When I surveyed friends and loved ones about what they'd think if I got my breasts augmented, many granted my potential decision more validity because I'm trans. There's an insistence that all kinds of surgeries are a necessity for a gender transition—for a trans person to truly feel at home in their bodies or to even be attractive—but that's not true, at least for me. While breast augmentation was something I thought I might want, it wasn't a prerequisite for transition. The truth is, while some trans folks can't see their lives going on without certain physical transition goals being met, I always knew that surgery wouldn't make me *more* of a woman—I'm a woman no matter what my body looks like.

But as a Black woman, it was difficult to embrace myself early on: I had a rail-thin body, no curves, and a flat chest. Black women with bodies like this are often seen as less valuable and desirable within the Black community, even if glorified in the mainstream beauty industry. You'll see thin Black models on runways and in magazines, but Black women with large breasts and butts have long been heralded as paragons of feminine beauty in music videos and Black media.

When it comes to the intersection of cosmetic surgery and Black womanhood, I can't help but think about the scrutiny constantly hurled at rapper and sex icon Nicki Minaj. She has the textbook example of what's considered the perfect Black woman's body: breasts that spill over most of her outfits, a cinched waist, and—the pièce de résistance—a full ass. Though many salivate over how she looks, others critique her body to the ends of the earth. And when they do, they speak of her alleged plastic surgery with disdain. Minaj, like all women, is held to a ridiculous double standard. On one hand, we're supposed to be able to say, "I woke up like this," but on the other, women who aren't conventionally beautiful and don't put in the exhaustive effort to appear so are derided and shamed.

Black women also live in the shadow of Saartjie Baartman, or the Hottentot Venus, a South African woman who was exhibited throughout Europe in the 1800s because of her voluptuous frame. Her historical presence, and what it meant to a society ruled by the white gaze, still affects how our bodies are viewed today. Black women without curves aren't valued—not to mention that Black women with "too many" curves aren't appreciated either. That celebration is reserved for women with a certain breasts-to-waist-to-hips ratio (or the "slim-thick" variety). Often, that's the kind of body many could get only from having some type of surgery. There's such a small box in which Black women can exist peacefully and without shame.

Beyond the self-esteem benefits a breast augmentation would bring, I anticipated being able to *pass* or blend in more easily among other women. And having a passable body would allow me to move through the world without drawing as much negative attention to myself. For so many trans people, living as closely to mainstream beauty standards as possible can be a major key to survival. Before hundreds of hormone shots, I didn't have that privilege. Walking out of the door was a daily game of Russian roulette. From awkward stares to rude interactions to a heightened threat of violence, the results of not blending in were hard to bear.

To eschew archetypal transition goals is courageous in a society that stipulates that we must all identify as either a man or a woman and fit into the narrow scripts of what those categories "should" look like. And even though I don't subscribe to the flawed binary of masculine and feminine, my own femininity is something I've reclaimed after spending much of my life being punished for it.

By considering breast augmentation, I wasn't intentionally seeking to fit more into a cisnormative, patriarchy-approved beauty ideal—but that's exactly the direction my surgery would push me in. And as someone so open about my trans experience who embraces owning this identity, I struggled with finding power and strength in this decision. But after spending so long asking others what they thought I should do and worrying what others might think, I'd stopped actually listening to myself or considering the power of my own choices.

Plenty of theorists critique choice feminism as both a tool of capitalism and an empty promise. But I still think the decisions we make for ourselves matter. What's the point of kowtowing to any kind of ideology that requires living with shame and self-hate? Yes, we live in a culture that bombards us with images of a perfect body—it would be ridiculous for me to act like I'm somehow immune to this phenomenon. But for this queer Black trans woman, the expectation to live up to the illusion of the perfect feminist—in an age of feminism that still privileges whiteness and cisheteronormativity—is just as oppressive to me. In the end, I made the choice to move forward with the surgery—for me and no one else.

I'm a few months post-op now, and I couldn't feel any happier about my breast augmentation. My life is hardly any different on a macroscale, but I feel more *real* to me, and freer than ever before. No more doubling up on too-small bras that leave deep, blush-red indentations in my skin; no more stuffing bras with balled-up socks and nearly suffocating from the pressure. No more angst. And outside of my family and close friends, I haven't really received a measurable amount of attention because of my breasts. This only makes me feel more confident that I made this choice for me and me alone.

I don't think most of us are given a chance to own our insecurities respectfully. For me, this decision was deeper than the surface. I wanted to be able to feel more at home in my body. I think of my body as something that was stolen from me, and my gender transition is a means to reclaim it. I had to endure most of my life feeling like an outsider, but with every transition milestone—changing my name, correcting the gender marker on my driver's license, hormones, surgeries—I have stepped more and more into a truer self.

How can we claim, as feminists, to believe in autonomy and agency when we so harshly critique other women's choices? We can't operate as if beauty is a level playing field. Intersectionality matters when we discuss beauty standards, and for a Black trans woman, the forces of anti-Blackness, the patriarchy, and cissexism are co-adversaries.

I am not a perfect woman, nor am I a perfect feminist, but not because I had cosmetic surgery. I don't believe that the perfect feminist exists, and I don't believe "realness" can be gauged. What's real for me is embracing my desires and goals for myself. I deserve to be happy when I look in the mirror, when I'm lying alone in my bed, or even when I'm getting intimate with another person.

My body is the house in which I live. I own it, and I will decide how to adorn it. I am no longer ashamed of my body, and you shouldn't be ashamed of yours. I am no longer ashamed of my desires for my body, and you shouldn't be ashamed of yours. This is what true liberation looks like.

Originally published on BuzzFeed *on June 30, 2016.*

Learning to Love It, Yes Even That:
Boob Sweat and More

Quita Tinsley

I live in Atlanta, or as some people (who are clearly not from Georgia) call it, "Hotlanta." This nickname doesn't come lightly. Summers in the South can be hot as hell. I spend many hours throughout the summer worried about "boob sweat": the sweat that accumulates under the breasts. I'm worried that it can be seen through my clothes and, more than that, I'm worried that others will smell it. Because of my past work in fragrance retail, I've learned the art of smelling like a fruit basket or floral arrangement to avoid that nightmare.

But why is it a nightmare? Why is the thought of someone being able to smell my body cooling itself down so frightening? It's normal (whatever "normal" means). Boobs, armpits, backs of the knees, and genitals all sweat because skin sweats. Does rejecting the notion that a bodily function is gross make me a radical feminist warrior? I am a radical Black feminist, but that's not why.

At some point, I made a commitment to myself to practice self-love, self-care, and body positivity. As a fat Black woman, I felt it was necessary to my life and work to be intentional in the ways in which I treat and think of my body. However, when we're talking about self-love and body positivity, we should also be challenging ourselves to discuss and critique the ways in which we neglect what we deem gross and yucky. We can't talk about embracing our fat without embracing the skin between our fat rolls. The yucky parts of our bodies aren't any less deserving of intentional love. We should devote more intentional time to caring for those parts of ourselves.

I can't lie; I'm not an expert at these practices. I still find myself not truly embracing body positivity when it comes to my own body. I still struggle with my own perception of my body and how I talk about certain parts of my body. I have to remind myself that my body is composed of many parts that are all deserving of love, even if society tells me that they are gross.

And sweat is not the only part of our bodies that is often considered gross. Body hair catches a lot of flak from society. Hair is not disgusting when it's growing from our scalps, but once on our legs, armpits, and genitals, it becomes gross. And let's be real: most of the prescribed notions surrounding body hair are assigned to feminine bodies. I tend to believe that if society is putting stipulations on a rule, those exceptions indicate that the rule is a complete farce.

I want to be clear that I am not insinuating that people who choose to shave their bodies are subscribing to the sexist norms that society forces on us. It was easier for me to give up the gender binary than to realize I hated shaving and only did it because it was "expected" of me. Body hair and sweat are small parts of a much larger conversation around body shaming and terrorism. We are all autonomous human beings who deserve the freedom to make decisions about our own bodies free from stigma.

What is it that you consider gross? Is it your facial hair? Is it the smell of your feet? Or are you like me, and it's your boob sweat? Whatever it is, you should know that it's a lovable part of you. You can and should love and care for those parts of yourself no matter how society has made you feel about them. Because at the end of the day, you aren't gross or yucky, but the oppressive systems that wish to break you very much are.

So, the next time you're about to call a part of you gross, pause. Take a breath and reflect; from there, think of the ways that you can love and care for that part of yourself.

And always remember the wise words of Queen Beyoncé: "You wake up, flawless."

Originally published on The Body Is Not an Apology *on September 25, 2015.*

I'm a Black Woman; That Doesn't Mean I Have a Bomb in My Hair

Taja Lindley

Following yet another awful terrorist attack, this one partially in an airport in Belgium, the topic of air-travel security and civil liberties is once again in the news. But my personal experience flying as a Black woman shows we still have a long way to go in balancing security and the rights of individuals—especially when those individuals aren't white.

I fly frequently. Between performances, workshops, retreats, and conferences, I'm typically on a domestic flight at least once a month. So I am no stranger to TSA flight requirements. I take my laptop out of my bag and put it in a separate tray. Take off my shoes. Remove my belt. Empty my pockets. Throw out my water bottle. Pack liquids under 3.4 ounces. Then I stand with my hands over my head for scanning.

And while I do my best to comply with TSA rules and policies, I am always stopped. Always. Why? Because their scanning machine says my hair may be, or possess, a security threat. Sometimes they need to "just take a look"—so I stand still while they walk around me in a circle to get a closer look at my hair. Increasingly, a TSA agent will need to pat down my hair, rake their fingers through my tresses and squeeze my scalp. And, of course, the so-called security threat is never found.

My hair is a critical part of my self-expression, my artistic practice, a celebration of my heritage, and my connection to spirit. So when TSA runs their dirty-ass latex gloves through my hair, it's an insult. It's racist. And it needs to stop.

A couple of months ago I headed to San Francisco from New York City for the annual Echoing Ida retreat. Unsurprisingly, but infuriatingly nonetheless, my hair needed to be inspected by a TSA agent at John F. Kennedy International (JFK) airport.

I had had enough. Like many millennials, I took to social media to vent my frustration. When I landed on the West Coast, I opened my Facebook app to find that a bunch of my friends had commented, mostly Black women. Many were outraged and others mentioned how they too go through this experience with TSA, wondering what we could do about it. I tweeted at TSA and their related Twitter account @AskTSA. Given my recent encounter with TSA at JFK, I was surprised to find this tweet from them for #BlackHistoryMonth:

I'm curious (and skeptical) about what changes, if any, have resulted from these partnerships. And the response from @AskTSA about my concerns was nothing short of underwhelming:

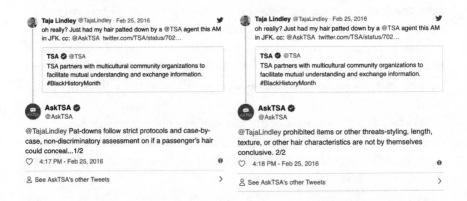

The TSA's current practice does little to respond to an agreement it made with the American Civil Liberties Union of Northern California (ACLU-NC) last year.[1]

The agreement was reached after the ACLU-NC filed an administrative complaint on behalf of Malaika Singleton, PhD—a Black woman with locs who experienced a hair pat-down after going through TSA scanning at Los Angeles International Airport and again at Minneapolis International Airport in December 2013. According to the agreement, TSA offered to ensure that "training related to nondiscrimination is clear and consistent for TSA's workforce," as well as track hair pat-down complaints "from African American females throughout the country to assess whether a discriminatory impact may be occurring at a specific TSA secured location."

Armed with this information, I vowed that the next time one of these TSA agents tried to touch my hair, I would remind them about the ACLU agreement, take names, and file a complaint. I didn't have to wait very long. I had my opportunity on Sunday, March 13, 2016, at the Raleigh-Durham Unified Airport in North Carolina.

I was on my way home after attending and providing healing services at the Black Youth Project 100 National Membership Convening. As usual, TSA needed to check my hair after scanning. I respectfully said no. When the TSA agent told me it was required, I asked for her supervisor. (Ironically, while I was waiting, another TSA agent complimented me on my hair.)

When her supervisor arrived, she said I had two options: (1) get my hair patted down where I was standing or (2) get my hair patted down in a private room. My heart was pounding. My ears were hot. I was steaming mad. It took everything I had to keep my composure.

Despite my anger, I calmly explained, "I don't want my hair touched. Every time I go through TSA security I get stopped for my hair, and other Black women experience this too." The agent replied, "It's not just Black women. Latina and Asian women get this treatment as well."

She said that if I refused, I would not be able to board my plane. It was twenty minutes until boarding, and I didn't want to miss my flight. After taking her name and letting her know that I would be filing a complaint, I "allowed" (can I even call it that?) a TSA agent to pat my hair down, only after I instructed her to change her latex gloves. She squeezed my bun, raked through my scalp. And what did she find? Nothing. What a surprise.

Being a Black woman while flying has meant harassment: consistent and constant rummaging through my hair searching for nonexistent threats and weapons. I understand that in a post-9/11 era there is a desire to be cautious—especially given the most recent terrorist attacks in Paris and Brussels. I too desire safety and security; however, I am not convinced that my hair is deserving of so much suspicion. Hair smuggling is not completely unheard of.[2] But there must be solutions to this security query that don't involve a breach of civil liberties, racial profiling, and humiliating pat-downs.

There are no bombs in my bun. Ain't no weapons of mass destruction tangled in my frohawk. I'm not smuggling drugs in my braids. No firearms are concealed in my pinned-up pompadour. No hidden weapons under my head wrap. I promise not to use my bobby pins to stab anyone. Nor will I use my head scarf to choke passengers. My twist-outs are harmless. My high ponytail will not kill you. My black kinky hair in all of its styles (trust, there are many) does not compromise homeland security.

My hair is my crown and glory. Raised by a single mother who had a hectic schedule, I became responsible for doing my hair at the tender age of nine. So you know I take my hair seriously. I've done every hairdo under the sun: from bobs to bangs, Aaliyah swoops to TLC T-Boz's "Crazy Sexy Cool" cut. Short and long. A full head of hair and a frohawk. Perms, weave, and natural. The list goes on.

My hair is a big part of who I am. That the TSA is ill-equipped to deal with it in a routine and noninvasive manner is symptomatic of systemic racism.

I'm not the only Black woman going through this. Melissa Harris-Perry, Solange Knowles, and other less famous Black women experience this travel degradation every day. And the problem isn't with TSA alone. TSA operates alongside a number of institutions within a framework of white supremacy that are both fascinated and threatened by what Black women do with our hair and heads.

In February 2016, a school administrator at a high school in Durham, North Carolina—not far from the Raleigh Airport—told young Black girl students to remove their West African–inspired head wraps because they violated the school dress code.[3] Black women in the workplace have been discriminated against for rocking natural hair in general and braids in particular, including Renee Rodgers, who filed a lawsuit (and lost) against American Airlines in 1981 because she was told that her cornrows violated the company's grooming policy.[4] And this is not just specific to corporate America: the US military made it a point to explicitly state that Black hairstyles were unauthorized.[5]

Although racial references may not be explicitly stated in their policies, the practice of implementing TSA policy is having a racist impact. It should be noted that not all agents who pat down hair are white. My most recent experience involved two Black women TSA agents. But to be clear: that is how systemic racism works. It's not just about the racial identity of the TSA agents implementing these dubious practices; it's about the races that are disproportionately and unfairly impacted by the practices of TSA.

More importantly, this isn't just about TSA agents. Their technology is questionable and ineffective. As Harris-Perry eloquently stated, "If your $170,000 machine can see under my clothes, but can't figure out I'm not hiding a bomb in my braids, maybe it's time to recalibrate the machine."[6] It seems logical but may not be a reality anytime soon. "We initially asked TSA to audit the scanner triggering false positives for African American hair specifically," said Novella Coleman, an ACLU-NC staff attorney who worked on the TSA agreement. "TSA was unwilling to take a look at that."[7]

Brittney Cooper, an associate professor at Rutgers University, says, "There is a long history of institutions regulating bodies in such a way that white bodies become the norm." Indeed. So when TSA says they do not engage in discriminatory practices, they only check hair with "anomalies," it is clear that what is outside of the norm is Black hair.

Notes

1. "Civil Rights Complaint on Behalf of Malaika Singleton against the TSA," ACLU-NC, January 12, 2015, https://www.aclunc.org/our-work/legal-docket/civil-rights-complaint-behalf-malaika-singleton-against-tsa.
2. Stuart MacLean, "Woman Caught Smuggling 1.5kg of Cocaine in Her Dreadlocks on Flight to Bangkok," *Daily Mail*, December 13, 2011, https://www.dailymail.co.uk/news/article-2073456/Woman-caught-smuggling-1-5kg-cocaine-dreadlocks-flight-Bangkok.html.
3. Taryn Finley, "Parents Demand School Let Their Kids Wear African Head Wraps," *HuffPost*, February 9, 2016, https://www.huffpost.com/entry/parents-demand-school-let-their-kids-wear-african-head-wraps_n_56ba2b43e4b0c3c5504ef267.

4. Maryline Dossou, "Natural Hair vs. Corporate America," *Ebony*, July 3, 2013, https://www.ebony.com/style/fighting-for-our-hair-in-corporate-america-032/; E.R. Shipp, "Braided Hair Style at Issue in Protests over Dress Codes," *New York Times*, September 23, 1987, https://www.nytimes.com/1987/09/23/garden/braided-hair-style-at-issue-in-protests-over-dress-codes.html.

5. Brittney Cooper, "The Politics of Black Women's Hair: Why It's Seen with Skepticism—and a Need to Discipline," *Salon*, April 22, 2014, https://www.salon.com/2014/04/22/the_politics_of_my_black_hair_why_its_seen_with_skepticism_and_a_need_to_discipline/.

6. Melissa Harris-Perry, "Black Women's Hair Becomes Targets in TSA's Security Theater," *MSNBC*, August 10, 2013, http://www.msnbc.com/melissa-harris-perry/black-womens-hair-becomes-target-tsas.

7. ACLU-NC, "Civil Rights Complaint."

This article first appeared in Salon, *a website located at http://www.salon.com, on April 4, 2016.*

Soft & Beautiful Just for Me Relaxer, No-Lye Conditioning Crème, Children's Regular

Kemi Alabi

DIRECTIONS

Snatch the could-be-girl-'cept-she-too-dark
-'cept-them-nigga-naps child by the braids.

Slice them open. Rake the comb through.
Cue the scalp pop, the scab-robed choir.

Teach the tribe dirge: staccato rip-rip
crescendo into sizzle and shred.

Litter the neck with butchered kinks,
a gutter-fur shawl, diseased offering.

Heatstroke, swamp drown, chemical spill,
decompose, exorcise, drag and prop

until brillo collapses, satin rises,
arabesques and curtsies with a snap.

Heaven's darkest halo is a high yellow.
On Earth, at last, a crown is cast in black.

INGREDIENTS

Propylene Glycol (Antifreeze)
These winters, nothing natural survives.

Helianthus Annuus (Sunflower)
Half the native wildlife, extinct.

Hydroxyethylcellulose (K-Y Jelly)
The rest tweaked to triple their bloom.

Citronellol (Repellent)
Teach her to burn

Salvia Officinalis (Sage)
all smoke, no fire.

Aqua (Water)
Refuse to call god by name.

WARNING

A child is made of water; a Black girl,
open flame. Product may catch fire.

Oshun may wrestle from her kitchen,
snap your comb in two.

There may be no Black girls.
Only burning gods.

There may be no Jesus.
Just empire.

You may be both the army
and the scorched earth below.

DIRECTIONS

What was the Atlantic
before it became
a graveyard?

Before crops meant
auction blocks,

which dance brought
the rain?

For best results,
cover her. Fall
in praise.

Be cloudthick
and unpartable.

Be tangled,
skystuck waves.

Originally published in BOAAT Journal *in the May/June 2018 issue.*

I Like My Unruly Eyebrows, Thank You Very Much

Cynthia R. Greenlee

I've never had my eyebrows shaped, plucked, threaded, waxed, filled in, tinted, drawn on, or otherwise groomed.

And I'm okay with that.

More than okay—I'm downright happy with it. It's other people who seem to have the problem.

Every time I enter a nail salon, overeager operators ask if they can do my brows before I sit down or offer one with my mani-pedi.

I get it: they're upselling, and I don't blame them. Brows are big business (up to $122 million annually in makeup products in the United States alone, according to NPD, a global research group[1]). And the nail industry flourishes on low-wage work.[2]

But one look at my eyebrows, and they assume that's why I'm there. Because who would want my irregular peaked brows?

They look surprised—and sometimes even disdainful or pitying—when I decline their ministrations. Or they look disappointed that we will not be co-combatants in this battle of nail salon versus nature.

I say, "No." Firmly. And then, "I like my eyebrows like this." End of conversation.

But it's a conversation I keep rehashing with solicitous friends who tell me I really "should" get my eyebrows done or share their stories of an eyebrow magician who cuts down shrubby eyebrows for a pittance.

It's cosmetic coercion, the idea that one "must" follow the trend just as surely as that threader follows the arch of a brow. Though I know that preferences and fashion don't develop in a vacuum, I'm suspicious of a beauty playbook that I didn't write and its rules: no white after Labor Day, no flats if you want to be sexy, no body-hugging dresses if you're not rail thin, and no sandals without a pedicure or polish.

Too many of these rules apply to women and our hair—and the

hair on our faces.[3] Sideburns and mustaches, no. There's a reason why bearded ladies were a routine feature in circus "freak shows."[4] Certainly, no impudent chin hair or peach fuzz unless you want to be mistaken for a crone or a woman too far gone to wield tweezers. But an emphatic yes to keeping up your eyebrows and keeping them in high style.

Having the "it" brow of the moment demands the support of a beauty industry that tells women we must design our appearances down to the finest hair.

If I lived my life according to the imperatives of women's magazines—and their frequent exhortations on brow upkeep—I would find myself guilty of gross neglect.

Since the beginning of 2016, Elle.com has published many eyebrow tutorials: shaping tips from a "brow guru," eight steps to filling in if you weren't born with the "perfect pair," the Cara Delevingne–esque make-over for us thick girls, and a feature about what celebrities look like without their brows.[5]

(I will never think of Zac Efron or Drake the same way again, and everybody's favorite no-dancing, in-his-feelings Canadian rapper Drake got a whole 'nother article about his barely noticeable—*to me*—brow evolution.[6] I will leave it to brow aficionados to demur.)

There are endless lists, and they often go something like this: shaping every three to four weeks; tweezing every two or three days to "keep things tidy"; threading/waxing, also every three to four weeks; trimming once a month; tinting every four to six weeks, based on how speedily the hairs grow back; and growth treatments from castor oil to Rogaine, as needed or instructed.

Here's the crux of my objection to the beauty regime that insists on the manicured brow: it's an endless cycle of care and cost.

Much like chemically straightening my hair and getting regular touch-ups to tame the "new growth" (which I no longer do either), a commitment to the acceptably symmetrical and balanced brow requires work that I'm just not willing to do.

I'm not interested in fighting hairs that grow outside a cosmetologist's approved route. For me, it's an expensive and unnecessary proposition—not to mention painful and short-lived. We know those wayward hairs will grow back however they want and whenever they want.

It was painful to watch a college roommate enact her Saturday brow-taming ritual. She'd rise early, soften noxious-smelling wax in my microwave, and slather it on the middle of her forehead. She'd grimace and pull the hardening substance away from her skin, taking with it the offending hairs that united her two brows into one. She'd turn, review her face in the mirror, and talk about how hard it was to be a hairy immigrant girl from the Middle East.[7]

Truth be told, I didn't like her much (or her zapping hair wax in my microwave). But I felt real sympathy as she struggled to maintain an appropriately haired visage. For her, having the right bilateral brow was a way to erase her otherness and maybe—just maybe—pass into whiteness.

"How many Americans girls have unibrows?" she'd ask. And by American, she meant white. That telltale single line across her forehead barred her from passing into whiteness or approximating something close to it. That eyebrow line might as well have been a color line because she believed it kept her from finding a suitable white mate. And maybe it did.

Passing into whiteness via brow modification was never an option for me as a Black woman—a visibly Black woman who politically and socially identifies as Black.

Nevertheless, I don't bow down to the brow orthodoxy that says "one shape fits all" or requires a full calendar of appointments and almost daily "face chores."

And, simply put, I don't subscribe to all the must-do maintenance babble because I like my brows as they are. I wish this didn't feel like a revolutionary thing to say. I like what I like, even when my preferences run contrary to fashion. All women must be able to like what they like about their physicality.

At least we should be able to choose that sculptural brow, or the fuzzy caterpillar look we were born with, or whether we follow the mandates of trend. Which is not to say that following trends indicates an unthinking devotion to herd-think but rather we must feel able to select what trends we follow, when we break with them, and how much we are willing to do for aesthetic belonging.

In fact, I love my eyebrows—as unfashionably pointy as they are—for another type of belonging. Funny as it may sound, my eyebrows are a bridge to my family.

They are the only visible facial feature I inherited from my father. I cock them just like he does—to question, to express disbelief, to show surprise—and lower them the same way he does in shade, concentration, or disapproval. My friends and family probably wouldn't be able to read my emotions without my expressive eyebrows. My eyebrows are punctuation for my glasses and my face.

My brows aren't uniformly full—the hair thins after the pointy part. What others see as a brow failing, I see as adding "visual interest" to my face. I don't want the uniform, slender, elegant arch that's supposed to be every woman's aspiration (unless you have a hankering for the "sensual" Brooke Shields–style brow or want to wait until the thick brow cycles back through popularity like bell-bottoms and platform shoes).

Admittedly, I'm not like many American women. I keep my makeup to a minimum. I wear a neutral lip gloss for the everyday and a bold lip every now and then. Eyeshadow is for special occasions. There is never an occasion special enough for foundation; my skin needs to breathe, and my Black has not yet cracked (melanin is a superb moisturizer, I hear).

I want my "natural" hair to be just that: natural and not coated in products that promise to yield that seemingly effortless 3B curl pattern. I don't pull out the gray strands that are making their presence known in a sea of darker hair.

Defining my own sense of natural brow and beauty is swimming upstream.

But Mexican painter Frida Kahlo bucked the culture with her hirsute monobrow—she didn't edit it out of her self-portraits. Feminist theorist and poet Audre Lorde had a jagged brow like mine. It's not a coincidence that these feminist icons had freewheeling brows.

Letting my eyebrows grow "wild" is too often seen as a sign—by other women—that I'm letting myself go. I don't judge women who love the artifice and creativity of makeup, the ability to remake themselves in front of mirrors. More power to them. But I'm letting go of this specific beauty standard that tells me my brows must be these graceful, flattened parabolas on my face.

So these brows are going to remain the way they are: free from teasing and manipulation. I won't be browbeaten into changing them.

Notes

1. NPD Group, "Eyebrow Makeup Dominates Total US Makeup Sales, Growth, Reports NPD," press release, July 2, 2014, https://www.npd.

    com/wps/portal/npd/us/news/press-releases/eyebrow-makeup-dominates-total-us-eye-makeup-sales-growth-reports-npd/.

2. Sarah Maslin Nir, "The Price of Nice Nails," *New York Times*, May 7, 2015, https://www.nytimes.com/2015/05/10/nyregion/at-nail-salons-in-nyc-manicurists-are-underpaid-and-unprotected.html.

3. Ellen Friedrichs, "4 Reasons Why We Should Stop Stigmatizing Women's Body Hair," *Everyday Feminism*, October 14, 2014, https://everydayfeminism.com/2014/10/stop-stigmatizing-womens-hair/.

4. Little Bear Schwarz, "Yes, I'm a Bearded Lady—and, No, I'm Not Grateful for Your Attention," *Everyday Feminism*, June 5, 2015, https://everydayfeminism.com/2015/06/yes-im-a-bearded-lady/.

5. Julie Schott and Christiana Molina, "How to Get Thicker Brows in 8 Easy Steps," *Elle*, September 5, 2017, https://www.elle.com/beauty/makeup-skin-care/tips/g8496/how-to-define-eyebrows/.

6. Julie Schott, "A Close Analysis of Drake's Eyebrow Evolution," *Elle*, December 22, 2015, https://www.elle.com/beauty/g27441/drakes-eyebrow-artist/.

7. Sabah Choudrey, "Being Seen as a Hairy Brown Girl—There Was Nothing Wrong with Me Then and There Is Nothing Wrong with Me Now," *Everyday Feminism*, March 31, 2015, https://everydayfeminism.com/2015/03/hairy-brown-girl/.

Originally published on Everyday Feminism *on May 20, 2016.*

"Are You Just a Plaything of Nature?"
Amina Ross on the Politics of Beauty

Kemi Alabi

Amina Ross is chopping butternut squash in my kitchen. Though they're used to being interviewed—about their solo art exhibitions; their multidisciplinary arts festival, Eclipsing and their "alternative domestic venue," Femme4Femme (F4F)—this conversation space feels a bit uncharted. Instead of fielding questions from a stranger about a debut project, they're chatting with me, their partner, about beauty and pleasure. Intimacy and art often collide, especially in our work, but this—our private rapport pinned to print—makes us both a little shy.

A self-proclaimed "undisciplined" artist, Amina's generous making practice includes curating a vibrant workshop series called Beauty Breaks—a series that saved me from isolation as a friendless transplant bumbling around Chicago only a year before. The irregularly scheduled workshop, hosted in F4F's attic and performance space, brought together an earnest and dynamic group of young Black queerdos intent on building community in a notoriously challenging city. I learned how to use tarot as a tool to cultivate my intuition. I built small sculptures from recycled goods. I meditated, wrote poetry, cocreated impromptu group performances, and refreshed my spirit in ways I could not have imagined. It was diametrically opposed to any of my former interactions with "beauty," and I wanted to talk about why.

"I set up a framework to talk about Black beauty and health through hands-on, skill-based learning," Amina explains. "Someone could come, for example, wanting to learn about a braiding technique, but then we leave also talking about intimacy and community building, or talking about hands and care and memory. It [starts as] this really surface thing, and then [goes] deeper. A makeup tutorial, but then beyond makeup. We're talking about our relationship to our face. Alteration. Presentation of your face, body, gender."

Yoga to start Beauty Breaks session "Mark Making." Photo by Ally Almore.

As the Beauty Breaks website explains, the workshop series aims to "forge new language around what it means to be black, beautiful and well." But Amina isn't sure if Beauty Breaks will continue, and I struggle to hide my disappointment. As we prepared butternut-squash soup—much like the one that warmed me and a roomful of once-strangers at my first Beauty Breaks—we talked about how and why this series began. These are edited excerpts from our conversation.

Kemi Alabi: You've had workshops that deal with the aesthetics of the body, workshops that are more theoretical about joy, hands-on food making. What's the through line?

Amina Ross: It started with beauty, health, and wellness as a magazine category. It's amorphous, really—but a "lifestyle magazine." If I say that to you, you can imagine what it is. It's about what a proposed lifestyle is, what a lifestyle should be, quote unquote, by this magazine industry that's selling ideals that are oftentimes aspiring toward whiteness and class ascension. Then they label it beauty, health, and wellness. I think about [Beauty Breaks] in the way I imagine editors think of what goes into a lifestyle magazine, which can really be anything. But I think about beauty, really interrogating that as a concept.

Kemi: What would you describe as success in Beauty Breaks?

Amina: Transferable skills and community. I've seen people make relationships and go on to work with each other. That for me is exciting. Seeing people feel joyful and then connected is success for me.

Kemi: What catalyzed your fascination with beauty, wellness, and the lifestyle magazine concept?

Amina: I had this residency, and I had to utilize one of their collections. The collection I chose to focus on was the Johnson Publishing library because I've always been interested in *Jet* magazine—for mainly aesthetic reasons, seeing all these beautiful Black people on these covers. They would have this Beauty of the Week photo of a really beautiful femme person in cute clothes on a hot, electric background. I was obsessed with feminine figures. I'm really queer. [*laughs*]

I went to school in the middle of all these modeling agencies in New York City—great place to be in fucking middle school. Going out to lunch and seeing these famous models who don't eat, you know. Just tiny, tiny, tiny—and majestic. Small gods to me.

[The magazines] presented an opportunity for me to examine similar materials that were from a Black-owned publishing house with a more critical lens. Advertisements are oftentimes the most visually compelling and have some of the strongest use of typeface. Even when the magazine got more radical in terms of the articles they were publishing—they published the first natural hair article, and not in a derogatory way—the advertisements always stayed the same because that's where they got their funding to print. Skin-lightening advertising even went alongside articles that were about reclaiming Blackness.

There is one advertisement for a relaxer [with] my favorite tagline. It was, "Are you just a plaything of nature?" It was this sad-looking person. "Are you just letting nature toss you around and be the boss of you? Adopt this technology to be able to tame your body, to tame your savage ways, to civilize yourself."

That was from the 1930s and 1940s. In the eighties and nineties, there was a lot of stuff around independent women—in order to gain financial freedom, buy this hair relaxer. "Was it her résumé, or was it

Journaling and drawing card interpretations for Beauty Breaks session "Tarot as a Tool." Photo by Ally Almore.

Raveen?" That's my other favorite one. There's this businesswoman, smiling with her perfect teeth on this big blocky cell phone.

There were a lot of things around saving yourself and being a powerful woman but becoming powerful through products. You can see the ideals around femininity, around what people believe would get them free in that time.

I was gonna take all this information, these taglines or slogans, mash them up and make something new.

Then I was like, "I hate this material, I don't want to do anything with it. How do I generate new language? Okay, through what way can I get people to have these conversations? Ooh, through hands-on learning." That's how it started.

Kemi: You're someone who loves aesthetics. It's not like you're rejecting beauty in your work. You saw a formulation in the advertisements: beauty is freedom. I'm wondering if you have your own personal idea of how beauty and freedom are connected and how you hope it's connected for others.

Amina: Maybe pleasure? The advertisements say you access beauty through changing yourself. Shaping yourself in the images they provide you. [Beauty is] already accessible where everyone is right now. It's just embracing what already exists. We have so many things, from school to internalized messages—from media, friends, family—that don't allow space for our goodness to *be*, to expand, to grow, to play. So just giving it space to be. To witness it.

Kemi: What are some of the ways that you play with beauty and locate pleasure there?

Amina: I have such a complicated relationship with my own appearance. I don't love fashion. I love clothes. It's different. I love the colors, the form, the questions, the textures, the shapes. But I don't love the industry.

With myself and my own presentation, I've just allowed myself a freedom: wearing what feels good, playing with color, texture, and shape. Then beyond my own presentation, in my work, I think about trance and the hypnotism of video—which is a similar propaganda machine to magazine, just selling you ideals and lifestyle through movies and all this stuff—wanting to use some hypnotic elements of that medium to open up space for imagination and playfulness.

Kemi: Are there other ways in your art practice that you play with the idea of beauty?

Amina: This is something I'm not invited to talk about a lot. That's really interesting to me because it's clearly there. No one ever talks to me about it. They only talk to me about the political or power—as separate things, which they're not for me.

Kemi: You don't separate beauty and pleasure from the political space?

Amina: No, not at all. They're completely together.

Kemi: Could you tell me about some of the ways in which they've been forcibly separated?

Amina: For utility. This idea that in order to work, you do away with the frilly stuff. Even thinking about budgets, the first budgets that are cut oftentimes in schools are art class. Like it's not needed, not necessary, not practical. But it is.

If you live somewhere where you have trash all over your street, buildings are falling down all around you, you still see how in those places people will still—to *survive*—make beautiful things. Because it is a part of living, even in the most dire circumstances. Even in the middle of wars, you see people carving out space for themselves,

Shani Crowe demonstrates braiding techniques on hair model. Photo by Ally Almore.

putting up their hair. It's a part of living in this world that not only makes it bearable but possible.

Imagine everything from your life that brings you pleasure removed. If you didn't have it, I promise you, your life would be a shell of a life.

Kemi: It makes me think—who has ownership of what beauty and pleasure are supposed to be? These lifestyle magazines?

Amina: Yes, yes! That's why it's seen as luxury!

Kemi: And very gendered, targeted to a particular class, and completely bound to capitalism.

Amina: Completely bound. Then you have people who are trying to undo [capitalism] who also want to get rid of [beauty and pleasure]. I'm telling you, it's a shell of a life.

Kemi: The first idea for Beauty Breaks was to capture some new language for beauty, beyond what you saw in the lifestyle magazines. Even if that's not what the workshops have explicitly become about, have you arrived at some new language?

Amina: I collect from all facilitators a thing that asks them what beauty is. So I have all of these definitions.

Tarot became really important. The language of images and symbols. Being able to think about, from magazines to tarot, the way images and symbols are imbued with meaning and power, and the stories they tell. I think about the spatial arrangements in the room, people's facial expressions. When the room looks a certain way, I know that things are good. [Beauty Breaks photographer Ally Almore's] photos are a great language. There's one of you. You're so cute.

Kemi: What does that mean?

Amina: Oooh.

Kemi: [*Laughing*] Just unpack what you've said. I'm so cute.

Amina: I like how you move through the world and hold yourself. You're very beautiful, like astoundingly so. In that way people think people are . . . this is complicated.

Kemi: Say why it's complicated.

Amina: I don't know. I look at certain things like, "There is beauty there." But some things are not particularly moving. Just as I can look at certain people, and they could be not particularly moving. But it isn't a formula.

Kemi: Mm-hmm, mm-hmm. We can move away from this.

Amina: Because you don't want me to break down how I think you're particularly moving.

Kemi: Maybe not. I have a complicated relationship with beauty, especially my own. You named that earlier, that you do too. What is that?

Amina: Well for me, it's tough because this is when I get to my interest in form. In shape, color, texture, size. I don't find myself to be particularly beautiful in a conventional sense by any means. So what I do find to be beautiful is cultivated.

Kemi: What do you mean "is cultivated?"

Amina: Is taught. Or I train myself to see myself in a certain way.

Kemi: You know we walk down the street, and I've never been with anybody in my life who gets as much attention, attraction, compliments. [*Both laugh*] You're someone who cares deeply about aesthetics and are seen as you move through the world. Is that welcome? Is that confusing? Is that validating?

Amina: It's welcome. It's not always validating. It could never be.

Kemi: Why not?

Amina: It would never be enough to validate . . . to sway my thinking.

The author at Beauty Breaks, back perpetually turned to the camera. Photo by Ally Almore.

Kemi: But you compliment me and say that I'm beautiful. You're some-one who vocalizes appreciation for other people's aesthetics.

Amina: Yeah.

Kemi: I've responded in that way. 'That's not enough.' And you've laughed at me. [*Laughs*]

Beauty is something you say is definitely real. Something observ-able, and something necessary. Something that requires cultivation and appreciation by humans for us to move through life. Then there's the complicated addition of that being mapped onto bodies—

Amina: Mm-hmm.

Kemi: And gendered, racialized, and contorted to a particular shape and size.

Amina: Yeah.

Kemi: So I understand where the complication is coming from. I'm just asking you to say more about what informs the way you move through the world as someone who cares about aesthetics and is very visible.

Amina: I need to let go of the look of things. I'm more aware of how I feel. Or if I am paying attention to look, it's with a soft focus. Like,

Meditative movement at Beauty Breaks. Photo by Ally Almore.

"Ah, nice hues of pinks and purple, those dried flowers." But not, "The flowers are dry."

It's really tough because I have a constant desire to control my body, specifically around my weight. It's very hard work to be like, "I am going to be this way because this is how I am." I have put a lot of energy into destroying myself. What I have to do is resist impulses to control my body and instead enjoy it.

Kemi: In that way, I sense that connection between beauty and wellness a lot more. Then to zoom out in a more political sense, what it is to construct our human lives around pleasure. Because pleasure and play exist in a lot of really empty, gutting contexts.

Amina: Yeah, in ways that empty you out. That's why it's pleasure *and* wellness. Beauty *and* wellness. It has to be together because if you separate both of them, it goes too far.

Kemi: Talk to me about what freedom within desire, beauty, and pleasure feel like to you when it's all uncoupled from harm.

Amina: The best answer is soft focus. It reminds me of mindfulness because you're not saying "I like this tree" while you're meditating.

You're experiencing it as color, shape, and just its essence. You're not pinning it down as a thing.

It's best to do that also with people. Not "I like this nose, and this, and this," which is also how video has treated specifically the female body in advertisements: tits, belly, ass, head, like you're only in parts. We learn to have gazes that objectify people. It makes you want to possess, own, and control. You can begin to look at the world as "I want that," and "I had that. I got that; I smashed that; I fucked that."

Kemi: Parts to be possessed instead of a whole to be maintained and connected.

Amina: Exactly, yeah.

Kemi: You talk about connection as one of the central pieces of successes in Beauty Breaks. Bringing wellness and wholeness in. So that soft focus, it seems it's . . .

Amina: To see it all, not just the segments of. You're not pinning anything down, you're taking it in, and it doesn't have to be any one thing. It's just all being, you know?

FOR THE KULCHA

Introduction

Janna A. Zinzi

Culture: The customs, arts, social institutions, and achievements of a particular nation, people, or other social group. What you'll see in history textbooks or on Wikipedia.

Kulcha: The funk, flavor, and ferocity that Black folks create as an expression of pride and celebration of our brilliance. It's for us, by us.

If we weren't dope as fuck, cultural appropriation wouldn't exist. And the world would be hella bland. Our flavor transcends generations and borders.

Who keeps Twitter relevant and remotely interesting? Black folks. (And don't fuck with Black Twitter CSI!)

Who broke the internet and keeps breaking it? Beyoncé, a Black woman from Houston.

What is the best-selling genre of music? Hip-hop, created by Black folks in the projects of the Bronx.

It's undeniable. It's irrefutable. Black America makes shit hot.

It's also what unites us. It's a shared understanding and through line despite our diverse geographies, ethnicities, languages, and food preferences (#TeamSaltyGrits all day!).

While culture includes what music is popular or what Netflix show to binge, it also provides a snapshot of an era reflecting our values and priorities. Sometimes it represents a collective experience often grounded in anti-Blackness that can be as painful as it is transformative. Think about the big business of cannabis consumption and legalization. We've been criminalized and imprisoned for trying to survive, and now white men are making millions and blocking our access to the industry. Think about the memes and art inspired by the uprisings that followed George Floyd's murder during a global pandemic. They help us find joy in the horror and assert our humanity. Kulcha can be tangible, yet also a state of being.

Culture shapes history and defines who we are as Americans in a country that was designed to exploit us. While popular culture is fluid and our tastes change, Black women and nonbinary people are consistently responding to and subverting the white supremacist context that stifles us. It's how we process a world that sees us as disposable. Kulcha is where we make our own rules. It is where we can find *our* liberation, represent *our* truths, center *our* experiences; it's *our* outlet for freedom of expression.

We are creators on a global scale. People who have never met a Black American know our music, television shows, movies, and fashion. Our culture is our country's greatest export, shaping how the world views the United States no matter what the political landscape looks like. When we are not in control of our images, the world gets fed stereotypes about us. But social media gives us power and a voice. Because of it, "Black Lives Matter" became a global rallying cry, showing the realities of our lives in America beyond the NBA superstars, syndicated reruns of *The Fresh Prince of Bel-Air*, or Rihanna's latest Instagram post.

People all over the world want our style, our vernacular, our bodies (hello, lip injections and butt implants), our cultural capital. You know those folks who post "Black Lives Matter" on social media but then will try to touch your hair IRL. Blackface has made a comeback with white women online using dark foundation to look ambiguously Black, like Rachel Dolezal in complete denial of her Eurocentric ethnicity (ahem, she's white). It's all fun and games when you're not being targeted by police, jailed for having a joint, or paid less for everything you do.

Enough about them: Back to us and our legends. We love our Whitney, Prince, Big Poppa, our Queen Bey. The folks who represent us to the world. They show us what's possible. They demonstrate freedom, thriving over surviving, and courageous creative expression. Through them, we see and love our Blackness. They put themselves and their truths on the line (like the writers of this section do), all for the kulcha.

How Prince Helped Me Be Black and Genderqueer in America's Bible Capital

Jordan Scruggs

I still remember when Prince sang on *Muppets Tonight* in 1997. I was seven years old in Chattanooga, Tennessee. It was a few years after he started using a symbol instead of his name, which the Muppets played up for laughs. I remember him wearing overalls in one scene for a farm skit and a ridiculous chartreuse turtleneck for a music video in the next. Even the Muppet-ified Prince had a pompadour.

I watched him sing about Cynthia, a Muppet who didn't care what people thought about her: "If you set your mind free, baby, you'd understand." After that, I wanted more.

I looked for Prince in music stores and online. I'll never forget seeing the cover of his 1988 album, *Lovesexy*. Here was this naked Black man on the cover of his album with flowers behind him. And people loved him.

So did I. "Purple Rain" helped me to understand the turmoil I was going through when a relationship ended differently than I'd hoped. "Little Red Corvette" was there to remind me to take time with my life. But it's the opening line from "I Would Die 4 U" that knocked me out. It struck me so hard and stayed with me because it was my life. And when I heard it, I realized it was okay to feel that way:

I'm not a woman
I'm not a man
I am something that you'll never understand

As I went deeper into the catalog, I found Prince in similar poses with the same aura of pride as on *Lovesexy*. Prince had a magical blend of masculinity and femininity that I was searching for but couldn't find within my own community or anywhere, really. You see, Chattanooga is a very religious city. I went to church nearly every Sunday for about twenty years. We have more churches than schools. In fact, in 2016, the American Bible Society named my hometown the most "Bible-minded" city in America.[1]

My family encouraged me to be proud of being Black, proud of where I come from, and proud of the space I take up in this world. But I never felt as confident as other family members when it came to their identities. My parents surrounded me with people who are the definitions of strength.

But not like Prince.

I was at work when I heard the news. I checked Twitter offhandedly and saw a tweet about a death at Prince's studio. I gasped and stepped back from the computer. I refreshed Twitter over and over again, looking for a source other than TMZ. When the Associated Press confirmed the news, I screamed and sank to the floor. My white coworkers didn't understand how real I was being when I said my gut was torn and my heart was racing. I couldn't accept it. He had been such a big part of my childhood and adolescence.

Prince let me see a person who wore makeup and whatever clothes he wanted, not caring whether his choices fit the gender binary.

The only conversation about sexuality I heard growing up was about abstinence. There was no talk of gender identity or being queer. There was no place I could reach out to for more information besides the public library because I didn't have internet access at home. I didn't know how my family felt about anything beyond the heterosexual world where I was raised. They never shamed or spoke badly about people; they just didn't discuss it. So it wasn't until I got older that I was able to put a description of genderqueer on myself. I could see and understand this concept of not being a man or a woman in Prince. But I didn't understand what it was called.

I rarely felt comfortable in my own physical body. I felt isolated. I still feel isolated, even though I'm surrounded by love and support. Family and friends can support me in every way, but they'll never really understand my gender identity, which makes me feel apart.

Prince understood. He was what I was missing. He was unapologetic. Sexy. Proud. Genderless. It's what I'm still working on right now. Even as I got older, there was no one out there who was as confident about their beyond-the-gender-binary persona. There was no music I could connect to as much as I connected to Prince's.

I found a North Star in Prince because he showed me the power of my genderqueer body. Prince let me see a person who wore makeup and whatever clothes he wanted, not caring whether his choices were gendered. Prince created both transcendent music and his own identity and did neither for anyone's approval nor opinion. That's brave as hell.

He continued to inspire me when he joined Janelle Monáe on her second album, *The Electric Lady*. It was a perfect match. Like Prince, one of her musical forebears, Monáe is unapologetic about her Blackness and sexual identity. She too is a pocket-sized revolution who is changing the game in a creative and bold way—from the way she composes her album interludes to her dedication to her family's labor history in her outfits.

I was standing in the exact same place at my exact same job and on Twitter yet again when I read the tweet about Janelle's sexuality. It was two years and five days after the day that Prince died. But unlike before when I felt a sense of loss, I felt a sense of peace. I felt borderline euphoric. For years I had watched every Janelle Monáe interview where she talked around her personal life. I was satisfied without being able to explain it when she would say she was an android . . . that was into other androids. I couldn't explain to myself for years why I felt drawn to someone who didn't place a gender on who they were dating. But as soon as I read the first paragraph of her *Rolling Stone* interview, I understood.

It was another Black person existing and loving in this mysterious haze of purple in a world of red and blue. I felt represented. I felt pride. I could confidently tell people, "Yeah, queer as in Janelle Monáe, free ass motherfucker." Because it felt that way. It felt freeing. It felt like seeing Prince in the worst shade of yellow dancing with Muppets all over again. Something new yet familiar. It felt personal. It felt like me.

Her third album, *Dirty Computer*, was released the day after she released this statement, and I was thrown back into the comfort of what it's like for music to truly mean something in your life. I needed Prince when I was seven and curious about myself just like I needed Janelle Monáe, when I was twenty-eight, on the cover of *Rolling Stone* talking about being a proud queer and pansexual Black woman. I was already out and proud. But now I was out, proud, and loudly screaming that it was #20Gayteen.

I've been fed the music of Prince, Whitney Houston, and Michael Jackson since I was young. They have all helped me translate the emotions I was feeling when I couldn't find the words. People in my life know how much I adore Whitney Houston in particular. Her music is a huge part of my soul. What I don't state enough is that Prince was the person who gave me the attitude and the confidence to fully be that soul.

It's more than music for me. Living in a state where LGBTQ people are constantly attacked is draining. It's vital to me to have this connection to music created by these artists. They remind me of my power, beauty, and the possibility of the future we dream up together.

Notes

1. "America's Most Bible-Minded Cities: 2016," American Bible Society, accessed May 6, 2019, https://www.americanbible.org/features/americas-most-bible-minded-cities.

Originally published on Splinter *(formerly* Fusion.net*) on April 22, 2016.*

30 Years Later, 7 Ways *A Different World* Was Woke AF

Brittany Brathwaite

A Different World was an American sitcom that aired for six seasons beginning in September 1987, making it thirty this year (2017). The show focused on students attending the fictional historically Black college Hillman, the Virginia alma mater of Clair and Cliff Huxtable of *The Cosby Show*.

While the show has been cited as a large motivation for many in the eighties and nineties who wanted to attend college, mainly historically Black colleges and universities, it also played a major role in bringing difficult and contemporary topics to the fore, placing real historical, social, political, and economic issues within the context of young Black people's lives, especially Black women and femmes, and connecting to their gender, bodies, sexuality, and community.

The sitcom explored pertinent reproductive justice issues for Black women, including stereotypical imagery, like mammy; intimate partner violence; sexual harassment and assault; misogynoir; contraception and condom use; and young-adult pregnancy. *A Different World* was way ahead of its time in creating and shifting narratives about Black college life specifically and Black life in general.

1. HIV/AIDS was a reality for young people growing up in the nineties.

A Different World was one of the first television shows in the United States to address the HIV/AIDS epidemic. A 1991 episode[1] starring Tisha Campbell and Whoopi Goldberg spotlights Josie Webb (Campbell), a Hillman college student who discloses her HIV-positive status in her public speaking class when given an assignment to write her own obituary. In the aftermath of her sharing, some of her classmates don't want to be served by her at the Pit, the campus dining spot, or wear hand-kerchiefs over their faces to avoid contact with her. The episode dealt with HIV and AIDS very deftly by depicting how the personal affected the public sphere and the stigma surrounding AIDS.

First, the show made information available about how HIV was trans-mitted (*some* folks weren't quite sure if you could get HIV from kissing at that time) and dispelled outright myths about the disease. Second, *A Different World* portrayed how to treat folks through Mr. Gaines (Lou Myers), who was Josie's boss at the Pit. When Josie thinks that she needs to hide her status from Mr. Gaines out of fear that he would fire her if he knew, he shows her care and compassion. Though employment dis-crimination was and remains illegal, it is still a very real thing for many folks living with HIV.

Josie's disclosure causes her classmates to think about their sexual activity and consistent use of protection during sex but also dispels myths about what an HIV-positive person "looks" like. This episode was groundbreaking, not only because it was one of the first but because the writers chose to tell the story through the experiences of a Black woman, Josie, during a time when women's groups, AIDS Coalition to Unleash Power (ACT UP), and the HIV Law Project were fighting the Centers for Disease Control and Prevention (CDC) to include women's diseases in the definition of AIDS.

2. Sexual violence is never okay, whether it's on a date or in the workplace.

Season 2's episode "No Means No" tackles date rape, consent, and sup-porting survivors. The episode follows naive environmentalist and first-year student Winifred Brooks (Cree Summer), affectionately known as "Freddie," who has a huge crush on a charming and seemingly friendly star baseball player, Garth Parks. Dwayne (Freddie's former crush, por-trayed by Kadeem Hardison) soon learns that Garth isn't the man every-one thinks he is and that Garth has been sexually assaulting women at Hillman. Garth attempts to assault Freddie while on a date after the school dance.

A Different World addressed several issues here: First, it dismantled the false belief that women "really" want sex, but because society tells them they're not supposed to ask for it, it is a man's job to "let them off the hook" so that it doesn't look like their idea—so says Garth. Second, it illuminated the fact that survivors of rape and sexual assault do not always feel that they can report their assault and sometimes believe that if they consented to other things, including the date itself, then the rape was also their fault. Third, it showed that it is critical for men to have conversations with one another about sex, masculinity, and sexual violence. This is demonstrated through a powerful conversation between Dwayne and Walter Oakes (Sinbad), the male dorm director at Hillman, who is known for his jokes and making light of issues but who deals very sternly with this issue when Dwayne approaches him.

A few seasons later, the series looked at sexual harassment in the workplace when Whitley Gilbert (Jasmine Guy), working as an assistant art buyer, is sexually harassed by her supervisor.

The episode aired one year after Senate confirmation hearings involving Clarence Thomas and Anita Hill. Hill accused Thomas, then a Supreme Court nominee, of sexual harassment when she was working for him at the Equal Employment Opportunity Commission. This hearing struck up major controversies in the Black community and raised questions about intersectionality, specifically whether a person could have allegiances as a Black person and as a woman at the same time. In the episode, Whitley dreams of appearing before the Senate and is dressed in Hill's memorable turquoise-blue suit.

3. Safe sex is the best sex.

In season 4, the "Time Keeps on Slipping" episode follows Hillman students as they prepare a time capsule for students twenty years later. Hillman students compile everything from a medicine pouch for the earth to a sonogram of a "baby girl." They also decide to create a video for the time capsule, but it's Ron Johnson's contribution that Whitley stops the production for. As Ron stands in front of the camera, Whitley asks, "Where's your contribution?" and he says, "In my back pocket." It's a condom.

Ron is told that it wasn't a sex education video or a joke, and he responds that neither is AIDS or unintended teenage pregnancy or anything else a condom helps prevent. "My message is responsibility," Ron says. "You want to preserve the planet; I want to protect it." Interestingly, while Ron was allowed to talk about condoms, he wasn't allowed to show one on television.

The "protection" theme is a consistent thread throughout the series, whether it's the reference to the "Letti Stay Ready Date Pack" and the "Walter Oakes Date Pack," or Jaleesa Vinson (Dawnn Lewis) chasing Whitley around the living room trying to get her to take a condom for the first time she gets intimate with Dwayne. This frenzy around the room leads to older student Jaleesa (who was constantly breaking down gender norms and roles) talking about how it was everyone's responsibility to make sure that a condom is always used.

Unfortunately, because of declining condom use in the United States (CDC statistics show that in 2016, newly reported sexually transmitted infections in the United States were at an all-time high),[2] we might need to bring these episodes back. There are way too many television shows that depict people having sex and never reaching for a condom, including HBO and Issa Rae's *Insecure*, which came under fire this summer for the lack of condom use on the show.

4. Stereotypes about Black women, even mammy, hurt.

In the season 5 episode "Mammy Dearest," dorm director Whitley plans a dedication ceremony. In an attempt to celebrate Black women throughout history and to highlight the ways that Black women have struggled to survive in the United States, Whitley presents portraits of powerful Black women like Angela Y. Davis, Marian Anderson, Maya Angelou, Leontyne Price, and—to everyone's surprise—mammy. Mammy's inclusion in this constellation of powerful women causes a stir among the women at Gilbert Hall. For many of the women, especially Kimberly Reese (Charnele Brown), mammy represents stereotypical racial imagery. Whitley "instructs" her residents that in order to neutralize the stereotype, they have to reclaim it.

The mammy caricature is a fat Black woman who cared more about the white families she worked for than her own at home. While mammy had children, she was often presented as asexual and less of a threat to the white women she worked for. Mammy was a representation of Black female domestic workers who were constantly devalued and exploited for their labor.

By depicting a central image of the interlocking systems of race, class, and gender oppression, the "Mammy Dearest" episode opened up conversations about Black womanhood, colorism, and anti-Blackness. Kim, a darker-skinned woman, can't take the mammy imagery, but Whitley, a light-skinned woman, cannot begin to understand what mammy represents. The episode presents new questions for us, including, what is the importance of these racial stereotypical images? And can they be reclaimed?

5. How to get an A-plus in misogynoir and profiting off of Black women.

In season 4's episode "Ms. Understanding," sixth-year senior Shazza publishes his senior thesis (which was rejected by the thesis board) as a guide for Hillman women to use to understand Hillman men. Playing off the real-life book *The Blackman's Guide to Understanding the Blackwoman*, by Shahrazad Ali, which was very popular at that time, it captures the bizarre, misogynist messaging presented in the original book. Shazza presents an ahistorical analysis of the Black community, asserting that the Black nuclear family has degenerated because "Adam and Eve no longer respect one another—especially Adam" and that "a woman is not a doormat until she lies down."

According to Shazza, the Hillman woman (also read as "young Black woman") should be confident, know her self-worth, and be treated like a "queen"—but only if she adheres to stereotypical and dated gender norms and roles. Of course, all of this is coming from a person who has been socialized as a man and has been reaping the benefits attached to male privilege his entire life. His "popular" text offered no real analysis of class, social systems, or history's influence on the lives of Black people in the United States while generating a great deal of controversy between the sexes on campus. In short, *A Different World* was reading Hoteps and analyzing misogynoir long before we started calling them out on Twitter.

6. It's never just a "love tap"; relationship violence happens with college baes too.

Of all the episodes of *A Different World* that I have watched—basically all 144 of them—"Love Taps" in season 5 had to be one of the hardest to watch. This episode follows outspoken sophomore Gina Deveaux as she navigates an abusive relationship with rapper Dion, who is quickly rising to fame on Hillman's campus with his misogynist raps. Initially, it appears that Gina and Dion have a cute nineties relationship as she supports her man's rap dreams, but we soon learn that this relationship is anything but aspirational.

In the episode, Freddie tells the women of Height Hall gathered around a table in the Pit that she saw a woman she did not recognize being beaten on the roof while she was doing her moon meditations the night before (a typical Freddie practice). She demands that Whitley, the co-dorm director, call an emergency meeting. At first, Whitley hesitates, but is quickly reminded by Kim what happened when her employer, E. H. Wright, did not believe her sexual harassment claims earlier that year.

Meanwhile, Gina is coming up with excuses for the bruises on her body (she ran into a coffee table or her desk). She pushes away her best friend, Lena (Jada Pinkett), when she gives her an outlet to ask for help, and she tries to change the topic or make jokes whenever domestic violence is brought up. The episode highlights the textbook signifiers of an abusive relationship: jealousy, isolation from friends, and attempts by the abuser to "apologize" or make amends with expensive gifts. When Gina confronts Dion, asking him, "What do I do to make you so mad?" he promises not to hit her anymore. A few minutes into that same scene, she can be seen being thrown up against a wall.

An important talk with Mr. Gaines (Mr. Gaines for the win *again!*) encourages Gina to break it off with Dion. It takes a real community effort for Gina to be able to leave Dion. Gina decides to press charges against Dion, and he is shown being taken away by police. This episode attempted to demonstrate, in its twenty-two-minute run time, how complicated ending an abusive relationship can be.

7. Pregnancy and parenting in college can be tough, but it also can be done.

Although Bill Cosby would not let Denise Huxtable's character be shown pregnant on *A Different World* when actress Lisa Bonet became pregnant (ultimately leading to Denise's exit from the show and her "year-long trip to the Motherland"), *A Different World* did bring up pregnancy and young parenting through other characters.

For example, in season 2, "It Happened One Night" follows freshman Kimberly Reese through a pregnancy scare with her then-boyfriend, Robert. In the episode, Kim's roommate, Whitley, even offers to support Kim in paying for an abortion. She says, "If you need money for any reason, there is money." And while Kim says that she does not want to have an abortion (she actually says the word "abortion"), she is not sure what she wants to do. Robert also suggests that Kim have an abortion, which causes Kim to ignore his calls.

In the same episode, Jaleesa also shares her experience of having a pregnancy that resulted in a miscarriage. Freddie proposes a "village care" scenario, suggesting that Jaleesa, Dwayne, and she could be uncles and aunties if Kim decides to keep the baby. This episode demonstrated how nuanced reproductive decision making can be and the types of compassion and care that are needed for that to happen. It also shows the stress that comes with the precarious circumstances connected to becoming pregnant in college.

Season 3's episode "Delusions of Daddyhood" shows Ron dating a young mom, Elizabeth James, who is balancing attending Hillman, dating, and taking care of her son, Isaac. And while the episode focuses on Ron's attempts to play daddy, it also sheds light on the fact that some people do parent while enrolled in college, even at traditional four-year schools like Hillman.

Notes

1. *A Different World*, season 4, episode 23, "If I Should Die Before I Wake," directed by Debbie Allen, written by Bill Cosby and Susan Fales-Hill, featuring Jasmine Guy, Dawnn Lewis, and Kadeem Hardison, aired April 11, 1991, on NBC.
2. Centers for Disease Control and Prevention, *Sexually Transmitted Disease Surveillance 2016* (Atlanta: US Department of Health and Human Services, 2017).

Originally published on The Root *on October 28, 2017.*

How Statement T-Shirts Unite Black History, Culture, and Fashion

Cynthia R. Greenlee

Before anything went "viral," the "It's a Black Thing. You Wouldn't Understand" T-shirt went viral. During my nineties college years, everyone I knew had one or wanted one, or had an opinion about the message—whether the T-shirt was simply cotton printed with words, an emblem of Black pride, or a divisive tool that should be banned in schools. You could see it at historically Black colleges and universities, and it was sold on street corners or in stores that peddled leather Africa medallions, black soap, essential oils, and mixtapes.

Decades later, I still have my "It's a Black Thing" T-shirt as apparel-artifact. I bought one secretly at a Black expo, despite my parents' objections; they thought it would attract undue and unfriendly attention in my southern hometown (and they were right), but I thought I was grown, and I liked it.

Since then, other shirts with something to say have made their way into my wardrobe: at least three #BlackGirlMagic selections, an "Unapologetically Black" shirt from Black Youth Project 100, a ten-year-old "Black Nerds Unite" shirt, and a vintage purple jawn that features an iron-on decal (remember them?) of a melaninated Barbie with a Farrah Fawcett–style winged hairdo. And I'm not bragging or anything, but I do have a #BlackGenius one too.[1] Each one declares some facet of my identity: Black, female, bookish, quirky, unconcerned with dressing up, and more than happy to wear my support of Black institutions across my chest.

The statement T-shirt for, by, and about Black folks seems to be having a renaissance. In July 2017, celebrities like Serena Williams, rapper Remy Ma, and actresses Tracee Ellis Ross and Yara Shahidi donned Maya Angelou–inspired "Phenomenal Woman" T-shirts to promote Black Women's Equal Pay Day.[2] That same summer, Twitter erupted in memorable memes when a style writer discovered that online retailer Zazzle was using white models to sell T-shirts related to Black culture.[3] Their hypervisibility is also a matter of sheer volume: search Etsy for "Black Girl Magic T-shirt" and you'll get thousands of results, including sequined tops, "I Am Black History" shirts, and a Wakanda-themed "Classy Like Nakia, Fight Like Okoye, Invent Like Shuri" number. Amazon boasts even more options.

This form of material culture has always been a barometer of Black civic culture and creativity—think Black Power T-shirts in the 1960s. Now, in 2018, there are shirts that list the names of Black luminaries past and present, memorial shirts that mourn people killed by police and that demand justice, contemporary riffs on "Black Is Beautiful," and reprints of classic slogans like "Black by Popular Demand." So why has the humble T-shirt—an item that literally came out (from under men's shirts) in the early twentieth century—emerged as such a fashionable force of nature among all manner of "skinfolk," from millennials to fortysomething professionals?[4]

The answer lies in both the historical and the utterly contemporary, say experts in Black popular history, culture, and aesthetics. The T-shirt

Idas and editors Angela Bronner Helm, Taja Lindley, Cynthia R. Greenlee, Samantha Daley (top: left to right), Jordan Scruggs and Janna A. Zinzi (bottom: left to right) took a break from writing for a rustic photo shoot at a group writing retreat in Monterey, CA, in 2018. Photo by Bethanie Hines.

The joy of expression . . . and the ocean! Ida Jordan Scruggs shines their light during a sunset beach stroll and writing break. Photo by Bethanie Hines.

renaissance is part social media, part outraged expression at anti-Black violence, and the latest manifestation of a Black public sphere in which apparel is political.

Professor Tanisha C. Ford, a historian at the University of Delaware and author of *Liberated Threads: Black Women, Style, and the Global Politics of Soul*, tells me that the clothing Black people wear has long been subject to coercion, regulation, and derision—and co-optation. Fashion has been a method of control for a long time, Ford explains: "African American dress was restricted under slavery. Slaveowners determined what bondsmen and bondwomen could wear, and typically dressed them in the cheapest of fabrics. During Jim Crow, there was the idea that dressing nicer than a white person could cost you your life; it was seen as a willful rebellion. Black women were mocked for wearing silk stockings and hats, things that were supposed to be reserved for white women."

In response to such sartorial coercion, fashion became a terrain for struggle and self-representation. "Wearing what we want to wear, in this structure that tries to strip us of humanity, is a work of resistance," says Ford. So the autonomy to dress oneself, whether in luxury labels supposedly priced out of 'hood reach, Sunday finery, or casual wear like sagging jeans represented a facet of Black freedom.

Even being able to engage in the marketplace as a consumer has a deep significance. Traci Parker, a historian at the University of Massachusetts at Amherst, studies Black consumer behavior and how department stores themselves were early staging grounds for civil rights campaigns. Parker tells me that Americans of all backgrounds have frequently seen being able to buy and sell as fundamental rights, but department stores were often loath to hire Black sales staff and extend courteous service to African American shoppers. As protesters bore "I Am a Man" protest signs in the sixties, Black consumers also tacitly argued that their "Black" didn't rub off on their "green" and that they were equally deserving of employment in a variety of clothiers.

That translates today, Parker thinks, into the current desire to "buy Black" and support the scores of melaninated T-shirt makers; it can be retail therapy seasoned with a dash of racial pride and resistance. "Oftentimes, these are Black men and women who are setting up their own online businesses, especially now during the decline of traditional brick-and-mortar stores. It may be their side hustle, but we're supporting each other in a world where it can feel like there's little real connection."

So buying that T-shirt with a woman's Afro in silhouette or "Professional Black Girl" printed on the front can be a form of connection via commerce. "This was an Etsy moment that has gone beyond Etsy," says Parker. "But we can say for certain it's about the ease of making a T-shirt, the ability of Black folks to find a significant customer base, and [being able] to protest on a daily basis in a way that is visual and apparent."

Of course, wearing a sentiment across one's chest doesn't equate to having a coherent politics or translate into action. A T-shirt is itself neutral, only able to absorb the meanings we attach to it, and equally capable of spewing white nationalism as Black cultural affirmation (a frequent response to my "It's a Black Thing" shirt: "What would Black people do if I wore a 'white pride' T-shirt?"). Nor is it easy to figure out if the creator is actually Black or who they might be. And in a culture that has hated on Black culture and aesthetics, even while co-opting the "cool" and creative labor of Black designers, there's also something to be said for the basic freedom to wear something simply because you like its look, feel, and fit.[5]

So what does it mean to wear a T-shirt that reads with some Black-zeitgeisty slogan? Mark Anthony Neal, chair of Duke University's Department of African and African American Studies, says there can be a disconnect between fashion and principles: "When you start to see a proliferation of these T-shirts, you see a generation of young people thinking about politics. But they may not be able to actualize their politics—may not see the strategy, or the organizations that are doing the work" of making change. "We don't see any real complexity in politics from T-shirts. It's old-school sloganeering that's wrapped up in new slogans."

Still, Neal doesn't minimize the importance of the slogan T-shirt or its relationship with social media. Twitter—the most potent online vehicle for Black wit, outrage, and creativity—has created a prolific universe of the hashtag-able, and those hashtags will not be contained.

Statement T-shirts can function as true invitations for solidarity or provocations from the sincerely curious or merely conflictual. Neal himself has worn such shirts, and they've drawn varied responses from white people. One man in a hardware store asked him, "'Black Nerds Unite' against what?"—as if an army of Black bibliophiles were plotting a coup d'état—and women have stopped Neal to check his "This Is What a Feminist Looks Like" bona fides. In their minds, "If anybody doesn't embody Black feminism, that's a big Black man," he said.

Neal's younger tween-aged daughter has been known to take over her father's shirts; in particular, she appreciates T-shirts that reference history, like one featuring Emmett Till and Trayvon Martin, both killed by racist vigilantes during their all-too-brief adolescences. Wearing it gives his daughter the chance to explain things she, the child of an African American studies and literature professor, understands more than most of her peers.

When Ford was about ten years old, a T-shirt led her down a similar historical path. Her godmother brought her a T-shirt emblazoned with the Gil Scott-Heron quote, "The revolution will not be televised."[6] On the back, it read "No Justice, No Peace" and listed the names of Emmett Till and the Scottsboro Boys, among others.[7] "When she gave it to me, I wanted to find out whatever I could about the people on the shirt. It crystallized something in me, connecting the names of Black people murdered by the state or who had encounters with the state to the everyday racism I experienced growing up as a Black girl in Fort Wayne, Indiana."

Granted, identity won't be mass-produced, made, or broken by a T-shirt. But Ford's creative partner, Southern Connecticut State University professor Siobhan Carter-David—the two started Textures MC Lab, a pop-up that explores fashion and material culture—thinks that

Idas Emma Akpan and Gloria Malone are unapologetically Black and proud at a very white Monterey, CA, beach. Photo by Bethanie Hines.

the proliferation of public statements about Blackness have made this a moment when a critical mass of people are ready to proclaim their racial identity or solidarity. "It's not just about the clothing—it's about the celebration of our brown skin. Now it's trendy to wear our hair natural, it's not just for the conscious," she says. "I wouldn't underplay the importance of Barack Obama's presidency. When he first popped up on the scene, I remember the moment we found out he was actually married to a sistah. We spent a lot of time making sure we defended her image. We said: We are beautiful, Michelle's arms are just fine, and our melanin is popping.

"When women are wearing 'Black Girl Magic' T-shirts, we are reclaiming the word 'girl' and symbolizing something very sistahgurl and affiliation with Black women. We want people to know that Black women are amazing and beautiful. . . . But I'm interested to see whether these T-shirts are a long-lasting thing and not just a fad."

With African American buying power reaching the trillions (not to mention cash throughout the diaspora), T-shirts that are "unapologetically Black" will not wane anytime soon. "For us, by us" is not a new concept for Black creatives, consumers, or fashionistas.[8] It's an idea that holds tremendous emotional weight in Black communities, which have high rates of starting businesses (especially among Black women) but low wealth and a disproportionately low rate of homeownership due to discriminatory housing practices, such as redlining.[9]

Christen Smith, a University of Texas at Austin professor, has witnessed that very emotional pull. Like Ford and Carter-David, she's a

T-shirts can start conversations. Ida Bianca Campbell makes a statement flipping the script on abortion narratives. Photo by Bethanie Hines.

member of a small club: Black women with PhDs and tenure-track jobs. Only 2 percent of US residents have doctoral degrees, and a small sliver of those are Black.[10] That's one reason she created her Cite Black Women Twitter account and an accompanying T-shirt that urges the recognition of Black women's thought leadership and publications.[11]

"When I first started selling shirts, people came up and told me so many stories about their struggles as Black women being ignored in the academy, and also in life," Smith said. "Many Black women felt empowered by the shirts. Some even cried. I was also struck by the number of allies—non-Black women—who came to support, noting their solidarity, telling stories about how they try to decolonize the canon by incorporating Black women into the core of their work. When I came home from the conference, I felt even more energized."

The idea isn't limited to the academic sphere. "As Black women, we are often being silenced, particularly in public spaces," says Smith. "We are often told that we are too loud, too present, too, too, too. . . . But ironically, alongside being told that we are too visible, we are ignored and silenced. Sometimes it feels like we are screaming in the wind."

So some people express themselves on cotton or organic bamboo. They tether their thoughts about politics, beauty, and history to their bodies, anchor them with their flesh. "T-shirts allow us to be loud and bold and in your face without saying a word," says Smith. "We don't have to be given permission to speak or given our turn. If I am wearing a T-shirt that expresses an internal sentiment that I feel, when you look at me, I am heard."

Notes

1. "BYP100 Launches 'Unapologetically Black' T-Shirt Campaign," Black Youth Project 100, September 4, 2014, http://blackyouthproject.com/byp100-launches-unapologetically-black-t-shirt-campaign/.

2. Christina Coleman, "These Celebrities Are Bringing Much-Needed Awareness to Black Women's Equal Pay Day," *Essence*, July 31, 2017, https://www.essence.com/news/celebrities-awareness-black-womens-equal-pay-day/.

3. Mary Anderson, "This Brand Is Being Slammed for Using White Models to Sell Shirts That Say 'Black Girl Magic,'" *Insider*, July 27, 2017, https://www.insider.com/zazzle-shirt-controversy-2017-7.

4. Pagan Kennedy, "Who Made That Shirt?" *New York Times*, September 20, 2013, https://www.nytimes.com/2013/09/22/magazine/who-made-that-t-shirt.html.

5. Dominique Hobdy, "Why This Black Designer Is Accusing Kylie Jenner of Blatantly Copying Her Work, *Essence*, June 9, 2017, https://www.essence.com/fashion/kylie-jenner-camouflage-plagiarism-plugged-nyc/.

6. Gil Scott-Heron, Full Version of "The Revolution Will Not Be Televised," YouTube, accessed June 1, 2019, https://www.youtube.com/watch?v=qGaoXAwl9kw.

7. "Who Were the Scottsboro Boys," PBS, accessed June 1, 2019, http://www.pbs.org/wgbh/americanexperience/features/scottsboro-boys-who-were-the-boys/.

8. John Tucker, "The Road to $1.5 Trillion in Black Buying Power and Dispelling a Common Myth," *Black Enterprise*, November 13, 2017, https://www.blackenterprise.com/the-road-to-1-5-trillion-in-black-buying-power/.

9. Amy Haimerl, "The Fastest-Growing Group of Entrepreneurs in America," *Fortune*, June 29, 2015, http://fortune.com/2015/06/29/black-women-entrepreneurs/; Rakesh Kochhar and Anthony Cilluffo, "How Wealth Inequality Has Changed in the US since the Great Recession by Race, Ethnicity and Income," Pew Research Center, November 1, 2017, https://www.pewresearch.org/fact-tank/2017/11/01/how-wealth-inequality-has-changed-in-the-u-s-since-the-great-recession-by-race-ethnicity-and-income/; Tracy Jan, "Report: No Progress for African Americans on Homeownership, Unemployment, and Incarceration in 50 years," *Washington Post*, February 26, 2018, https://www.washingtonpost.com/news/wonk/wp/2018/02/26/report-no-progress-for-african-americans-on-homeownership-unemployment-and-incarceration-in-50-years/; Ta-Nehisi Coates, "The

Case for Reparations," *The Atlantic*, June 2014, https://www.theatlantic. com/magazine/archive/2014/06/the-case-for-reparations/361631/.

10. "Educational Attainment," US Census Bureau, accessed August 14, 2020, https://www.census.gov/newsroom/cspan/educ/educ_attain_ slides.pdf.

11. Sophie Inge, "'Cite Black Women' Campaign Gains Momentum," *Times Higher Education*, January 22, 2018, https://www.timeshighereducation. com/news/cite-black-women-campaign-gains-momentum.

Originally published in Elle *on March 2, 2018.*

Where's the *16, Parenting, and OK* Reality Show?

Gloria Malone

While they might never admit it, I firmly believe the negative ways in which the media—television, film, print journalism—portrays teen pregnancy and parenting influenced how the adults in my life treated me after I told them I was pregnant.

When I became pregnant at fifteen, the adults in my life believed my life was over. In addition to explicitly stating this to me, they began to treat me differently and even stopped helping me look into colleges because they believed I would not finish high school.

These stereotypes about teen parents also affected my self-image and already low self-esteem. Thankfully, over time, I was able to overcome my self-doubt, and my family members got over their issues and started supporting me. But not every teen has the same experience. The way the media represents teenage pregnancy and parenting has real-life consequences and effects on teen families, including depression and poverty because of a lack of support from society. By moving away from these stereotypes and featuring more positive story lines and outcomes, people in the media can make it easier for teens to create thriving families.

From films to public service campaigns, the representation of teenage parents is often inaccurate, sexist, classist, and racially biased. In order to change this, we must first examine the ways in which people in the media are doing a bad job and then look at how they can do better.

The media often focuses on female teens and their "inability to say no and keep their 'legs closed.'" Public service campaigns like the one from the National Campaign to Prevent Teen Pregnancy have featured the words "cheap," "dirty," and "used" across photos of young women to emphasize the narrative that pregnant and parenting teens are associated with these characteristics. Along the same lines, a New York City Human Resource Administration's pregnancy prevention ad campaign featured a young Black child asking her teen mother, "[C]hances are he won't stay with you. What happens to me?" "Are you ready to raise a child by yourself?" the ad asks, putting all of the blame and responsibility on the mom. These narratives absolve teen boys of any responsibility for the sexual activity that results in pregnancy.

"Inferring that a young mother is promiscuous, that a young father just won't be there for his child, and that they will forever 'live off the system' is harmful," explained Marylouise Kuti, a former teen mother and young parents' advocate who is part of #NoTeenShame, a national advocacy campaign—of which I am a part—that helps to counter the negative narratives of teenage pregnancy and parenting in society.

When teen pregnancy and parenting are presented as a "female problem," the financial obligations and responsibilities are placed solely on the woman. If the pregnant and/or parenting teen is a Black or Latina female, these stereotypical narratives are compounded with racialized biases: long-term poverty, single motherhood, and low education achievement. While white pregnant teens are often awarded celebrity status (i.e., they seem to more often become the "stars" of MTV's teen parenting shows), pregnant Black and Latina teens frequently see themselves and representations of their families in hurtful public service announcements.

Furthermore, as youth advocate Natasha Vianna told *Rewire.News* in an interview, "One of the biggest problems with the way teen parents are portrayed in the media has to do with where the media chooses to start the story. Teen pregnancy and parenthood has almost always been framed as the beginning of the end of a young person's life, so we don't get to hear much about what their lives were like before pregnancy— especially if their lives were much harder than [they are] now."

In choosing to begin the narrative at the time of pregnancy and ending it at the time of the child's birth, shows like the 2009 MTV reality series *16 and Pregnant* do not show viewers what the life of a teen who is pregnant actually is. We see the shame and stigma the teen experiences, the birth of the child, and, in some cases, an adoption before the show ends, as if that's all there is to teen pregnancy and parenting. The lives of the parents beyond the pregnancy are ignored unless they are sensationalized for programs like MTV's *Teen Mom* series.

But even these shows are unrealistic for several reasons, including that the cast is mostly white, cisgender, heterosexual, and predominately middle class. All of these women are also getting paid thousands of dollars to be profiled and have their lives edited for public consumption. From season to season, the living conditions of the mothers improve because of the MTV salary the women are receiving. The shows also seem to highlight the most stereotypical, hurtful teenage family stereotypes: the problematic "baby daddy" drama, the "party girl," and the irresponsible and disrespectful teenage mom.

Then there's the fact that the media often overrepresents adoption, especially when it comes to teenage mothers. "The adoption story line is often used as a way to fix the 'problem,'" sociologist Gretchen Sisson, whose work focuses on teenage pregnancy, parenting, and adoption, told *Rewire.News* in an interview. "Teen parenthood and abortion are both very stigmatized. So adoption is kind of the way out and a way for the character to redeem themselves. Before abortion was legal, adoption was a way for white women to 'undo' the sins of sexuality outside of marriage. Adoption is used as a solution for teen pregnancy and abortion, when really it is neither of these things."

In her research, Sisson found that less than 1 percent of women in the United States place children up for adoption. However, films and shows like *Glee*, *Juno*, *16 and Pregnant*, and *Saved* all have story lines that result in a pregnant teen giving their child up for adoption.

Marriage is also often viewed and used as a way to "make things right." In the 2001 film based on Beverly Donofrio's autobiography, *Riding in Cars with Boys*, Beverly states that she does not want to marry the father of her child. But after an emotional scene with her parents, who feel she ruined both her and the father of the child's life, she reluctantly agrees to the marriage. Characters on the MTV shows *Teen Mom* and *Teen Mom 2* also experience pressure from family members to marry the fathers of their children, as if that's their only option.

I can attest to this dynamic playing out in real life: when I became pregnant at fifteen, many people expected me to marry the father of my child since he "got me pregnant" and "marriage would make it right."

If one does not give their child up for adoption or marry the father of their child (if the father has not left them already, as the narrative goes in the media), the narrative often attributed to parenting teens is one of a desolate existence for both mother and child. Whether it is losing all of their friends, being disowned by their families, being kicked out of school, or being sent away by family, teenage mothers simply do not have positive narratives of themselves in the media, and the negative effects of this are very real.

Teenage mothers have a higher rate of postpartum depression than mothers twenty and older; they are often forced out of school by illegal policies or because of bullying from staff and students alike, and they are more likely to experience social injustices because of age, race, and socioeconomic background, which present unique barriers to social welfare assistance.

Media has a responsibility to accurately and holistically represent teenage families, especially those of color. There simply is not enough positive representation free of gaslighting when it comes to teenage families. All teenage fathers are not absent from their families' lives. Teenage parents are more likely than nonparenting teens to obtain their GED. And not all teenage mothers are kicked out by their parents or have as their end goal in life to attend college and get married.

To be sure, teen parents face several hardships since many teenage parents are already living in poverty before they become pregnant and face barriers to finishing their education, finding and obtaining work, and finding stable housing if they are in a situation that does not allow them to stay in their initial place of residence. However, teenage parents also often say their children served as a catalyst for them to do better in life, finish their education, stop mismanaging money, and get serious about discovering who they are as people and what type of contributing member of society they want to be. Not only are teenage parents capable of love, compassion, and good parenting—the parents of the pregnant and parenting teens are capable of the same through supporting, loving, and encouraging their children to remain determined to reach the goals they had before becoming pregnant and after having their own children.

There is no doubt in my mind that I am a better person today because I had my daughter at age fifteen. When my family began to unlearn the false narratives about what my teenage pregnancy would supposedly do to the family and me, they began to show love and support.

Why aren't there examples of *that* in the media? Where's the *16, Parenting, and OK* show to help teens see the decision doesn't have to lead to destitution?

While the media has taken on the role of "teaching" about teenage pregnancy, mostly through shame and stigma, media makers need to acknowledge that they are influencing how gatekeepers—including school administrators, healthcare providers, and other adults in a young person's life—perceive and treat young pregnant people. That was my experience, and I know through my work that I'm not alone.

We have to start asking ourselves, as former teen mother and #NoTeenShame member Christina Martinez recently mentioned to me, "What if we were to surround young parents with messages of hope, support, and encouragement? How might that alter the confidence in which they approach their role as parent?"

If my family and high school guidance counselor had responded to my decision to carry my pregnancy to term and parent my child in a more positive way from the get-go, with tips on planning for my future and for my daughter's future, I may have experienced a more healthy and positive pregnancy. And so I ask, how are others preparing teens to live the life they want for themselves and their families? We can and must do so much better.

Originally published on Rewire.News *on October 20, 2014.*

Lemonade Refreshed My Spirit. I Didn't Feel Exploited, Commodified, or Powerless, bell hooks.

Emma Akpan

I'm a woman who grew up in the church, and I have always struggled with my spirituality. I struggled because, for years, I was taught that if we prayed and had faith, we wouldn't experience pain.

As I got older and experienced more pain, my faith waned because that no longer rang true. However, experiencing Beyoncé's "visual album" *Lemonade* was theologically and spiritually freeing because Beyoncé expresses a tangible spirituality—a spirituality one might touch in our mothers, aunts, and sisters through words, songs, and foods, like lemonade instead of an ethereal God that lives in the sky.

It was like a slap in the face when I saw that bell hooks, the pioneering feminist writer who taught me how to find love in my community of sisters in her work *All About Love*, offered a reproachful critique of the album in her 2016 essay, *Moving Beyond Pain*.[1] hooks claims that Beyoncé used a drink, lemonade, to simply sell a false feminist narrative. For hooks, Beyoncé's rejection of a male God and embracing her mothers and sisters and herself as God doesn't go far enough; she thinks Beyoncé should reject men and capitalism completely.

I disagree. As Beyoncé elevated herself to God status by finding God in her womanhood and using lemonade as the unifier, she elucidated the obvious need for women like me to consider finding love and liberation through my community, instead of in a male-identified God.

bell hooks missed the spiritually liberating elements of the album when she dismissed it.

My spirituality was once defined by an intangible hope that everything would work out, just by speaking, crying out, or praying. At times, it appeared that this particular style of spirituality worked.

During winters in Toledo, Ohio, where I grew up, mornings were spent scooping large piles of snow from the car and shoveling our long driveway just to get to school. Because it was so cold, my mother had trouble almost every morning getting her '89 Buick to start. But I have the kind of mother who is so devoted to God that every morning, she would instruct us to shout "JESUS!" as she turned the ignition. When the car started, we were supposed to say, "Thank you, Lord!" Because of her, in our minds, Jesus could fix anything.

So when my mother told me that she had prayed at a church altar for ten years to save her marriage, I imagined her trying to fix a broken marriage like a car that wouldn't start.

As a family, we found that praying to God for a marriage doesn't work. My parents divorced after fifteen years of marriage, leaving me to wonder if the damage to our family would have been mitigated if she had simply stopped praying and left.

Like my mother, many Black women wear spirituality and devotion to faith as a badge of honor—until it fails them. We model devotion to our churches and church leadership, devotion to our marriages and heteronormative relationships, and devotion to our homes and our children. Anything but devotion to self. Yet like my mother, many end up feeling let down after all this devotion—abandoned in the face of their prayers.

In the opening scenes of *Lemonade*, Beyoncé appears to come to the same realization as my mother and so many women before her did. She provides vague, poetic descriptions amounting to trouble in her marriage, invoking spiritual practices like fasting, praying, avoiding mirrors, and abstaining from sex in order to fix it. But, ultimately, she realizes that her prayer isn't stopping her from drowning. She breaks free of the spiritual hold her marriage has over her and places her godlike status into her own hands.

In a Judeo-Christian context, indeed, in most modern cultural contexts, such independent self-worship is heresy. Christianity teaches us that in no way should we be comparing ourselves to God. Instead, we should aspire to qualities that good Christian devotees possess: meekness, forgiveness, playing by the rules.

But men are almost never raised, socially or culturally, to have those qualities. Instead, they are taught to use spaces unapologetically with the assumption that they have the right answers, the right interpretation of Scripture and theology, and the confidence that they belong (including on the pulpit). Men are celebrated when they are outspoken and give "strong" direction, while we as Black women are expected to be devoted to them, like we are to God.

Rejecting and subverting this narrative, Beyoncé instead questions why her husband wasn't devoted to her because she is a God. She says in "Don't Hurt Yourself," *"Bad motherfucker, God complex, motivate your ass, call me Malcolm X. . . . When you hurt me, you hurt yourself. Don't hurt yourself. . . . Love God Herself."*

Beyoncé shows us not only that women can easily be stand-ins for God but that, in fact, this is a necessary subversion of Scripture in our patriarchal society, because most of us brought up in Western Christianity imagine God as a man or have been taught that God is a man.

She both declares she is a God and asks why men are God, placing God back into the hands of Black women.

In Beyoncé's *Lemonade*, God is no longer the man we worship in the sky. God does not exist in marriage. God does, however, exist in sisterhood. Despite what Black theology teaches us—that women must pray to God and have God be our stand-in for husbands while we wait for men to propose—Black women do not depend on God alone in the absence of men. We also depend on each other, which she highlights in the magical realism of our grandmother's kitchens. She knows that Black women create delicious and love-filled meals with little resources, heal wounds without medicine, and provide comfort and joy with a laugh and smile,

This is why Beyoncé's *Lemonade* was so freeing, and I found bell hooks's assessment surprising. Beyoncé offers us an alternative, connecting our spiritualities to our bodies and to the bodies of other women. We see an artful display of other women, but it does not intend to commodify us for the gaze of white mainstream culture; it is for Black women to see ourselves and God in our sisters.

And we do see God in the bodies of women because Beyoncé celebrates Black women's spiritual practices and beliefs by showing us God in her many forms. While most godlike devotion is singular, Beyoncé buckshots the devotion and directs it to our bodies (whether that means our style of dress, our control of our sexuality, and where we choose to enter to our mothers, grandmothers, sisters, sister-friends, and to our own gods, whether they be the Yoruba goddess Oshun or other deities).

Ultimately, Beyoncé forgives her husband and stays in her marriage. But that isn't the point. There is no "clear" outer change to her life circumstances or the state of her marriage. But as anyone can attest who has taken the ride through *Lemonade*, everything is actually different due to the inner shift and spiritual awakening that has happened.

Because of the journey of truth that Beyoncé takes us through, we ultimately realize that whether she stays with or leaves her husband is not the point of the visual album. Instead of linking our spirituality to men, our husbands, our fathers, our pastors, and other church leaders, Beyoncé links our spirituality to our own healing and the healing of our mothers, grandmothers, and sisters.

She did this for my mother. She did this for me, and for all the women who grew up in church envisioning our men as stand-ins for God. Beyoncé reminds us that we do not have to do that. But what we can do is find God in our sisters. Find God in our cooking, our land, our healing kitchens.

Find God in ourselves.

Notes

1. bell hooks, "Moving Beyond Pain," bell hooks Institute, May 9, 2016, http://criticaltheoryindex.org/assets/MovingBeyondPain---hooks-bell.pdf.

Originally published on Medium *on May 12, 2016.*

I Became a Black Woman in Spokane.
But, Rachel Dolezal, I Was a Black Girl First.

Alicia Walters

Rachel Dolezal has become a symbol to many African Americans of the separation of Blackness from Black people; to me, she is an example of how American society simultaneously devalues the individuality of Black women and us as a community to the point that the performance of Black womanhood is preferred over the people.

If Blackness can simply be worn or performed, then every white woman with a weave and a cause, every white girl with a snap and a little attitude, can supplant the lived experiences of what it is to become a Black woman: the journey of discrimination, the camaraderie of sisterhood, discovering the deep sense of responsibility and weight of the world, and, ultimately, finding the inner strength and acceptance that can only be built through struggle.

Rachel Dolezal may have perfected her performance of Black womanhood, and she may be connected to Black communities and feel an affinity with the styles and cultural innovations of Black people, but Black identity cannot be put on like a pair of shoes. Our external differences from the white majority might be how others categorize us as Black, but it's the thread of our diverse lived experiences that make us Black women.

Dolezal's specious claims to Black ancestry and faux Black identity could not have been sustained, and she would not have been able to pass if Black womanhood were seen and understood as more than skin—or weave—deep. Wearing Black womanhood was apparently even enough for Dolezal's "fellow" Black leaders in Spokane, Washington, who turned a blind eye to what the wider world now recognizes as her all but laughable claims of racial identity, whether out of fear of rocking the boat or plain northwestern niceness. Her charade could have only been maintained in a town (and within a society) with simplistic, stereotypical conceptions of Blackness—that Blackness is a shade on the range of olive to dark chocolate, a set of idioms delivered in a cadence from which American English derives its slang, and any number of bodily character-istics or mannerisms familiar across the globe, among others. And yet, while Black Americans have long embraced a diverse array of lineages as kin, simply looking the part and faking the rest doesn't cut it.

Whenever I tell people that I grew up in Spokane—a city in which only 2 percent of the population was Black—I usually neutralize their confusion with a joke about how I was one of about seven Black people, and five of us made it out.

You see, Black people aren't supposed to live in small towns in the Pacific Northwest of this country; Blackness has been defined as an "urban" identity. But while the majority of Black people in the United States do still live in the southern states,[1] and concentrations of Black folks outside the South tend to be around metropolitan areas, neither fact accounts for the constant migration of Black people toward eco-nomic opportunities, including to places like Spokane. Their migration to Spokane in particular may just have been the inspiration for the estab-lishment of the original headquarters of the Aryan Nations[2] thirty-seven miles away.

I was born in 1983—right in the middle of Spokane's first (and only) Black mayor's tenure, which spanned 1981–1985, cut short due to ill-ness. A celebrated leader whom Black people worked hard to elect, and an example of "acceptable" Black leadership, Mayor Jim Chase once told the local paper that he "never knew much discrimination in Spokane."[3] While that was perhaps true for him, it was not my family's experience, nor the experience of the Black people who lived through segregation through the 1970s in Spokane.[4] Though segregation was no longer enshrined in law in the 1980s when I was growing up, Black folks still lived almost exclusively on the East Side of town and in the his-torical neighborhoods built for railroad laborers. My Midwestern white mother and Black Puerto Rican father had moved to Spokane for col-lege and defied the unspoken segregation by starting their family in a working-class North Side neighborhood away from the Black enclave but hoping for the best. My father left the picture shortly after I was born, and my mother navigated the discrimination we faced in school and throughout town. I became familiar with the meaning of "nigger" quite early in life.

As one of just two Black girls in my elementary school, my kinky-ish hair, brown skin, and athletic build were uncommon. Before natural hair was considered cute, little white girls would shame me about the size of my "poofy hair." Throughout elementary school, in the confines of my bedroom, I put champagne-colored slips over my head to mimic the straight blond hair I thought I needed to fit in, gently swayed it back and forth, and dreamed of belonging—but I knew Black girls could never be white. When I was ten, my father, to the surprise and disgust of my mother, took me to the JC Penney salon in Seattle (three hundred miles away) to chemically straighten my hair and get my eyebrows and upper lip waxed. The first Black man in my life, he taught me that being a Black woman meant trying to conform to white standards of beauty.

But when I was fourteen, I gave up the relaxers and transitioned into rocking my natural kinky-ish afro. It instilled a new kind of confidence in me: I could not hang my head and wear this beautiful crown. My mother had not raised me to be an invisible, go-along-to-get-along gal, and, though I still harbored jealousy of my white peers with their incessant hair flipping, I decided to stand out instead of try and fail to fit in. I wore bright, creative clothing; I embraced my love of dance, of song, of sports, of speaking truthfully about race with little care for whether people attributed any of it to my Blackness or to me. Being able to get to a place where I could be myself made me feel powerful: I wanted to do and be everything, and, as I learned more about the history of the Atlantic slave trade, African diaspora, and white privilege, I wanted to tell these white people about themselves.

Realizing that I was hypervisible and yet never truly seen, I started a club called Helping Overcome Prejudice Everywhere (HOPE) with my brother. Each semester, my Spanish teacher would let me take over her class to lead my classmates through workshops on white privilege; it eventually became an established leadership course.

On the surface, I was successful, but I also longed for the recognition of fellow Black people, including my few Black male peers, for whom I was seemingly nonexistent: all of them, including my brothers, were busy chasing the hair-flippers. We may have been teammates in track, or they might've been my brother's friends, but the boys who I thought would be my best chance at external validation as an attractive woman left me wanting.

In Spokane in general, I rarely saw Black men coupled with Black women; more than a few men in our small Black community had white wives and girlfriends, while the Black women always seemed to be single. Naive, I imagined that, on the tightly knit East Side, there were churches full of Black women who were coupled with and loved by Black men. But on the streets of Spokane, in the public spaces at festivals, in restaurants, and wherever else I looked, Black and white men alike were always more interested in white women than women who looked like me. What I took from those years was that Black women were far from desirable partners.

To be a Black young woman in Spokane was, for me, to be rejected, isolated, and left to find my own way. Becoming the Black woman I am today was not about learning a performance, it was not about certain clothing or my hair texture; it came from first being a Black girl, from the trauma of rejection and isolation and its transformation into a kind of self-taught solitary pride from learning to preserve my own sense of true self.

Dolezal managed to put on an identity—that of a Black woman—in a way that renders invisible the experiences that actually forged for us our identities as Black women. She presented to the world the trappings of Black womanhood without the burden of having lived it for most of her life. She represented us and gained status in both Black and white communities as one of us, even though she could have worn her white-ness and talked to white people about their racism—something sorely needed in a town like Spokane.

Had she really understood the history of Black women in America, Dolezal would have recognized that she is perpetuating a fetish for Black women's bodies that devalues actual Black women while celebrating our parts when attached to the right (white) form. But she was not alone in this act of playing Black and benefiting from it.

Since Black womanhood is apparently all in the look, our society would rather have white former Disney pop stars twerk, talentless celeb-rities with enlarged backsides and their equally talentless siblings with swollen lips than celebrate the Black woman's form with the person who carries it. Black women learn that we are not desirable, that we are invis-ible, and yet we are imitated by the world's Dolezals and in our popular culture. Little Black girls like me could never have passed for white—and would've been ridiculed if we'd tried—but anyone with the right accessories can now seemingly claim to be a Black woman when it suits them.

Spokane was, for once, perhaps just ahead of the curve: we might be moments away from declaring that simply wearing "Black Woman" is enough to *be* a Black woman . . . or even preferable to it.

Notes

1. Sonya Rastogi et al., "The Black Population: 2010," US Census Bureau, September 2011, https://www.census.gov/prod/cen2010/briefs/c2010br-06.pdf.
2. "Aryan Nations," *Spokesman-Review*, accessed August 14, 2020, http://www.spokesman.com/topics/aryan-nations/.
3. Jim Kershner, "Spokane's Black Mayor Left His Mark," *Spokesman-Review*, September 21, 2008, https://www.spokesman.com/stories/2008/sep/21/spokanes-black-mayor-left-his-mark/.
4. Jim Kershner, "Segregation in Spokane," *Columbia Magazine* 14, no. 4 (Winter 2000–2001), https://www.washingtonhistory.org/wp-content/uploads/2020/04/winter-2000-01_001.pdf.

Originally published on the Guardian *on June 14, 2015.*

Weed for Period Pain? Yes, but I Want Equity in the Marijuana Industry Too

Jasmine Burnett

March 2016, *Vanity Fair* announced that Whoopi Goldberg is colaunching a line of cannabis (marijuana) products in April that will provide holistic alternatives for menstrual cramps.[1] Yes, you read that correctly.

As a Black woman of reproductive age who uses cannabis daily, I was excited to hear about Goldberg's venture, especially as someone whose uterus has seen an abortion and a myomectomy (a surgery to remove fibroids) and who currently manages symptomatic fibroids once or twice a month.

But I also have questions.

How will Goldberg and her business partner help to expand access to all of the people who suffer during menstruation?

And can Goldberg's influence create more opportunities for other Black people who have always been invested in cannabis but who have struggled against stigma and fear of criminalization?

It is no secret that the cannabis industry is increasingly becoming decriminalized in some cities across the country.[2] At the same time, it is rapidly becoming big business in states where it has been legalized.

However, it is rare that emerging weed entrepreneurs represent the diversity of the people who use it.

Goldberg's products, for example, could help counter the racial disparities in the business and, at least in a small way, help to shift the health disparities of Black people suffering from debilitating cramps.

What we know about Goldberg's holistic cannabis business for cramps is that she's launching it with Maya Elisabeth, a white "canna businesswoman." Elisabeth founded the Om Grown Collective, an all-woman growing business, and owns Northern California–based OM Edibles. Together, the women partnered to create Whoopi & Maya, a brand of products including edibles, tinctures, topical rubs, and a "profoundly relaxing" bath soak infused with THC, the chemical responsible for many of marijuana's properties.

In an interview with *Vanity Fair*, Goldberg said she wanted to create a product that was discreet, provided relief, and wouldn't leave us glued to our couches. The Whoopi & Maya brand is launching in California. For those of us who are interested in the product but live in states where cannabis is not decriminalized or legal, we'll be left without access to it.

Since 2014, Whoopi Goldberg has been outspoken about her use of medical cannabis to deal with glaucoma and headaches without resorting to "eating [handfuls of Advil] every day."[3] Goldberg also mentioned that her inspiration for this product comes from her grown granddaughters and the way that they suffer from menstrual cramps.[4] What this tells us is that she approached the solution to a health and wellness issue from a position of empathy, unconditional love, generosity, presence, and a willingness to listen. Those characteristics should be central in how the medical establishment addresses the health disparities of Black women and people who suffer from debilitating cramps due to fibroids and endometriosis.

Fibroids are noncancerous tumors that grow on the uterus and can cause heavy bleeding and cramping, and endometriosis is a condition where cells from inside the uterus are displaced, growing outside the uterus, which can cause scarring and can lead to heavy bleeding and intense abdominal pain. The burden people with these conditions must carry can extend beyond physical pain.

The Burden of Uterine Fibroids for African American Women study outlines the medical, emotional, and economic challenges faced by this group of women who are nearly three times more likely to be affected by the condition than other women.[5] The real economic challenges resulting from fibroids are witnessed by African American women, who are 77 percent more likely to miss work due to the condition than their white counterparts. These effects, among other things, further reduce the already disparate earning potential of Black women and limit opportunities for them to care for their families: we also know that Black women of reproductive age tend to be the heads of households for their immediate and extended families.

In the United States, menstruation starts when girls are, on average, twelve years old and typically ends anywhere between fifty and fifty-five years old. According to a survey conducted by the Association of

Reproductive Health Professionals, this means 450 periods averaging two to seven days or more for people who suffer with fibroids and endometriosis.[6] That leaves women, queer, and trans folks who suffer from menstrual pain bloated, moody, irritable, fatigued, angry, and in pain for the duration of their period.

For Whoopi Goldberg's part, she said in *Vanity Fair* that her product would help to meet a need among people with a monthly discomfort: "You can put the rub on your lower stomach and lower back at work, and then when you get home you can get in the tub for a soak or make tea."

As MSNBC reported, while Goldberg is not the first celebrity to lend their name to a cannabis product, she is, to date, the most mainstream celebrity who isn't necessarily associated with drug culture to take the plunge.[7] Her decision to lend her name to these products is also significant because so few people of color have been able to puncture the sellers' market in this burgeoning industry.[8] *BuzzFeed* reported that fewer than three dozen of the more than three thousand legal marijuana dispensaries (or 1 percent) in the United States are owned by Black people.[9]

The reasons behind this phenomenon are diverse. There are documented reports of how people of color are intentionally being shut out of the cannabis business. Black farmers, in particular, are forced to deal with laws that require expensive legal representation and financial resources above their incomes.[10]

Then there is paranoia about embracing an industry that is still perceived as criminal in many parts of the country. And more religious or conservative members of the Black community still promote the concept of marijuana as a kind of gateway drug to more dangerous substances.

According to Art Way, state director of the Drug Policy Alliance office in Colorado, African Americans have historically been disproportionately arrested and prosecuted for possessing marijuana.[11] But now that lax laws are spreading in some parts of the country, there has been a palpable change in perceptions surrounding the recreational use of the drug.

And so the questions I started with still need answering: How will Whoopi Goldberg and the industry create more opportunity for all of the people who suffer during menstruation or who are interested in being part of this flourishing industry? For those with answers, I'm ready to go into business, and I know at least a hundred other Black people who are ready to throw down for cannabis wellness and business expansion opportunities.

Notes

1. C. J. Ciaramella, "Whoopi Goldberg Launches Medical-Marijuana Products Targeted at Menstrual Cramps," *Vanity Fair*, March 30, 2016, http://www.vanityfair.com/hollywood/2016/03/whoopi-goldberg-marijuana-company.

2. New York Marijuana Policy Project, accessed August 20, 2020, https://www.mpp.org/states/new-york/.

3. Whoopi Goldberg, "Whoopi Goldberg: My Vape Pen and I, a Love Story," *The Cannabist*, April 17, 2014, http://www.thecannabist.co/2014/04/17/whoopi-vape-pen-love-story-column/9571/.

4. Ciaramella, "Whoopi Goldberg."

5. Elizabeth A. Stewart et al., "The Burden of Uterine Fibroids for African-American Women: Results of a National Survey," *Journal of Women's Health* 22, no. 10 (2013): 807–16, http://www.ncbi.nlm.nih.gov/pmc/articles/PMC3787340/.

6. Camran Nezhat, Anjie Li, Sozdar Abed, Erika Balassiano, Rose Soliemannjad, Azadeh Nezhat, Ceana H. Nezhat, and Farr Nezhat, "Strong Association Between Endometriosis and Symptomatic Leiomyomas," *JSLS* 20, no. 3 (July–September 2016), https://www.ncbi.nlm.nih.gov/pmc/articles/PMC5019190/

7. Adam Howard, "Why Whoopi Goldberg's Weed Business Matters," *MSNBC*, March 31, 2016, http://www.msnbc.com/msnbc/why-whoopi-goldbergs-weed-business-matters.

8. Chandra Thomas Whitfield, "Capitalizing on Cannabis: Meet Colorado's Black 'Potrepreneurs,'" *NBC News*, April 20, 2015, http://www.nbcnews.com/news/nbcblk/capitalizing-cannabis-meet-colorados-black-potrepreneurs-n344556?cid=sm_tw&hootPostID=67fee1a8fe6a04e2dbaf3c49c7ad6744.

9. Amanda Chicago Lewis, "How Black People Are Being Shut Out of America's Weed Boom: Whitewashing the Green Rush," *BuzzFeed*, March 16, 2016, http://www.buzzfeed.com/amandachicagolewis/americas-white-only-weed-boom#.jy2pPKzq5Z.

10. Carolyn M. Brown, "Black Farmers Shut Out of $10 Billion Medical Marijuana Business," *Black Enterprise*, November 10, 2015, http://www.blackenterprise.com/small-business/black-farmers-shut-out-of-legal-marijuana-business/.

11. ACLU Foundation, *The War on Marijuana in Black and White* (New York: American Civil Liberties Union, 2013), https://www.aclu.org/report/war-marijuana-black-and-white.

Originally published on Rewire.News *on April 21, 2016.*

Tourmaline* Wants Her Just Due

Raquel Willis

Silver-tongued filmmaker and artist Tourmaline modeled complexity and vulnerability when she revealed that noted director David France lifted major source material for his award-winning documentary, *The Death and Life of Marsha P. Johnson.* The documentary is quite possibly the highest-profile work ever released on Marsha P. Johnson, the foremother of the LGBTQ rights movement who sparked the legendary 1969 Stonewall Riots by throwing a shot glass and demanding liberation in a Greenwich Village tavern in New York.

On October 6, the day France released his documentary, Tourmaline defiantly published an Instagram post explaining the disparity between her financial status after years of working on her yet-to-be-released film *Happy Birthday, Marsha!* and his "multimillion-dollar Netflix deal." She believed *The Death and Life of Marsha P. Johnson* was born from a "grant application video" that she and fellow artist Sasha Wortzel submitted to the Arcus Center for Social Justice Leadership at Kalamazoo College.

"This kind of extraction/excavation of Black life, disabled life, poor life, trans life is so old and so deeply connected to the violence Marsha had to deal with throughout her life," Tourmaline wrote. "So I feel so much rage and grief over all of this."

The accompanying selfie displayed her in #BlackGirlMagic form: tilting her head back with her eyes closed, fully exposing her shimmering emerald-green eyeshadow. It was as if she was basking in the glow of the sun and "paying it no mind," as Johnson's iconic catchphrase commands. In the left corner of the portrait, a figure almost peeks over the frame. It's a tattoo collage featuring Johnson herself. Tourmaline's piercing shot at

Editors' note: This article originally ran with Tourmaline's previous name, Reina Gossett.

the cisgender, white, well-connected and heavily resourced France mirrored, at least outwardly, Johnson's lifelong stone throwing at the status quo. Her accusations may have seemed out of the blue, but behind the scenes, there had been a long tussle between her and France.

"One of the things that's so interesting is that this dynamic with David France had been playing out for a while. There were a number of egregious things over time," Tourmaline said. "At moments, Sasha [Wortzel] or I would say that we should say something, but there was also a dynamic in which he had a lot of institutional power and closeness to power structures, recognition, and resources."

By calling out France, the *Happy Birthday, Marsha!* filmmaker moved from documentarian to subject. Her David-and-Goliath moment fell within a larger context of accountability during the first official year of the Donald Trump era. From women organizing en masse against the predator in chief and the ever-violent patriarchy to widespread discussions on white supremacy and systems of privilege and power, her vulnerable and risky admission came during a time of rapid raising of consciousness.

"I think [2017] included a lot of stuff being unearthed or made plain around what harms and violences are happening in private, intimate ways and publicly without everyone knowing it," Tourmaline said in a phone call. "A lot of people are coming out and sharing truths in all different kinds of ways. I shared something that was very hurtful and violating and happened not just to me. I put it out there and had people respond to it in ways I never dreamed of."

A bevy of trans activists and artists expressed their long-held doubts on the conception and production of *The Death and Life of Marsha P. Johnson* while others simply showed disappointment. Most notably, trans author and activist Janet Mock amplified Tourmaline's claims in a comment on her Instagram post. She wrote, "I love you, Reina. You remain my heroine. Thank you for introducing us to ourselves with your vital life-giving work. You've helped me and I'm sure thousands better see ourselves. I love you."

For many, *Happy Birthday, Marsha!* was the people's choice since it had been financially backed through crowdfunding and featured numerous trans actors, including Spirit Award–winning Mya Taylor. Given Tourmaline's presence in the trans community as an organizer and public scholar, transparency around her project was much greater than

France's. With *Happy Birthday, Marsha!*, Tourmaline drew on community power—something that was instilled in her at a young age.

Social justice has been stitched into the fabric of Tourmaline's family
for generations. Both of her parents were community organizers: her
mother, Maureen Ridge, worked with unions such as Service Employees
International Union, and her father, George Gossett, worked with the
Invaders, a Memphis-based Black Power activist group inspired by the
Black Panther Party. She carries stories from her parents and grandparents about their time in the civil rights and Black freedom movements with every step she takes. She further credits her politicization to
George's interactions with state institutions in her hometown of Rox-
bury, Massachusetts.

"I got involved [with social justice] when my dad had a disability and
multiple psychiatric illnesses. For long periods of time, he was frequently
in [psychiatric] hospitals and prison," she said. "Right around when [for-
mer president Bill] Clinton cut welfare, there was increased criminalization of poor people. Friends in my neighborhood would ask why they'd
see my dad at the [psychiatric] hospital.

"I felt shame around visiting my dad in [those facilities] and dealing
with what that meant."

When Tourmaline enrolled in Columbia University and moved to
New York City in 2002, her activism became more deeply informed by
the experiences of people who were or had been incarcerated. She was
greatly involved in transforming campus culture but always knew there
was greater work to be done beyond the ivory tower of academia. One of
the ways she kept a foot on the ground was by teaching creative writing
classes at the infamous and inhumane Rikers Island. Though she was
thriving in many ways, her father continued to struggle.

"My dad passed away in 2010 in a violent and sad way. He passed
away in a field and wasn't found for many months. No one knows how
he died," Tourmaline said. "It was really a story of Memphis and Black
life in the United States. Part of my art is really around experiences of
loss and grief and dealing with how people heal around violences. We
can't even talk about them because they're so heavy."

There are stark parallels between the deaths of Tourmaline's father
and Johnson. Both dedicated much of their lives to lifting the veil off of
harmful power structures through their organizing work, suffered the
neglect of their needs due to systemic anti-Blackness, and died under

mysterious circumstances. On July 6, 1992, Johnson's body was found in New York City's Hudson River. Although investigators ruled her death a suicide, her family, friends, and community have long called for a deeper investigation.

"The circumstances of Marsha's death really remind me a lot of my dad's death. It's also like a lot of Black folks' deaths. It's clear that structural abandonment of services and care in the United States is causing so many of our deaths," she said. "It's a part of so many people's stories who are deemed not worthy of tending."

After graduating from Columbia, Tourmaline delved into the progressive LGBTQ nonprofit world. She worked as the director of the Welfare Organizing Project at Queers for Economic Justice, where she produced *A Fabulous Attitude*, a documentary on low-income LGBTQ New Yorkers surviving inequality and thriving despite enormous obstacles. She was also the director of membership at the Sylvia Rivera Law Project. Tourmaline mixed this experience with her growing passion for video blogging.

In a 2015 interview on Mock's former MSNBC show, *So Popular!*, Tourmaline shared how Johnson's own art-fueled activism encouraged her to pursue filmmaking as a natural extension of her own work. "Marsha was an activist and also an important performer. She was in a group called Hot Peaches. She wore flower hats and had this aesthetic that was its own kind of activism. I think [trans people's] art is its own kind of activism," Tourmaline said. "[Making *Happy Birthday, Marsha!*] was a moment for me to just get lost in the beauty of filming and storytelling."

While bridging the gaps between academia, activism, and art is at the core of Tourmaline's work, connecting the current movement of resistance and liberation to historical moments is also key. She doesn't believe that we need to rewrite our politics but tap into the power of historical figures like Johnson and living legends like Miss Major Griffin-Gracy. She believes more needs to be done to elevate the people most targeted by the prison-industrial complex, particularly mass incarceration, HIV criminalization, and anti–sex work legislation.

"Without demands for the most vulnerable, this moment of increased visibility is only ever going to be tied to increased killing. I think the two are so tied together. In my experience, for a long time before the trans tipping point, we had a set of really radical demands, and they were inescapable," she said. "Our survival was a demand in and of itself. I think it's really important to always name that it's all of us or none of us. If it's going to be all of us, we need to always center and demand the things that will affect the most vulnerable of us."

In May 2014, writer Katy Steinmetz referred to Black trans actress Laverne Cox as an "unlikely icon" when she appeared on the cover of *Time* magazine. If that was the "tipping point" for trans representation, we are in a much different era now. Actresses such as Amiyah Scott, Jen Richards, and Angelica Ross have made breakthroughs on the small screen while Mock was recently announced as a producer and writer for *Pose*, a Ryan Murphy–produced eighties-era drama that is slated to feature the most trans series regulars ever for an American television show. Tourmaline wants us to grapple with what it means to live in a time where trans narratives seem more mainstream than ever before.

"I think we're at an interesting point where we are moving with a lot of beautiful contradictions. [We are] seeking to disrupt and be unruly to assimilation into structures and systems that are not for us and aren't doing anything for us. It's violating and harming us," Tourmaline said. "As I have more of a platform and visibility, it's important to be constantly naming structures and systems and the violence of assimilation. What about dis-respectability?

"So often when we seek out mainstream representation or inclusion, we have to leave so much of our beautiful selves at the door. Naming those exclusions and violences is so key."

It is not lost on Tourmaline that, as she has been elevated in this current boom in entertainment and media for trans people, it has also been one of the deadliest times on record for people on the ground. In 2017, the average age of Black trans victims was thirty years old. Beyond her cultural work, she wants to remind others of the historic radicalism of the trans community and that, even in the contradictions of survival and success in a capitalist system, the liberatory intentions and actions must be ever present.

Toward the end of 2017, Tourmaline's shine emanated as her work was feverishly boosted. In November, she accepted the Queer Art Prize for Recent Work for *The Personal Things*, a short animated film featuring voice-over by Griffin-Gracy. There's no doubt that *Happy Birthday, Marsha!*, which is slated for a 2018 release, will receive similar accolades. With much care, the film's team is brainstorming on the most fitting way to honor Johnson's legacy and involve the community. With an air of powerful defiance against a world that still devalues Black trans power, Tourmaline hopes her work will be just one brick in the long road to liberation.

"It takes me being in space with other Black trans people to have a collective imagination around reparations. In order for that to keep happening, we must demand a shift from the prison-industrial complex. We can't fully shift space when so many of us are incarcerated just for surviving and living. We need adequate housing or safety to even go outside of our housing," she said. "That imagination happens upon the ground of our ancestors. It's got to happen in a way that doesn't leave anyone out. In the center are Black trans people who are disabled, undocumented, formerly or currently incarcerated."

Originally published in Bitch *magazine on June 12, 2018.*

The Word Is "Nemesis": The Fight to Integrate the National Spelling Bee

Cynthia R. Greenlee

In 1962, teenager George F. Jackson wrote a letter to President John F. Kennedy with an appeal: "I am a thirteen-year-old colored boy and I like to spell. Do you think you could help me and get the Lynchburg bee opened to all children?"

The long road to the National Spelling Bee has always begun with local contests, often sponsored by a local newspaper. Nine publications, organized by the Louisville *Courier-Journal*, banded together in 1925 to create the first National Bee in Washington, DC.

Decades later, Jackson was protesting the policies of the local newspaper that sponsored the Lynchburg, Virginia, contest, which excluded Black students from participating in the official local competition—the necessary step that might send a lucky, word-loving Lynchburg child to nationals. There was more at stake than a coveted all-expenses-paid trip to the capital, an expensive set of *Encyclopedia Britannica*, and a $1,000 cash prize. For local and national civil rights activists, keeping Black children from the spoils of spelling fame was an extension of Jim Crow educational policies that should have ended, in theory, with the Supreme Court's decision in *Brown v. Board of Education of Topeka*.

While the Warren Court decided in 1954 that "separate but equal" would no longer be the law of the land, there were still "Negro" schools and white schools educating children across the South less than a decade later. A patchwork of local responses met the desegregation orders that followed the Supreme Court ruling, including deliberate foot-dragging, some real confusion about how to undo what years of white supremacy had wrought in the nation's schools, and full-throated defiance to educational equity.

In the summer of 1959, when public schools in Prince Edward County—not far from Lynchburg—were ordered to integrate, the local government decided to close their schools instead of integrating them.[1] (They remained closed for more than three years.) The Lynchburg public school system, which educated five thousand white students and one thousand Black students, slowly but steadily contemplated its own integration. Lynchburg had been Virginia's capital for part of the Civil War, and some of the city's boosters continued to fight Reconstruction-era battles over memory and public space, bragging that the city had evaded Union capture during the "War Between the States." In 1960, six years after the Supreme Court decision, the city finally began to consider concrete plans to integrate. One proposal suggested taking it incrementally, one grade level at a time, until Black and white seniors were in high school together.

A year before the city opened the doors of E. C. Glass High School to Black students, the policy of the spelling bee sponsor, the *Lynchburg News*, threatened to roil an already fraught racial climate.[2] The newspaper ducked the federal mandate for fairness by cloaking racism as a private business matter, arguing for "tradition." Lynchburg's spelling bee controversy was past, present, and prologue rolled into a single contentious conflict. It pointed back to Jim Crow and demonstrated the small ways that segregation could still thrive, even after it had been ruled unconstitutional by the nation's highest court.

*

The Lynchburg spelling bee's separate and unequal practices came to light through a timely clerical error. Just before Christmas 1961, principals and teachers of fifth- through eighth-grade students in Black schools received a document that outlined the rules for the Lynchburg spelling bee. After the holiday, when school reconvened, the document was retracted. "Spelling test materials were distributed to Negro schools through the error of a new secretary in the office of a city school supervisor . . . Negro participation is not expected." A green employee may not have known the lay of the land when it came to spelling bee policy, but Lynchburg's Black educators, students, and families were surely aware that the courteous un-invitation was a statement that the local spelling bee that had served whites only since the 1940s would continue to do so.

Lynchburg's National Association for the Advancement of Colored People (NAACP) president W. T. Johnson sent a letter to the bee's national sponsor, the Scripps-Howard Newspaper Alliance, laying out the facts and closing with a one-two punch. Of course, Johnson demurred, the Lynchburg branch of the civil rights organization did not "want to believe that the Scripps-Howard Newspaper Alliance would wish to become involved in a segregated Spelling Contest. . . . We are certain that holding the finals of a Jim Crow contest in Washington would be courting disaster." Understanding the power of public shaming and building off the *Brown v. Board of Education* victory—which had marshaled evidence that segregation was harmful to Black children— Johnson followed with the explicit threat of "possible legal action and publicity in Washington and elsewhere."

The NAACP's team of lawyers and nationwide army of activists were not to be trifled with. Since its founding in 1909, the group had protested the release of *Birth of a Nation*, blocked a Supreme Court nomination, pressured President Harry Truman to ban discrimination in federal employment, and launched dozens of legal challenges to the many-headed hydra of segregation. They would picket on street corners and petition in courtrooms. The Scripps Alliance, one of the nation's powerhouse publishers, worked to quell the damage for their premier event, but its response varied from no-nonsense to irritated.

Responding to the NAACP, National Spelling Bee director James Wagner fired back that "some of the statements indicate you are being misled, or are ignoring the facts insofar as the conduct of the National Spelling Bee . . . a program that has enjoyed the respect of the public and educators alike since 1925." He explained that each participating newspaper "determines its own rules and procedures, and otherwise operates completely independently." But Wagner refused to identify all newspaper sponsors—including fifty that weren't Scripps newspapers— and said the only rule regarding the spellers themselves was that they had to be of appropriate age and grade. Wagner clarified the national contest's nondiscrimination policy. He noted that several Black students had competed in the national bee in recent years and had performed well.

The National Spelling Bee—at least the finals in Washington—wasn't formally segregated and hadn't been so "long before the Supreme Court decision regarding segregation." MacNolia Cox, a thirteen-year-old from Akron, Ohio, is believed to be the first Black child to advance to the finals in 1936. According to poet A. Van Jordan, who wrote a book about

MacNolia partly based on her mother's journals, the straight-A student memorized ten thousand words in preparation.[3] Traveling from Ohio, Cox had to board a segregated train to Washington, DC. She wasn't lodged with other participants, and when she arrived at the bee, she was sent to a separate table. During the contest, when she continued to spell words correctly and advanced to the final rounds, she was given a word that wasn't on the official list: "nemesis." The young Akron girl who wanted to be a doctor ended her spelling bee run in defeat. MacNolia went on to work as a domestic, like so many African American women of her time.

The Black and white competitors of the 1960 National Spelling Bee stayed in the same hotel—though it's unclear if they shared rooms— boarded sightseeing buses together, and broke bread together at banquets during a time when Americans had recently watched white southerners mob the interracial Freedom Rides with vile heckling and unrepentant violence. The complaints against the Lynchburg bee came a few short years before the Civil Rights Act of 1964, which mandated that public spaces, such as hotels, restaurants, and theaters, had to open their doors to African American sleepers, diners, and consumers.

By contrast, the National Spelling Bee appeared to be a feel-good story of meritocracy and sportsmanship, a contest that was unafraid of "social amalgamation." In the perpetually sex- and race-obsessed minds of some whites, sporadic interracial contact could trigger "social equality," which meant sex, interracial marriage, the inevitable arrival of biracial children, and nothing less than the catastrophic decline of white civilization. Because who knew what one chance encounter dealing with a Black person on an equal playing field could do?

Even as the National Spelling Bee promoted itself as a bastion of progressivism, however, its rules of "each contest for itself" sounded like a more polite translation of the argument for states' rights that retained local (read: white) control. While the National Spelling Bee had an open-door policy, local school systems and newspaper sponsors governed exactly which students would get a crack at the "big dance" in Washington.

Indeed, when national NAACP officials investigated how many of the participating sponsors discriminated against Black students, they found that the Memphis *Press-Scimitar* held an annual Shelby County Negro Spelling Bee at Booker T. Washington High School but barred

Black participants from the regional qualifier, the pipeline to the Washington finals. The editor of the Tennessee newspaper promised verbally it would "take steps." ("Whatever that means," wrote an NAACP official in a February 1962 memo.)

The Memphis approach of sponsoring separate, segregated contests was echoed across dozens of cities, where Black spelling contests had been established decades earlier. In 1905, Baltimore community members organized a spelling bee because African American students weren't allowed to take part in the white-only competition. The mayor showed up to the festivities, and a Black businessman made sure that the top prize was an exact replica of the trophy awarded in the white competition. (Similarly, in Birmingham, Alabama, Black insurance broker and hotelier A. G. Gaston filled the void by personally bankrolling a statewide Black spelling bee beginning in 1954.) By all accounts, these segregated Black-only bees appear to not have been eligible as qualifiers for the national bee. But that didn't stop problems when white southern students traveled to northern bees where they encountered Black students who sometimes out-spelled them.

In 1908, readers of New Orleans's largest newspaper, the *Picayune*, were apoplectic when a spelling delegation traveled to a National Education Association bee in Cleveland, Ohio. When the Louisiana spellers came in third behind Marie Bolden, a thirteen-year-old Black girl, the *Picayune*'s pundits suggested that the New Orleans competitors had been so distracted by the "dusky maid" that she was able to best them by writing out four hundred words correctly and spelling another one hundred orally. Before the contest, Louisiana school superintendent Warren Easton consulted with a handful of school board members. His question: What should he do if his students were faced with competing against Black students in the northern city? The reply from a school board member: "Knock the nigger out."

The fallout from the spellers' defeat by a young Black Ohioan continued in vitriolic letters to the editor, some of them strident cries that the superintendent should be fired for putting white students in the inappropriate position of competing with Black students. The flap revealed white southerners' deep commitment to the hard work of maintaining white supremacy. It exposed, in stark terms, the danger of interracial spelling bees: a mundane contest that happened in schools everywhere, the spelling bee was a merit test that could provide evidence that African

Americans' memories and intellectual prowess rivaled, or even exceeded, the smarts of their white neighbors.

"Certainly in the days following the National Spelling Contest, the race problem was in evidence, if it ever was, in New Orleans and the South!" wrote a New Orleans clergyman about the fracas over the spellers' brush with Marie Bolden. "Did it show itself, then as a problem of Negro crime, or brutality, or laziness? Assuredly not! Of the Negro's personal repulsiveness? By no means! There is no evidence of Negro criminality, or brutality, or laziness, in the Negro child's victory. . . . The 'intense feeling' can be explained on one ground only: the Negro girl's victory was an affront to the tradition of Negro inferiority."

With its notion of meritocracy, the spelling bee was innocuous and purposeful—clean educational fun for all. But it also suggested that Black Americans could be "improved" by educational opportunity—and sometimes outpace whites along the way. When twelve-year-old Gloria Lockerman, described by *Jet* as a "fat-cheeked, blasé little girl from Baltimore" and "television's million-dollar baby,"[4] appeared on *The $64,000 Question* game show four times in 1955, she wowed audiences by spelling a tongue-twisting sentence—"The belligerent astigmatic anthropologist annihilated innumerable chrysanthemums"—and won $16,000 for her college education. A pickle company gave her a lifetime supply of her favorite treat, and she made the rounds on TV variety and talk shows. In a later moment of racist candor, one of the show's writers described her as "Cinderella in blackface."

A few years later, allegations surfaced that *The $64,000 Question* was rigged and that the youthful spellers (not just Gloria) who delighted TV viewers were given a word list and coached. An English professor from Northwestern who wrote for the show explained that he would only ask Lockerman words she could spell or that were seemly. "We discarded words like 'nephrectomy,' for instance, because it wouldn't do to have a little girl talk about a kidney operation. Similarly we wouldn't use a world like 'niggardly' because some viewers might think it had something to do with 'nigger.'" Gloria's victory, her detractors suggested, was a fraud, though show producers conceded she was an exceptional speller, coached or not. During the investigation, Gloria was a sixteen-year-old college freshman at Morgan State University. When media sought her out on campus, she ran from a journalist, screaming, "I'm not saying a word!" and reportedly had to be quieted with sedatives.

What a hard, heavy weight for Black children to bear, to be the person who literally spelled trouble for white supremacy.

*

Black leaders, educators, and activists valued the spelling bee as proof positive that their children were just as capable and gifted as white pupils. National magazines like *Jet* and the NAACP's *Crisis* continually shared celebratory notes of Black children's achievements, pointing out that middle-class African American youth could play piano sonatas, recite Latin oratory, and spell as well as anyone else.

Months after the NAACP began agitating for equity in the qualifying rounds to the national bee, Jocelyn Lee, a twelve-year-old seventh grader at Tulsa's Marian Anderson High, became the first Black winner in the Oklahoma City bee's twenty-five-year history. In 1965, the April issue of *Jet* showed fifteen-year-old Clorrine Jones, wearing a smile, a glistening beehive, a checked jumper, and a banner—the winner of Memphis's first integrated spelling bee, three years after NAACP officials had blown the whistle on the segregated local contests. She won in the last round with the word "campanile."

Adolescent spelling bee champions like Lee and Jones were pioneers of desegregation, even if they never attended truly integrated schools. They were descendants of enslaved people for whom literacy was forbidden and whose educational institutions were built from the ground up with community support. It was no coincidence that one of writer Paul Lawrence Dunbar's most popular poems was "The Spellin' Bee."[5] Written in dialect, the poem follows the drama of a Black church spelling bee, complete with flirting, finery, and a narrator who throws the contest so his sweetheart can win. There are lawyers, the shabbily dressed, a pastor whose "speeches were too long fur toleration," farmers' daughters, and the everyday laborer like Ole Hiram who was disqualified for bungling the word "charity." But all were united in the quest for community and a coveted spelling book:

> The master rose an' briefly said: "Good friends, dear brother Crawford,
> To spur the pupils' minds along, a little prize has offered.
> To him who spells the best to–night—or 't may be 'her'—no tellin'—
> He offers ez a jest reward, this precious work on spellin'."

A little blue-backed spellin'–book with fancy scarlet trimmin';
We boys devoured it with our eyes—so did the girls an' women.
He held it up where all could see, then on the table set it,
An' ev'ry speller in the house felt mortal bound to get it.

The vision of an entire town turning out in pursuit of a spelling book is quite a different picture of community than that described in the 2006 film *Akeelah and the Bee*, the fictional story of an eleven-year-old girl whose family and friends largely don't understand her quest for learning.[6] This is a modern misunderstanding. Historically, African Americans have understood the spelling bee as a contested racial space, where mastering a word list was a feat of skill, motivation, and racial resistance through direct competition with one's "social betters." If Black spellers weren't actually sparring with white rivals, each word memorized—the letters, language of origin, possible meanings—was another symbolic brick building a Black community hungry for the book learning denied to them in slavery and segregation.

While George Jackson's letter to President Kennedy was published in newspaper articles across the country, George remained shut out of the Lynchburg bee. When a *New York Times* reporter called the school's chief administrator to cover the controversy, the journalist asked the official to spell "apartheid"—a request denied after a long pause. The school system similarly refused to budge on having an open, integrated spelling bee. Because everybody knows that spelling can be dangerous.

Notes

1. "The Closing of Prince Edward County's Schools," Virginia History Explorer, Virginia Historical Society, accessed June 5, 2019, https://www.virginiahistory.org/collections-and-resources/virginia-history-explorer/civil-rights-movement-virginia/closing-prince.
2. Darrell Laurant, "50 Years Ago: Two Students Cross Stubborn Segregation Line at E.C. Glass," *News & Advance*, January 29, 2012, https://www.newsadvance.com/news/local/years-ago-two-students-cross-stubborn-segregation-line-at-e/article_420dc4b9-9114-5ba1-b998-6e1403ab0abe.html.
3. Michael Romain, "The Tragedy of MacNolia Cox," *Wednesday Journal*, May 20, 2015, https://www.oakpark.com/Community/Blogs/5-20-2015/The-tragedy-of-MacNolia-Cox-/.

4. "Gloria Lockerman: Television's Million Dollar Baby," *Jet*, November 10, 1955."

5. P. L. Dunbar, "The Spellin' Bee," in *The Complete Poems of Paul Laurence Dunbar* (New York: Dodd, Mead, and Company, 1913), https://etc.usf.edu/lit2go/187/lyrics-of-lowly-life/3651/the-spellin-bee/.

6. *Akeelah and the Bee*, directed by Doug Atchison (Santa Monica, CA: Lions Gate Films, 2006).

Originally published on Longreads *on June 5, 2017.*

We Will Always Love You: Why Whitney Houston Was Our All-American Gurl

Jordan Scruggs and Janna A. Zinzi

On February 11, 2012, singer-diva Whitney Houston died at the Beverly Hilton, hours before the legendary annual Clive Davis pre-Grammys party she was set to attend. She was making a slow comeback, climbing out of addiction, and focusing on sobriety. Houston blessed the world with decades of music, multiple record-breaking hits—memorable ballads, such as "I Will Always Love You"; her rousing rendition of the "Star-Spangled Banner"; bubblegum pop anthems like "How Will I Know"; soul-moving covers, such as "I'm Every Woman"; and a deep catalog of songs that still make us dance (even though Whitney famously couldn't). Her death—along with those of other Black megastars like Aretha Franklin, Michael Jackson, and Prince—hit many of us hard, including Idas Jordan Scruggs and Janna A. Zinzi, who had this conversation about what Whitney means to them. And she wasn't just one thing. Whitney Houston was an all-American girl (with melanin!), the tortured songstress who couldn't be herself, the musical genius who could master a song in one take, and the ideal fairy godmother who could heal Cinderella and help a real queer southern kid navigate their relationship with God and the world. Amen and aché, Whitney.

Janna A. Zinzi: We both share this deep love of Whitney Houston because of how she impacted our childhood and how we identify with Blackness. There are so many golden, pivotal moments throughout her career. What's one of your favorite tracks of hers that embodies her spirit and makes you smile?

Jordan Scruggs: "I Wanna Dance with Somebody." It's that joyful type of love. It has that Carly Rae Jepsen–type of thing . . . that energy of, you know what, like we're crushing on each other. I like that forthcoming part. "I always liked this person, I didn't really do anything about it, but I kinda wanted to do something. I want to have fun, want to be carefree. Maybe want to flirt, maybe didn't want to flirt. But I just want to be joyful and be loving in this space, in this energy, in this vibe."

That's so perfect, just across every generation. I feel like every single time you hear it, you can't help but move and forget whatever. Be stress-free for the three minutes and thirty-five seconds that this track is playing.

Janna: Prince Harry and Meghan Markle: Apparently, that was their wedding song! I love that so much. One, because, you have Whitney. And Whitney's royalty, right? So it's bringing her music to that royal wedding, which was such a . . . however you feel about the British monarchy . . . it was still a Black-ass moment to have Meghan Markle in there marrying Prince Harry with a Black-ass preacher, choir, and this after-party with all these Black celebrities like Serena Williams there dancing to Whitney.

I've always been dancing my whole life, and dance is how I connect with feeling, with spirit, with myself, with love, really. Her videos were so much of a foundation of my upbringing and how I processed love. Music and music videos, that's where I learned a lot about love and relationships for better or worse, a lot of the songs are very much about unhealthy models of love.

But this song is so lighthearted for me. I resonate so much with that idea of feeling that connection when you dance with somebody. Whether it's for that temporary three minutes vibing on a dance floor or whether that's a foundation of a relationship of love. Just the idea of people dancing with somebody who loves you and who you love is way different than I'm gonna grind it up on somebody. I sound old. I like to grind, but I'm just a romantic. It still feels like my North Star of like, "What does love feel like? Oh, dancing with somebody who loves me!" That's the ultimate. It's also basics, you know what I mean?

Jordan: So my jump-off and intro to Whitney started with *I'm Your Baby Tonight*. That album came out the year I was born in 1990. There are very few albums I specifically remember being played nonstop, and that's one of them. I remember not being able to walk and dancing on my dad's feet around this table in our living room on these hardwood floors to "I'm Your Baby Tonight." When people are like, "How did you get into Whitney?" I didn't really have an option.

It was such a good album for me to grow up with because she had all these different styles. It was the peak nineties. It has a heavy R&B and pop feel with these killer vocals. Then she looked like the all-American girl. And it's not Cindy Crawford. It's not some Brady Bunch. It's Whitney Houston in these ripped jeans with a leather jacket and . . .

Janna: Yes, I remember the leather jacket!

Jordan: And then she transitions to where she's wearing a full suit. Her and Annie Lennox were the first time I ever saw women wear suits, and it was just like amazing for me.

Janna: Yeah, my entry point was even before "I Wanna Dance With Somebody." My mom had Whitney's first tape where she's on the cover, and she has a low-cut . . . she's damn near bald. That wasn't what we were seeing because it's the early eighties. My mom in her wedding picture has the same haircut. So there was something about the album cover, that cassette cover, I connected with and was just like, "This woman is so beautiful." There was just a soft, innocent elegance to her.

"How Will I Know" was probably the first one that I was just like, "Yo, I'm into this." I would watch the video, dance around with it, doing the steps. Just being older now and thinking about it, that was so much of a marketing technique, a reframing of what the American girl looks like.

People bought that image of her, "She's American. Yeah, she's Black. But she's a good Christian girl." That was even to the point where she got booed at the Soul Train Awards because they were like, "Oh, she's not Black enough." I didn't even realize this. Al Sharpton had a whole campaign against her, calling her "Whitey Houston." I'm like, "Damn, Al Sharpton." Really, was it that deep?

I know your relationship with the church and growing up Christian—and then your love of Whitney and then also being queer. It's so interesting how her image was crafted very specifically for us.

Jordan: I tell people all the time, "I think God is a Black woman." I legitimately think that God is a Black woman who looks and sounds like Maya Angelou. But just like I think of Maya Angelou, I hear Whitney Houston when I think about images of Blackness and Christianity. *The Preacher's Wife* soundtrack is literally the top-selling gospel soundtrack of all time. She didn't even say, "Hey, I'm gonna do a gospel album."

When I started realizing that I was queer, people always assumed that you can only be queer, or you can only be a person of faith. And that's never been true for me. I watched *The Preacher's Wife*, and I was like, "Oh, everything." And if you go through the time line, this is already after she's getting into alcohol. In interviews from that time, she's like, "Pray for me like you would pray for anybody else." Her faith never wavered, and that's what happened to me. I tell people all the time, "I never lost faith in God. I lost faith in Christians."

Janna: That's really powerful.

Jordan: There're pivotal moments in my life where Whitney Houston is just right there. I'm like, "Yup, there we go, yup, I needed that." When was *Cinderella*? I was just fascinated with this concept of Whitney Houston being a fairy godmother.

Janna: I love that. It's the same for me, even as we're ten years apart. Even though we're different generationally, there's that same connection. So, for me, before Whitney was "Little Red Corvette, "Let's Go Crazy." "Purple Rain" came out in 1984. This was shaping our images of Black excellence. You have Prince coming out at the same time, but for me, the main woman that was out before Whitney was Madonna. I was about Madonna. Mad hard. But she doesn't look like me. The funny thing is, I'm half Italian, so I felt connected to her, but also, she was sexual and rowdy, and I was feeling it.

But then there was just this difference of Whitney in terms of the soul of her voice and the sweetness of what she was bringing.

Jordan: She almost didn't do *Cinderella* because she was like, "I'm not the right age." And Brandy was like, "I'm only gonna do it if you're my fairy godmother." When Brandy met her, Brandy immediately burst into tears, screamed, and ran away, which honestly is relatable. I would probably do the same.

Janna: I would('ve) freak(ed) out.

Jordan: And Whitney was just like, "Hey darling, your pretty face, you're good. We're gonna be great" in the behind-the-scenes clips of her helping Brandy with her vocals. Then you jump five or six years later when she was doing the track "Heartbreak Hotel" with Faith Evans and Kelly Price. Kelly was like, "Oh, the sound people told me not to sing to my full potential," whatever, because you don't want to outshine Whitney. Whitney went off. She's like, "No, I want you to give a hundred percent of you. I don't care about me," and that was the thing.

Janna: I'm thinking about this a lot in my life, right, about Black women and martyrdom. Black women are always showing up, expected to give our best, and fully wanting to give our best. What was that cost to her? Having such a powerful gift and knowing you have to open this up to the world and a world that's not gonna nurture you and just really sees you as a cash cow. She's working in one of the biggest capitalist structures: the music and entertainment industry. What does downtime look like? What does the self-care aspect look like? And how those means of escape, all those drugs, because . . . she was doing the drugs before Bobby. It's the work schedule and the having to be "on" and having to produce all these things.

Jordan: I was listening to every single Whitney Houston album that came out without ever thinking about how her first album came out in '85 and her last album came out 2009. That's twenty-four years.

Whitney deserves to have a break, to say, "No, I'm done performing for the people." My entire concept of heaven is literally just all of my favorite artists just relaxing. Singing when they want to. Not performing but expressing themselves. I just imagine just tranquility for them.

Because to be always on the go . . . honestly, I watched one of Prince's last interviews when he was on Arsenio Hall. Arsenio asked, "Who are you listening to now? Do you go see live performances?" It stuck with me how stressful this must be because Prince was like, "It's really hard for me to listen to new music and to new artists because I'm constantly recomposing the music in my head to make it sound better."

To always have your brain be in that "on" position creatively, I can't. I would need a nap every five minutes.

Janna: Me too! And that's why you can understand folks using drugs, whether they're prescription or cocaine or marijuana. Whatever it is, to be hyperstimulated all of that time because of the way that your brain works and processes these things and not being able to turn that off. You can see getting on Prince's level where he was throwing the rule book out the window like, "Fuck y'all's capitalist bullshit. I'm gonna make my own shit. I'm gonna do it on my own terms."

Janna: It broke my heart at the end of Whitney's career, when she was broke and had to go on tour. The tour was a mess. People booed her; media tore her apart. She ended up doing a TV remake of *Sparkle*. That was her way of crawling out of a hole financially and spiritually when she was getting off drugs. A gift can be torturous too.

For Whitney, there was a lot of unresolved trauma from her past, from her family, from needing attention, from abuse that she experienced while her parents were on the road. How her father was a hustler and ended up suing her. He was stealing her money and then sued her for $100,000,000. So you have that fraught relationship, and then she spiraled in ways that, let's say, Beyoncé obviously hasn't.

Jordan: Something that I've been trying to do as a fan of brilliant Black artists is go beyond the album. I remember when Gary, her brother, was being interviewed with their mother, Cissy Houston, and said, "I was the one who gave her drugs for the first time." I was devastated because this is her big brother. He's her backup singer for those first early years, her right-hand person. Whitney was a modern-day Job for me because everything came flying at her: drugs, rumors, Bobby cheating, losing money, working harder than she wanted to. It went from being good and great and perfect to not being good, great, or perfect.

Janna: She was that good. "The Star-Spangled Banner" from the Super Bowl . . . that was the first take that she had done of that arrangement. The music director who made the arrangement was like, "I sent her the tape and never heard anything back for a few weeks. We are on the way to the Super Bowl and she listens to it; she nods her head and says, 'Yeah, I got it; let's go.'" And he's like, "Wait, we're not going to practice?" She's like, "I got it." And she gets up there and rips it. That is spirit and is divine.

You don't have to be religious or go to church to experience that or know what that feels like. And people around her [did] not know how to support. She had to be a church girl; she couldn't be hanging out with a lesbian. That was a whole fucking drama.

There're just so many things that she could not be and could not express, like her having to, and wanting to, be in this marriage with Bobby for her image. Not just her image, but not wanting to be a divorcée like her mom was and acting like, "I have to uphold this marriage because the public thinks it's gonna fail, and everybody around me thinks it's gonna fail. But I don't want to be a failure because I'm such a superstar in my career. But this love thing. I'm that, too, and I have to have that."

You can be Whitney-fucking-Houston and the best singer in the world, but you're still a failure if your marriage falls apart? It's really powerful to me as a thirty-eight-year-old single woman. That's some cautionary shit.

Jordan: Yeah, it's the same thing if we go back to Aretha Franklin's funeral. The fact that this grown man had the audacity to shame single mothers. Yes, Aretha had children at the age of fourteen. Aretha Franklin was Aretha Franklin. That Black women can exist to the capacity of Whitney Houston or Aretha Franklin and still be chastised beyond the grave. People are still like, "Yeah, but she did this." When will Black women be enough?

Black women deserve to be, to get their coins, their sunshine, their praise, and their roses while they're here. No one's perfect but Jesus Christ. Can we give them a moment to just exist in whatever capacity that they can? The Papa Pope thing on *Scandal*: you have to be twice as good. If we have to be twice as good, and we have to do twice as much work, other people will need to be twice as gentle, twice as healing. And we'll need to be twice as patient with ourselves to heal ourselves because, otherwise, we're going to burn out, be destructive, and we're going to not be our best if people don't give us the space and capacity to heal ourselves.

BLACK LOVE AND BLACK FUTURES

Introduction

Cynthia R. Greenlee

#BlackLove. #BlackFutures. The first nourishes the second.

There is more to the present than Black suffering. There is something more than the present.

And there is more to the hashtag #BlackLove than a handy social media discourse, the expression of heterosexual relationships, or visuals of pretty, smiling chocolate people. Just as Afrofuturism invites us to untether our imaginations from current environments, we think about the relationships that sustain us in the now. But we also strive to create better days, pregnant with possibilities dreamed of but as yet unrealized.

Our #BlackLove is a many-splendored thing. As Charmaine Lang writes in her piece about the correspondence between Black feminist luminaries, such as Audre Lorde and Toni Cade Bambara, it's the sister-friend who writes you letters about the fatigues of the activist grind or the friendship breakup. It's knowing that binaries are aggressively unloving and reduce us to only the tiniest sliver of ourselves or human experience. Jasmine Burnett says it's rescuing our senses of self, joy, and bodily eroticism from the vicious pleasure snatchers that abound: the church, rampant sexual violence, homophobia, fear of Black bodies.

But let's not trade in ideals and inaccurate positivity: Our #BlackLove is a work in progress. Inherently queer in that we have always formed families the way we want but often afraid of queers. Some in our communities are moving toward a love that is radically inclusive, embracing those of us who have always been here but have been excluded from the family. Some of us lag behind.

As Miss Major, a living legend and "trans visionary" told Raquel Willis in an interview, "If [it] ain't right, fucking fix it, whatever it takes."

Perhaps justice—wanting everyone to have what you have and all of us to have more of what we need to thrive—is the highest expression of love. We can create that here on earth without waiting for spaceships to beam us up and out.

Journey to Me: How I Came Out and Embraced All of Me

Charmaine Lang

I saw her sitting in the room during a morning break at a conference. Beautiful, with big hair framing her face. I was drawn to this woman. I had, before then, never been instantly drawn to anyone, especially a woman.

She was sitting at the table with two other women of color and a white woman. I went over and introduced myself. I would see her throughout the conference, almost as if something was bringing us together. I wanted to get closer to her. And, at the same time, I did not want to get closer, for fear of what it would mean to my pretense as a straight woman.

She invited me to dinner the next day, and I gave her every excuse as to why I could not accept her invitation. At the time, I didn't even know her intentions. I didn't know if she was attracted to me or just wanted someone to accompany her to a restaurant. At dinner, she stared at me. Making me even more uncomfortable. I would not return her gaze, though I admired her beauty from my peripheral vision and quietly wondered how it would feel to hold her hand or run my fingers through her hair.

I had to excuse myself from the table and go to the bathroom and have a talk with myself. It went something like this. "No, ma'am. You cannot like this woman. End of story. Get your life together." Further denial.

I had denied my attraction to women since I was younger. It was safer to parade around as heterosexual given how homophobic society and my family could be. I remember seeing my younger sister's journey to coming out as a lesbian and how some members of my family isolated and ridiculed her. I recall seeing our mother's struggle with blaming herself for having a gay daughter, compounded by one of her sisters declaring that my sister was going to hell for her "deviant" behavior.

I was considered the good daughter. The one who did everything she was supposed to do.

So I paraded around as a heterosexual Black woman until I decided that I no longer wanted to deny my queer identity. I had to go through the process of coming out to myself.

This woman and I stayed in touch mostly through texting. I kept my responses minimal and vague, as I didn't want to lead myself on or make her believe I was interested. I didn't want to ask questions of her, nor of myself. I had settled into a sense of denial of my intimate desires for Black women, and I was comfortable with that.

But then I saw her again.

It wasn't until three months later at yet another conference that she asked me straight out if I liked her. I shifted around in my seat a little, trying to decide how much to reveal, how much to hold on to. I ended up telling her that I was attracted to her. It was not an easy thing to admit to myself, let alone say out loud, on a bus with other folks on it at that. But I felt free to look at her in all her beauty, to take it in, and appreciate it. I felt free.

At thirty-three, I finally felt free to admit that I am emotionally, sexually, and romantically attracted to Black women. I mean, I am still single. A band did not start to play after this admission, and life largely remained the same.

What did change, though, was how I began to move about my world. Allowing myself to be open to whatever the universe has for me. I no longer have to pretend anymore. I don't have to worry whether or not my friend saw me checking out a woman. Hell, I no longer have to question or justify why I was checking out a woman. I know now what I've always known: I am attracted to women.

Yep, I said it.

Accepting my queer identity has allowed me to further explore my creativity, to lift boundaries I have set due to my fear of falling in love with a woman. I have reexamined what life could be like with a woman, or a man for that reason, because I'm still very much attracted to men too. It's created a space for me to be open to possibilities, open to the universe, open to myself. When we deny any parts of our true selves, we neglect that which is most beautiful and that which makes us whole human beings. Perfectly complex.

I am perfectly complex.

It took a while to accept it, to bask in what makes me human—my complexities. But here are some of the pieces to my journey to accepting my queerness.

1. I speak to the universe.

I prayed for guidance and support with self-love and love from a partner. As I prayed, I began to realize that people were coming into my life who were supportive and loving, and they challenged me to go deeper with my love for self. I also noticed that my descriptions of an ideal mate became genderless. I no longer prayed for a man, but I prayed for genuine love from a beautiful soul whom I could share experiences and a lifetime together.

2. I keep a journal.

I write about what I want to experience. How I want to feel. I think deeply about love, hurt, and lessons learned. I try to write every day, as it helps me to relieve stress, to clarify my thoughts, and to explore what I want in life. What I write in my journal often signals for me what I need to release, what I need to usher into my life, and the progress I have made.

3. I surround myself with open-minded people.

The people in my life are accepting, allies to the LGBTQIA+ community or are queer themselves. So when I came out to folks, it was mostly a beautifully supportive experience. There were questions, of course, but no one made me feel bad for coming out. In fact, I felt more affirmed and at peace as a result.

4. I write poetry.

In *Poetry Is Not a Luxury*, Audre Lorde asserts, "Poetry is the way we help give name to the nameless so it can be thought." It was through my poetry that I could write about my attraction to women without fear of who would judge me. I wrote poetry as a way to organize my thoughts. To survive. To dream. And to embrace all of my intersecting identities as I moved to action.

5. I am in nature.
There's something about being among the trees, the green hills, and the ocean that opens me to all of my senses. I can smell the lavender and rosemary. I can see the vastness of the rolling green hills. I hear the sounds of the waves from the ocean, and at once, I feel the water pull at my feet. I am in love with nature. It was actually on a trip to Sonoma and Los Angeles where I was so entirely engrossed in natural beauty that I felt at peace and was quiet enough to hear what my spirit was telling me. It was also here, in nature, that I began to awaken to all of me and see my queerness as a part of who I am.

6. I cry.
Sometimes shit gets rough. Meditating, great friends, or journaling may not be what I need at the time. Crying may very well be what I need to do. And so I cry when I need to. Too often, we, as young people, are taught to stop all that crying. And as grown folks, especially women of color, we are made to believe that to be strong means to deal with it all with a smile on our face. I realize that there is no strength in denying how I am feeling. I honor my feelings and let them pass through me, realizing at the same time that they are just emotions needing to be processed and released. Crying is therapeutic.

Accepting all of me, and loving me unapologetically, has been revolutionary. I realize that there is no freedom in denying any part of me, so I acknowledge that I am the one I have been waiting for to love me, hold me, and set me free.

We are worth loving all of what makes us complex, full, beautiful human beings. What are some of the pieces to your journey of self-love and acceptance?

Originally published on For Harriet *on July 3, 2015.*

"Overworked and Underpaid": Organizing, Black Womanhood, and Self-Care

Charmaine Lang

As a researcher, I am interested, indeed positively obsessed, by the long tradition of Black feminist organizing in the United States. Outspoken activists like Echoing Ida's spiritual foremother Ida B. Wells, Anna Julia Cooper, Fannie Lou Hamer, Toni Cade Bambara, and Frances Beal embodied their values to center the voices and thought leadership of Black women. They wrote and delivered speeches about the duality of sexism and racism Black women encountered in this nation, garnering in some cases accolades and honors.

But awards do little when a culture of martyrdom—the discouragement to prioritize one's own emotional and mental health—reigns in the lives of activists.

I have found in my research that not much has been written about how women of color organizers made space for joy, wellness, and love while fighting against white supremacy and other forms of oppression. With activists today facing a similar struggle, I wanted to know what we could learn from our Black women activist foremothers to avoid burning out.

So I went to the archives—that special place where I could touch a letter or a newspaper. At the University of Wisconsin-Milwaukee, I examined *Triple Jeopardy*, the 1970s newspaper of the Third World Women's Alliance, a radical women of color organization. I saw themes of struggling against oppressive structures and the fatigue that often accompanied the work. For example, the committee responsible for editing and publishing *Triple Jeopardy* described themselves in the last two editions as "overworked and underpaid."[1]

Similarly, during archival research at the Spelman College Archives, I came across a letter from writer-activist Toni Cade Bambara to writer-activist Audre Lorde in which the closing simply, yet very tellingly, read "overwhelmed Toni."[2]

For me, this admission that they were tired, human, and affected by the oppressions they fought makes room for Black women to name their feelings and share their stories. That vulnerability and space needs to be continuously created because it would allow us to express that we are in need of change, and in need of assistance as we work under multiple pressures—deadlines, limited resources, the constant hovering of oppression, and age-old representations of Black womanhood.

The "mammy" trope—which depicts Black women as perpetual asexual servants loyal to white supremacy—is particularly damaging to Black women. It holds that Black women are happiest when they are serving others, which means that they all too often are expected to delay their own self-care and joy. This trope gained popularity in the nineteenth century, but its remnants remain with us as Black women continue to be thought of as strong. If we take the mammy trope as an example, a Black woman's only role is to be in service to everyone outside of herself. Black women activists then become the depository for any affliction that ails people.

Many Black women have tirelessly fought to resist ascribed roles. *Triple Jeopardy* and the letters of Bambara and Lorde taught me that Black women used activism and writing as forms of self-care. Self-care is antithetical to the mammy trope, which represents Black women as self-sacrificing. Black women's ability to write each other about their personal, creative, and organizing lives was deeper than just catching up. Letter writing served as a tool of survival, as the authors reimagined their lives as Black women. They also supported each other, as they provided feedback on each other's poems and stories; they uplifted each other and made plans for meetings and celebrations.

Many of the letters I came across in the collections of Bambara and Lorde expressed gratitude to the sender from the recipient whose spirits were lifted after receiving a personal letter. "I got your lovely card, and it picked up my dropping spirits—just like your fiction does," scholar Mary Helen Washington wrote in a letter to Bambara. In another letter addressed to Bambara, the writer (signed only as "G") said, "Girl—I just got your letter—and was it ever on time."

Black women writer-activists also did some form of consciousness-raising via letter writing. They expressed rage and humor at the audacity of people, mostly white male publishers, trying to define them through a white, masculinist, and heteronormative lens. And they sought understanding and reconciliation from each other as Black women and feminists.

In a letter to scholar Evelynn Hammonds, Lorde writes,

> Please forgive the delay in this reply to your letter . . . I wanted to think about issues you raised in your letter reaching beyond the material ones. . . . Evelynn, it is not clear to me the exact nature of the conflicts underlying the history between you and Barbara and Cherrie, nor does it need to be. But the bitterness on both sides is quite obvious . . . I do not like this. It makes me very sad because I feel it is unnecessarily destructive for us all. We have so little time, and there are so few of us doing real work, and under so much pressure. . . . I ask you to consider: WHO PROFITS FROM THESE SEPARATIONS BETWEEN US, THESE ACRIMONIES, THESE FEUDS? So, I am wondering if there is any way possible for each of the three of you, having been separate now for over a year, to re-examine your relationship to the personal conflicts between you . . . and consider what some of the real bases are upon which you can deal with each other with some amount of respect and trust?[3]

They gathered strength from each other as they talked of how things are and how they wanted them to be.

These letters challenged the narrative of the strong and everenduring Black woman. They serve as an example of the importance of quality of life for activists and how they can best be supported.

In order to have sustainable movements, social justice movements and organizations need to center the care of activists.

Organizations and movements can make sure that they are creating space for self-care by prioritizing wellness and encouraging activists and movement builders to take the time to do the same. I know that the work to destroy all forms of oppression requires all of our time. We are, after all, fighting to bring about a more just and equitable society. However, it is possible to do the work and prioritize health and wellness at the same time.

I know that conversations around self-care can sometimes be elitist and classist. Yoga classes can cost an average of eighteen dollars per session, and massages sometimes start at seventy. Self-care can quickly become about who can afford to relax and release some tension. But costs don't necessarily have to be a barrier to relaxation.

Community care is essential to the lives of activists. Activists and organizations can host massage and healing circles, journal together, check in with each other regularly, and seek authentic and honest relationships that affirm them. Instead of being seen as more work, this actually can be an essential part of a wellness routine that can aid activists in their work.

Love for each other and an investment in our individual, as well as collective needs, will help us as we navigate and work to dismantle hostile environments. Activists can encourage each other to take care of their emotional, spiritual, mental, and physical selves. Managers and executive directors can create wellness as part of work culture by checking in with their employees. Some already do. I hope others will catch on.

Notes

1. *Triple Jeopardy* 4, no. 2 (January–February 1975). *Triple Jeopardy* Collection. Special Collections, University of Wisconsin-Milwaukee Libraries.
2. Toni Cade Bambara to Audre Lorde, letter, September 14; Audre Lorde Papers, box 1, folder 011, series 1.1; Spelman College Archives.
3. Audre Lorde to Evelynn Hammonds, letter, April 8, 1983; Audre Lorde Papers, box 1, folder 4, series 1.1; Spelman College Archives.

Originally published on Rewire.News *on April 15, 2016.*

We Should All Go to Rehab

Yamani Hernandez

Turning forty cracked me open. On Christmas night, the day before my birthday, I had a first-trimester miscarriage in the emergency room. I was alone. Days earlier, I dropped a person I once believed to be the love of my life at the airport so he could visit his mother. I'd sat with him through her open-heart surgery six weeks before. He rubbed my belly and said, "Goodbye, peanut. Daddy will be back soon."

Unbeknownst to me, he flew to spend the holiday with another woman, his other long-term off-and-on girlfriend. A woman he told me he had broken up with six years ago.

He took a week to return to me while I bled out the pregnancy we planned. He said we would try again.

Two weeks later, in grief counseling, he broke up with me because he viewed my coparenting commitments to my existing two children as too supportive of their father, a man he never met during our six-year relationship but claimed to hate. Six weeks after that, through a coincidental overlap in Black feminist professional connections, I spoke with his other girlfriend and discovered he had been living a double life for the bulk of our relationship. He'd left me with the $1,400 hospital bill and went back to her. She said that she thought he "was just fucking" me and had known him to be "a sleaze and psychotic" for twenty years.

Desperately trying to make sense of it all, I looked up one of his friends on social media and asked her if she knew the labyrinth of lies he'd been weaving. She responded that I "needed professional help, as it was pathologically inappropriate to contact [her] for something that had nothing do" with her. She threatened to pursue legal action if I contacted her again.

It still cuts like a knife to read those words, but I've now learned that abusers usually have a community of enablers who never know the full story of the terror they've caused. In any case, it was all too much, and it broke me.

In retrospect, I had been breaking for a long time.

Since childhood, actually. I am like the one in four people who have experienced physical and sexual abuse as a child and like the one in eight adults who is the adult child of an alcoholic.

People who have suffered trauma after trauma need a rehabilitation process. I know that now because I went to rehab.

The Misery and the Magic

My life is stressful, and it has been from as long as I can remember. I became a caregiver for my alcoholic custodial parent and younger siblings at age five when my father abandoned us and withheld income during a four-year divorce. When my mother was sober, she was an extraordinary, dreamy mom who made life fun on $1,800 in child support, once ordered, a month for a family of four. She was enthusiastic, creative, affirming, and physically loving. When she was drunk, she was lewd, mean, and cruel. I would often have to tuck her in after she passed out. Sometimes I would do this after she'd yelled insults at me or beaten me with a chair leg.

Now that I am an adult, my work stress consists of leading a national organization on a politically charged issue. The job comes with regular harassment and death threats. My home stress consists of being a single coparent of two children, one of whom has obsessive thoughts that I am contaminated and a threat to him. Other than my children, I am estranged from my biological family.

My last romantic relationship, while not completely ideal, was my only place of solace and respite. My partner was many things: extremely handsome, funny, an amazing cook, a brilliant writer, a skilled organizational and communications strategist, an expert on educating Black boys, and much more. Like his other girlfriend, I'd met him in college and had a "thing" for him for two decades. Besides intense physical and romantic attraction unlike any I'd ever experienced, I relied on him daily for executive coaching and a listening ear to my parenting struggles with two Black boys. He was my best friend, and I wanted to be with him forever.

I would have done anything for him, and I almost did. He had full access to everything in my life. Keys to my house, clothes in my closet, use of my car, full trust with my body with no protection. I introduced him to every friend, family member, and even coworkers. He often met me on the road when I was traveling. I supported him financially for the last year we dated when he quit his job and "retreated to another city to live with his uncle" to focus on writing a book.

I visited his uncle's home, and they both lied about him living there. He had actually moved with his other girlfriend to a city and a campus I spoke at, just miles from their home. She told me she sent money monthly to his mother, the same woman who called me her daughter-in-law when I visited her daily in the hospital.

Even without knowing the details of his infidelity, the relationship was also a source of endless confusion and angst. We broke up temporarily every year, often over differences in commitment. But we were never out of touch longer than a couple of months. I would try to date other people, but it never lasted. Like moths to a flame, we always came back to each other.

With each reunion, he would make bigger promises. Couples counseling. Engagement. But the problems also became more disturbing. He insulted me and sometimes said worrisome, weird things. He wanted a cult, he told me, and said he considered himself a pimp. I told myself he was joking. I was built like a linebacker, he said, and he imitated my limp and my son when he had mental health breakdowns. He said I was abnormal and that he didn't introduce me to his friends because he was embarrassed to be with me. He learned my passwords for my devices and repeatedly breached my privacy to read emails from times he and I hadn't been together. He berated me for not telling him about those things once we reconciled. Once he'd interrupted me at my desk during a work crisis to ask, "Can I pour water on your head?" When I'd ask why he'd say such a thing, he'd say I couldn't take a joke.

I was always confused about the ever-moving goal post of his love. I stopped taking care of myself and fixated on convincing him to love me the way I needed. Six years, I had loved. Waited. Invested. Endured. And he'd been sharing his life with someone else the whole time.

I had given all I could give and now I needed someone to take care of me. So I went to rehab.

Rehab was like going to college again and majoring in self-love and worth. Or like being born again but into a whole community that is conspiring for your wellness. We all deserve that. Especially when we are unraveling.

Technically, rehab is inpatient treatment for people seeking relief from addiction, chronic pain, trauma, and mood and eating disorders that have negatively impacted their lives. The stigma I had about the word "rehab," what it was and who was there, did not match up with the gift of my experience. I thought that rehab was somewhere celebrities and wayward teenagers went when strung out on heroin and cocaine. I wasn't sure what happened there, and I thought it was a cross between hospital and jail—and, unfortunately, some are. I thought there was something wrong with people who went. The fact is there was something wrong with me. I had been deeply harmed as a child and as an adult. I wasn't a celebrity. I wasn't ordered to go. But I needed help, and I didn't know what else to do.

I learned that there is not much difference between all of the reasons why people end up at rehab. Trauma either causes or is the result of whatever has brought people there. People go for mental, physical, and emotional help to retrain their minds, bodies, and spirits. With healthier habits, beliefs, thought patterns, tools, and relationships, it is possible to mitigate, if not end, cycles of harm and change for the better. For me, it was a rigorous, magically intense reset.

My recovery will be lifelong. But for thirty days, I was held with love, care, and every possible type of therapeutic intervention. In my four decades, it's the best I've ever been taken care of. It taught me about a quality of life I had not been living and what is actually necessary to heal. Yoga and positive thinking alone are not enough.

The Road to Rehab

Between Christmas and late March, I tried to manage the layers of my loss: the pregnancy I'd wanted, the man I loved, and my senses of pride, stability, and self as a "strong Black woman." Ultimately, my strength reached its limit. In the vein of Solange Knowles, I tried to sleep it away; I tried to work it away; I tried to wait it away; I tried to train it away. I tried to social media it away. And I tried like hell to love it away with a partner who insulted me daily, lied and gaslighted me for years about being in another relationship while accusing my coparenting of being a problem and a threat to his happiness in our partnership.

I couldn't comb my hair. I couldn't bathe or eat. I mostly just cried and obsessed over questions about his duplicity and my own worth. I wrote more than one thousand notes in my phone trying to hash through my shock and pain. I did not want to live anymore.

I needed a medical intervention, evaluation, and care that wasn't going to be possible while continuing to be at work or at home with my kids by myself. I texted my therapist an update on what had happened. "I need help." I said. "I feel like I have been beaten with a hammer, thrown over a building, and run over with a truck. I cannot sleep or eat or see straight. I am spiraling, and I cannot function. I can't do anything, and I don't know what's real anymore. I need to go somewhere. Residential."

He texted back, saying this kind of deceit was intimate partner violence and sent a list of rehab programs. After hearing my symptoms, one in Arizona told me to come immediately.

In the midst of uncontrollable grief and shock. I reached out to my board members at my job to let them know I would be unable to work, and I needed to take medical leave. I reached out to a friend for my first favor ever: Would she buy me clothes and toiletries to take to treatment? I knew I'd be unable to prepare.

I also wasn't prepared for the cost of rehab. It cost $100 per hour for thirty days. Grand total: $72,000. My insurance covered 75 percent of it, but the remaining $18,000 was on me. In the midst of crisis, I committed to a payment plan once I left rehab. The minimum payment allowed was $1,000 a month—a difficult amount of money to spare each month. This payment is less than the cost of my student loan payment, which I traded for ten months (and will default on) to pay for rehab. It was worth what it took to save my life. I am privileged to make a six-figure income, but if I did not, I'm not sure if or how I would have survived.

Everybody who has suffered trauma needs to go to rehab, and it should not only be possible for those who can afford it. How many suicides and homicides and abuses could be prevented if everyone had access to this care?

Once there, I was diagnosed with major depressive disorder, severe anxiety, and post-traumatic stress disorder (PTSD) for short-term trauma due to the rapid succession of a miscarriage, a cruel breakup, and abuse. Though my providers speculated, only a medical professional with direct contact could formally diagnose my past partner with sex addiction and antisocial and narcissistic personality disorders. Combined with the stresses of childhood physical and sexual abuse and parenting a child with mental illness, it was a wonder I hadn't collapsed before.

The first several days were the hardest. It was more like hospitalization. We were quarantined from the rest of the campus to be monitored at all times to prevent self-harm. We went outside only three times a day for fifteen minutes. After this initial period, we moved into a resort-style accommodation with a pool and view of the mountains. Our days were packed with all kinds of therapy: individual and group, with art or horses; meditation and massage; and appointments with general practitioners, psychologists, and naturopaths. We had lectures on Brené Brown's work weekly. I had exposure to some therapies I'd never heard of that are specifically for PTSD, including eye movement desensitization and reprocessing, which uses rapid eye movements to take the emotional charge out of traumatic events.

Looking "Together" but Barely Holding It Together

While there, I learned that I am what mental health professionals call "worried well." In my therapist's words, other people view me as a "high-functioning" person who doesn't display stereotypical signs of distress. I'm conventionally successful, well-groomed, and have material possessions and markers of superficial success. I take care of my parental duties, in collaboration with a devoted coparent. My host of badass friends adore me, though I rarely ask them for help.

Underneath the pretty pictures and stereotypes of happiness, I struggle with perpetual sadness, low self-esteem, overwhelm, never-ending responsibility, sleeplessness, incontinence, and sensitivity to certain kinds of touch, space, and sound. I navigate these things alongside all the systemic barriers that every other Black queer woman navigates in life.

My problems are not only systemic. In my month at rehab, I learned more about my comprehensive mental, physical, and emotional health than I had in forty years. I got my mental health diagnoses, learned what treatments specifically work for them, and how often I need to access them to maintain stability. I now know I have hyperandrogenism, an intersex condition that means I have a resistance to insulin and more testosterone than most women. This explained a lot of things about my gender perception that I thought were psychological but that are actually biology and had been ignored by medical practitioners for my entire life when I asked for endocrinology testing. I have very light periods; I am very hairy, and some of my other physical features are more stereotypically masculine. I have always struggled with feeling like I fit or having comfort as a "girl." I haven't felt like I was a boy exactly but maybe something in between. The fact of the matter is that I may not be like most girls biologically. I'm a little bit different.

I learned that, like most children of alcoholics, I developed my own addiction. However, my addiction isn't substance based. For the first time, at rehab, I found myself facing the realities of my own compulsive and dysfunctional behavior around love. Because of insecure and damaged attachments to my caregivers as a child, I am predisposed to look for love in places that do not serve me. I mistake crushes for love, and if I authentically fall in love with someone, I have a destructive habit of loving my partner more than I love myself. Despite clear signs of unavailability, isolation, neglect, cruelty, insults, and lies, I have the uncanny ability to see the best in people, even when they are harming me.

My childhood trained me well—to care more about losing love-avoidant people than my self-worth. It trained me to have a high threshold for abuse.

I believe we are ALL broken, that we need to recover, and that the world might change when we all get the care and commitment we need, regardless of cost.

In the absence of systems that ensure our care and survival, we all need rehab for the harm we have endured. It was there that I learned for the first time what it means to be taken care of and what it takes to heal.

In Betweens

Jordan Scruggs
Illustrated by Bishakh Som

Some things are better said with images.

"In Betweens" is a collaborative minicomic with words by Jordan Scruggs and images by Bishakh Som.

We created this piece for Trans Day of Resilience 2016, in memory of TGNC people killed by anti-trans violence and in celebration of trans, gender nonconforming, nonbinary people of color everywhere.

"In Betweens" is made possible by Echoing Ida, Strong Families, and Forward Together.

echoingida.org
forwardtogether.org
forwardtogether.org/strong-families

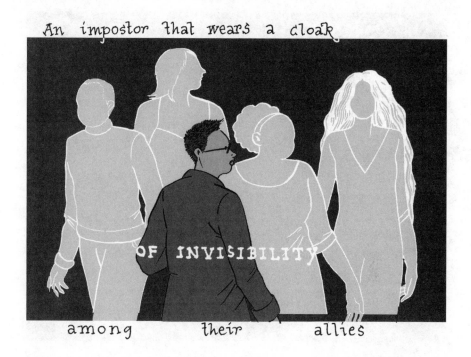

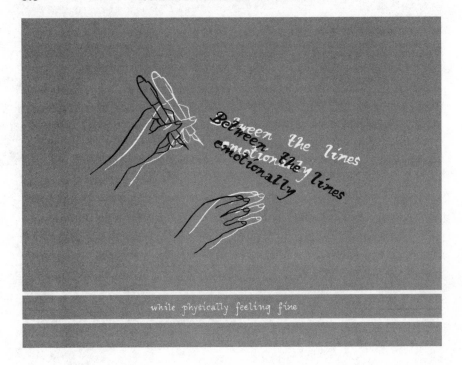

Between the lines
Between the lines
emotionally
emotionally

while physically feeling fine

some

times

Originally published via Forward Together
for Trans Day of Resilience in 2016.

Trans Visionaries: How Miss Major Helped Spark the Modern Trans Movement

Raquel Willis

Raquel Willis is more than a writer and activist. She functions as a trans archivist preserving and publicizing the still-too-often hidden histories of trans communities. In a series of articles for them.*, she's profiled HIV/ AIDS advocate Cecilia Chung and Atlanta's DeeDee Chamblee, a mother of the Movement. Here she interviews the incomparable Miss Major.*

As we celebrate International Women's Day, we must elevate the brilliant and powerful transgender women of color who have paved the way for today's social justice movements. Miss Major Griffin-Gracy has spent more than forty years advocating for the marginalized, whether in prisons or on the streets. Born and raised on the South Side of Chicago, the trans activist came to know herself in the 1950s and '60s, when police raids of queer bars were rampant and the thought of LGBTQ+ people speaking out against oppression was novel. She, alongside other vanguard activists like Marsha P. Johnson and Sylvia Rivera, emerged from the perilous 1969 Stonewall Riots with a commitment to support her sisters and other trans family.

Though Miss Major's lifelong leadership is now widely acclaimed, the road hasn't always been smooth. She spent several stints in prison during the 1970s and credits her radical political stance on issues like abolition and Black liberation to those experiences. Despite her own run-ins with white supremacist and cisheteronormative systems like the prison-industrial complex, she has always played a role in building up and motivating the trans community. In *MAJOR!*, a feature-length documentary that chronicles her life, many of her close friends and confidants share the positive influence she has had on their lives and the various local communities she has lived in.

In 2005, Miss Major joined the San Francisco–based Transgender Gender-Variant and Intersex Justice Project as a staff organizer, and later as executive director, to lead its advocacy for incarcerated transgender women. She officially retired ten years later, but her fire continues to burn. She is currently developing House of GG, a safe haven and retreat house for the transgender community. We caught up with Miss Major to discuss her long fight for liberation, her self-care, and her thoughts on the current political climate and what it means for trans activism.

Raquel Willis: What does it mean for you to be forty years into your activism and to be an elder now after getting involved in the movement at such a young age?

Miss Major Griffin-Gracy: When you're doing this out of care and concern, you really don't think about it as activism or a movement. You think of it as—for me—protecting my girls. Getting to this age is interesting because things are better than they were when I was growing up. There's still the stigma of being a trans person, but the world is changing, and we are more prominent than we've ever been, in a semi-positive light. They're still killing us; they're still throwing us underneath the jails, but there are people that are not a part of our community who are bitching about the injustices that they are doing to us. That's a major step.

Raquel: You're right: So much is different now. There are so many young folks who are owning their identities at single-digit ages. What were the dynamics of your family, and how did you understand yourself as a kid?

Miss Major: At that point it was, as it is now, a matter of survival. It's interesting to think about when I was younger—the constraints and the way I had to negotiate through in order to maintain breathing every day. My family would say, "Oh, that boy is acting way too femme, chile," or "You need to beat the 'shim' out of him." They tried, but you know us trans people are some tough sons of bitches. We don't take that shit, especially the Black girls. We understand what we've had to go through as a culture and as a people. It becomes a matter of standing up for who we know we are. It's not that we *believe* we're this or that. We *know* that's who we are. When the dust settles, I want my trans girls and guys to stand up and say, "I'm still fucking here!"

Raquel: You grew up on the South Side of Chicago. Do you have any family still there that you see?

Miss Major: Well, everyone else is dead. My father's family was small, and my mother's family was large. All of my aunts are gone. I may have some cousins here and there. Of course, they're not going to keep up with me. As I was living my life, I didn't have time to hold connections to people who would rather I die than breathe and be successful.

Raquel: You've lived in a lot of places, but you most recently moved from San Francisco to Little Rock for your current project. What is it, and how did you come up with the name, House of GG?

Miss Major: The technical name is Griffin-Gracy Historical Retreat and Educational Center, but that's a lot for people to remember. When I came up, there were houses that developed in New York, like the House of Crystal Labeija and the House of Xtravaganza. They started in order to help the younger girls who were on the street. They helped them learn the things they needed to do to survive, like how to negotiate with the cops and what to do if they got busted. I thought in honor of them and all they've done and tried to do, I would keep the thought and feeling of them alive with the House of GG. I want it to be a retreat where I can bring the girls here and help to create a sense of family for our community.

Raquel: We saw each other about a month and a half ago at the Creating Change conference when you received the Susan J. Hyde Award for Longevity in the Movement. I know that was complicated because you talked about the weirdness of having white, cis, gay people honoring you in that way after all of these years.

Miss Major: Yeah, these white, overprivileged, entitled, stick-up-their-ass motherfuckers who hate us, nudge each other when they see us, talk about us as we walk by no matter what city we live in. It's not that all of them are bad. There's about three out of the thousand that have some sense and respect people for who they are. I had a lot of personal issues over this. I said in my speech, "It took forty years for me to get up here. You motherfuckers are late." They want to rant and rave and act like, "Oh, this is the thing to do!" Miss Major is not your token. You need a token? Well, go to the subway and buy one and get on a fucking bus. In accepting the award, I wanted to make sure that I stood up for my community and who I am [by letting] them know that they have been doing this shit to me since I was a kid, and it hasn't stopped. The only reason they don't do it to me now is because I'm an older woman.

Raquel: We are in a moment of trans visibility like never before. What does that mean to you with the political backdrop of the Trump administration?

Miss Major: This president wants to eradicate us from the face of the earth. He doesn't have a belief system, and he's not a politician. When he won this, my worry was that our community would become so fearful of what he may do that they [might] run blindly into the closet and hide. This is a time that we can't hide. We need to have our presence known. I don't want to see trans people on the endangered species list. I'm hoping being out there myself that people will see me going on and believe that we can do this.

Raquel: There are a lot of younger organizers and activists coming up now. Do you have any tips for folks doing this work?

Miss Major: We have a right to be angry, but you have to be angry in degrees. You use your anger to come up with ways to dismantle the bullshit that is oppressing you in the first place. There has to be a way to manage this so you accomplish the goals you set out for yourself. It's not an easy thing, but you must nurture, take care of, and look out for yourself too. If you don't take the time to heal your wounds and soothe your ills, you cannot be of any benefit to anybody else.

Raquel: What do you do for self-care, Mama Major?

Miss Major: I'm a person that likes music and TV. I liked Big Band Era stuff like [George] Gershwin, Count Basie, Peggy Lee, Martha Washington, Dinah Washington, and Billie Holiday. On days when I'm feeling kind of icky, I'll curl up with my dog, Moose, and watch TV. We've had her since my kidney surgery. If I need a little masculine attention, I'll go get it.

Raquel: Were you ever married? Was there a desire for you to have that kind of life?

Miss Major: You know, I did [have that desire] when I was younger. My closest friend at the time was Crystal Labeija. She had the most beautiful wedding, and I was one of her bridesmaids. Then, I said that's what I wanted. Eventually, I thought, "Well, I'm an ex-hooker. One man? I don't have time for that." I liked having long, engaging romantic affairs for maybe three to six months [at a time]. Then I would bring somebody else in.

Raquel: I didn't realize you and Crystal Labeija were so close. Y'all are both such legends. How did you meet her?

Miss Major: At the time, we didn't think of each other as legends. We were just young girls out there trying to have a good time. Crystal and I met on Thirty-Fourth and Eighth Avenue, getting ready to jump into the same car to turn a trick. He made a really sarcastic comment saying, "Well, I want the light-skinned girl." I got pissed the fuck off and so did she. We walked away and went to eat at Dunkin' Donuts.

Raquel: After all is said and done, what do want your legacy to be?

Miss Major: I would want my legacy to be if it ain't right, fucking fix it, whatever it takes. I'd want to be remembered for trying to do the right thing and care for all people. We're all part of one another. I would want people to understand who we are as human beings. I want us to look at the similarities more than the differences.

Originally published on them. *on March 8, 2018.*

Pleasure Politics Part I:
Employment, Economic Justice, and the Erotic

Taja Lindley

Too often we are led to believe that work must be something separate from pleasure: that we are to do what we love on the side in our spare time, that pleasure is an extracurricular activity, a hobby, a side gig. As if only a privileged few are supposed to do work that is fulfilling and passion driven. As if pleasure is a luxury, not a necessity.

Know: these are lies.

In the United States, we have been conditioned to work to survive, to get by, to pay bills, to stay afloat, living a day-to-day and paycheck-to-paycheck existence. We have been conditioned to work most of our lives so we can enjoy pleasurable activities in our free time, predetermined holidays, limited vacation, and, if we're lucky, during retirement. Says Audre Lorde, such a system "reduces work to a travesty of necessities, a duty by which we earn bread or oblivion for ourselves and those we love."[1]

Listen closely: when policy makers, public figures, and the media talk about the current status of the economy and high unemployment, the discussion revolves around jobs. As it should: people are looking for work. But when the narrative around jobs is unconcerned with how work connects to the passion, purpose, ambitions, and talents of workers, our economy does a disservice to our humanity and creativity. The conversation reinforces a narrative that implies that any job will do. What about purpose? What about passion? Yes: we've got to feed our families; we've got to keep roofs over our heads, and there are bills to be paid. Survival is a primary need.

But we are so much more than our basic needs. In a world of haves and have-nots, with widening disparities in wealth and income, the travesty of our global economy makes pleasurable work challenging to access. An economy organized in this way serves only the elite and powerful, whereby the majority of workers are employed and/or exploited to fill the vision and pockets of those who are already in power.

In short: systemic inequality makes pleasurable work more accessible for some than for others.

As a policy and research fellow at a grassroots economic justice organization, I witnessed firsthand how this played out for long-term unemployed people on public assistance in New York. The sentiment that "any job will do" pushed many people on welfare into low-wage jobs with few (if any) benefits and with little to no room for upward mobility. Caseworkers were generally uninterested in helping people find the professional development and training programs that could help them move into the careers of their choice, opting instead to fulfill short-term goals of job placement. Many caseworkers were informed by stereotypes of the "undeserving poor," their job responsibilities informed by public policies concerned with getting people off public assistance, not into satisfying work.

Beyond the safety net, there is still an indoctrination of working for necessity where people are encouraged to chase power, money, and prestige and reserve pleasure for happy hours and vacation time. People are encouraged to embrace a lifestyle that costs just as much as their salary. It has its advantages: in exchange for a weekly commitment of at least forty hours, you can pay off that exorbitant student loan debt and possibly save some money and accumulate wealth. Certainly, a savings account and strategic investments can pay off in the long run, but high income and wealth do not equal happiness. What is our life worth when we sell it for only a few moments of pleasure?

In her essay, Lorde explains that the erotic is neither frivolous nor a luxury. She defines the erotic as

> a measure between the beginnings of our sense of self and the chaos of our strongest feelings. It is an internal sense of satisfaction to which, once we have experienced it, we know we can aspire. For having experienced the fullness of this depth of feeling and recognizing its power, in honor and self-respect we can require no less of ourselves.[2]

Erotic autonomy, Lorde suggests, is to live a fully embodied life where we are living our purpose and passions and creating from our unique talents with an undeniable feeling of satisfaction. The erotic is the lens we use to scrutinize our choices so that we make decisions that support the fullest expressions of who we are.

So when we talk about the erotic as it applies to our work, it is about (re)claiming power over our lives and how we operate in this economy. It is a radical notion that values the talents, creativity, and contributions of everyone, even those who have been marginalized and deemed unworthy of pleasurable work—work that satisfies our internal desires and financial needs.

Wealth and purpose-driven hustles are not mutually exclusive. Imagine how different our world would be if people performed work they were excited about and not what they thought they had to do to get by. How might our economy change? What would the meaning of work be? How might there be more support for innovation and entrepreneurship, even among historically and currently marginalized and exploited communities?

Creating spaces and products that encourage people to feel good in their bodies is a critical part of my reproductive justice framework and an extension of my life's work. So when I founded Colored Girls Hustle, it represented that erotic space for me: a place where I could be my authentic self as an artist and do work that affirmed women and girls of color. Part of Colored Girls Hustle's work is to redefine "hustle" as passion and purpose-driven. We create original media and feature women and girls of color who hustle hard for their communities as artists, entrepreneurs, healers, and activists. Colored Girls Hustle is actively contributing to a conversation about erotic expression and autonomy being integral parts of economic justice.

I hope you'll join me in defining erotic autonomy within the context of work, prioritizing the erotic in economic justice for women and girls of color, and articulating the financially lucrative and sustainable ways this can manifest.

Notes

1. Audre Lorde, "Uses of the Erotic: The Erotic as Power," in *Sister Outsider: Essays and Speeches* (Berkeley, CA: Crossing Press, 1984), 53–59.
2. Lorde, "Uses of the Erotic," 54.

Originally published on Feministe *on June 10, 2013.*

Herbs That Fortify Us

Carib Healing Collective

We can reach toward healthy Black futures by recovering the medicine of our pasts. Bianca Campbell, Samantha Daley, and Ruth Jeannoel discovered a shared history of herbal wisdom while in Echoing Ida. Together, they formed the Carib Healing Collective, a home for stories and medicine rooted in Caribbean healing practices. Through workshops, zines, and social media, they've shared their knowledge with an audience ready for (re)new(ed) modes of self- and community care. Here are some of their favorite remedies.

Bianca

I owe much of my life to my grandmother's wisdom with plants and her unconditional care. As a child, I had weekly, daylong vomiting fits. Even now, when I am extremely stressed or nervous, my body seizes up with nausea. Doctors didn't know what to do and sent me home without a diagnosis.

My grandmother put me on a routine of peppermint tea. During my fits, she would hold me and comfort me until I fell asleep. She would reassure me that everything was going to be okay. It took roughly one year of this weekly therapy, and I was forever changed. With even more time, I went from an incredibly nerve-racked child to a moderately less anxious adult who no longer has her wonderful grandmother—but can calm her mind down on her own.

When stress grabs hold of my gut, I mentally reset myself. I do mindfulness practices as I boil my peppermint. I thank my body for its concern. I thank my body for trying to communicate to me using tactics that worked in my youth. I let myself feel my fear deeply and fully. I pinpoint it. I clarify with my body, "Is this where and why it hurts?" The loss of someone I love, an unexpected pregnancy, my job, a bill I can't pay this month? Then I ask, "But is this where we end? What's actually happening right here and now?" The answer is usually no. It hurts, but I'm not in immediate danger.

I say, "Body, if you let me, I can help us. But I can't do it doubled over in pain. I'm okay. We're okay."

I am usually folded over in a deep stretch once my kettle of hot water starts to whistle. I'm usually in a better place by the time I am sitting down, curled up with my cup. But ending with the tea is the essential, practical, and spiritual end to my anxiety-reducing ritual.

Peppermint tea has been used in the Caribbean for centuries. The menthol in the tea is said to be a mild muscle relaxer and antispasmodic. This means mint can stop the spasm of involuntary muscle, like your gut and your mind. It is also anti-inflammatory, helps relieve gas and bloating, and has a lot of antioxidants. Peppermint is just one of the five main types of mint used in Jamaica, where my beloved grandmother is from. While my grandmother can no longer hold me physically, there is an ancestral spiritual warmth from her hands on mine whenever I have a cup. I drink as an offering to her and to others who have paved my path, whose wisdom, joys, and horrors I inherited. I thank them all for their concern. I reassure all of them how tallawah I've become. I let myself move forward.

Bianca's Anxiety and Nausea Tea Recipe

- Cut up roughly 5 slices of ginger.
- Place ginger in a pot with 4 cups of water.
- Bring water to boil for 10–20 minutes to taste.
- In each cup you are serving, place a 1/4 cup of fresh peppermint leaves.
- Pour ginger tea over the peppermint.
- Steep for 5 minutes.
- Enjoy!

Ruth

We are an extension of the herbs that surround us.

In a dreamy part of the land sat this beauty: her roots were thick, covered by small purple flowers with beautiful long stems standing strong. Her leaves carried veins from her deep roots.

I asked my godmother what her name was and what her purpose was. She shared with me that her name was Vervain and that this herb was for Yemoja, the goddess of the ocean. She shared that she had many strengths but that it was really good for the womb.

After a while, I began to see vervain everywhere I went. I began to notice her more and more. I finally was able to taste her, and she was so sweet. She helped me release stress and even helped me have fluid dreams. I later learned that vervain is a natural sedative and relaxant that many people find useful for sleep troubles and anxiety. She also has been used to improve lactation for nursing mothers and as a natural treatment for painful menstruation. Vervain became my go-to herb, and she still is.

Preparing Tea

Recognize the vervain in nature, ask permission to have a piece of her, and tell her what you would like.

Example: *Good morning, Vervain, you are looking so beautiful and radiant today. I'd like your permission to have some of you so that I can make some tea. The tea will be for me so that my womb may be healed from any past trauma. I pray for clarity. Thank you so much!*

• Gently grab 2–3 stems of the herb.
• Wash it with warm water, place water in pot until boil, turn stove off, and place vervain in the pot.
• Cover it for 10–15 minutes.

You can add sugar if you'd like. I myself prefer honey as a sweetener.
Happy brewing!

Samantha

Herbs have been healing me and sustaining me from the womb, but until the Caribbean Healing Collective (CHC), I didn't feel connected to them. Learning the rituals and wisdom through herbs is a part of uncovering my history, and as a wise doula, Carmen, said, "[It's a part of] coming for all my grandma's shit!"

My relationship with herbalism is very much from my Jamaican background and began with herb and liquor elixirs to ease my asthma. I think it's crucial to realize just how much nature and herbs sustain us all in our daily lives. They've helped me heal from injuries both mental and physical and have pulled me up from the depths of depression when I felt like I wasn't enough. Herbs have poured into me, and a part of my journey with the CHC is to pour back into them and to thank them for all the ways they've kept me and continue to keep me. My offering is a tea that both relaxes and fills me with warmth, desire, and a deep restfulness.

Sam's Calming and Relaxing Tea

- 1 teaspoon of lavender (helps nausea, headaches, upset stomach, and bloating)
- 2–3 teaspoons of rosebuds (detoxifies, an anti-inflammatory, good for skin)
- 2–3 teaspoons of moringa (an anti-inflammatory full of nutrients)
- 1–3 teaspoons of lemongrass (relieves anxiety, pain, and has a lot of antioxidants)
- Optional for sweetness: honey (rich in antioxidants)
- Also optional: gotu kola and chamomile (to intensify the feeling)

Add herb ingredients to a cheesecloth or tea strainer and place in boiling water. Steep for 4–5 minutes, then let sit for an additional 5 minutes to ensure that all the herbs have been thoroughly released. Then you can add honey to temper the sometimes spicy taste of the lemongrass.

Feel free to accompany this tea with some candles, a good book, and any other items that help you de-stress after a long day.
    Enjoy!

Lessons in Queer Community Building: Fear, Yearning, and Loving in Milwaukee

Charmaine Lang

My partner, Lynnae, and I were driving, engaged in our usual griping at the utterly reckless ways some Milwaukee drivers shit on safety laws while behind the wheel.

It's become a car game of sorts. I'm usually the one who points out disregard for red lights and how numerous cars bogart the bike lane. But I realized, as we complained about unsafe drivers, that I wanted to step back from our traffic complaints and imagine a community where we feel truly safe, seen, and connected. Underneath the surface of this routine conversation lurked deeper concerns that here in one of the nation's most segregated cities, Milwaukee, we—a Black queer couple—always feel unsafe.

We often talk about our future but from a more practical standpoint: moving to a warmer climate, career goals, which one of us will carry a pregnancy, the type of home we want to create together. I wanted us to envision living our dreams but in conversation now.

Lynnae indulged me, and we discussed everything from community gardening and neighborhood cookouts to working and living alongside our colleagues. But it became clear that we yearned for a queer, safe, and affirming community. And it became clear that my partner, who was not out as bisexual at work at the time, wanted to live a more integrated life where safety as a bisexual woman was not only guaranteed but was the norm. Where she could easily be herself at home, work, and play. This world we were envisioning together consisted of joy, fun, and connection—words we rarely feel in our current city, a place committed to centering privileged white people.

In this place called home, we are vulnerable to racist, sexist, or homophobic attacks. How do we access joy, I wondered, if we aren't consistently dreaming about it and making portals for its existence in our lives?

Talking about joy and desires easily forgotten when stressed, our tones softened. Our body language shifted. We smiled.

I was curious about how other Black, queer Milwaukeeans create community. So I arranged a brunch at my house with two people I adore: my partner, a thirty-nine-year-old teacher from the Midwest, and her best friend, Kwame, a queer thirty-three-year-old doctor and Milwaukee native I've come to know better through thrift shopping and over salmon BLT sandwiches from a shared favorite restaurant.

This is not the first time we convened over food at my place; it's become a ritual for us to eat, play games, and talk about work, romance, and travel.

Over plates of scrambled eggs, crispy bacon, sautéed spinach, and cherries, I asked them what it means to be queer, bisexual, Black, and professionals in this place.

Charmaine Lang: How do you all find community here in Milwaukee?

Lynnae: I come to your house and invite people over for food. But I don't have a place that I go, where I like to mingle with people. I was going to the gym pretty regularly, but I didn't make the effort to meet people or to expand the relationship beyond "I recognize you; you're the grunting guy."

Kwame: How Charmaine has formed community is pretty impressive for me, here in Milwaukee. The first time I came over here I was like, "Look at all these beautiful Black people."

I can sense that there's some queerness here, but everyone's definitely not queer. But it's queer-comfortable. If someone from California came and did this, did that here in my city, what am I doing wrong?

Charmaine: Absolutely nothing. How did I meet those folks? The person who is central to me is my friend Akua, and she's no longer in Milwaukee. And before she and her family moved, they used to always have community functions at their house, which is where I met many of the people who I am still in community with and where I learned how to build community in the first place.

I learned through my friend and her gatherings that community making is consistent and compassionate. I always try to have a self-care component in the gatherings I now have, whether that's making essential oil spritzers or meditating. It's so important that we get grounded with ourselves and each other when we build community.

Charmaine: How do you find community with LGBTQ people?

Lynnae: I don't do anything specific. I don't really have a community that's specifically gay. My community is specifically Black, but not gay.

Kwame: I relate with what Lynnae is saying. I don't take special care to develop a Black queer or gay community. I probably more often than not just do things that I'm really into, like going dancing, taking dance classes, pursuing a Bible study class, being active in the community. And then in those spaces, community forms naturally.

Charmaine: So, Lynnae, you identify as bisexual?

Lynnae: I do. I do. But I'm not as out as. . . . I would consider myself not out, but, apparently, some of my mannerisms and my interactions with [Charmaine] specifically are outing me more and more. I'm having difficulty not being affectionate in public. Or I want you to come to different spaces with me, where it's clear like, "She's [repeatedly] bringing the same person as her friend. Something is up." But if I was as out as maybe I could be, maybe I would make more effort to connect with the queer community because my only interaction intentionally with queer people is when I go out dancing, which is rare because I'm so busy these days.

Even when I was a student, and I had all the time, my only interaction for years was when I joined a queer discussion group. That was a very safe space for me, very warm space for me. I was upset with myself that I had waited so long to connect intentionally with queer individuals and specifically queer people of color. I felt like I thrived in that environment.

And then I was nominated for the community awards. I declined it because I wasn't ready to be out in that capacity, and I was [job] interviewing at the time as well.

All I could think about was because you have this ceremony and you get your picture, you're going to be on the university website, and if a potential employer did a Google search and it popped up, how would that affect my chances of gaining employment?

It was like very shameful for me to admit that I didn't want that . . . because the community was there for me, and I wasn't there for them.

Kwame: Do you experience concern right now about your interactions with Charmaine? People in Milwaukee, I believe, could reasonably be expected to react very negatively to same-gender loving expression in public. Is that on your mind?

Lynnae: Never. Never. The thing that I've grown used to hearing, which is a form of violence, is men asking for me and my partner to do things for them. Like if they approach one of us, it's like, "Oh no, that's my girlfriend." They say, "Oh, word? Kiss her. Let me see some shit." Or "You all should make out, or why don't you all come over to the house?" Things like that. But I'm never concerned about my safety in the sense of someone's going to attack. I do get concerned when you're telling men no, and they just don't want to hear no as an answer.

Kwame: Being a woman in a world where men are aggressive in that space?

Lynnae: Mm-hmm [affirmative].

Charmaine: That's a good question, Kwame. Have you ever felt any threat of violence or just concerns of safety?

Kwame: Growing up, I think I've never been a fully straight, "hetero-appearing" kind of child. So, yes, as a kid, I experienced some violent things, even though I wasn't kissing someone or holding someone's hand. I was merely walking or listening to music or whatever. But coming into my life as an adult, no. Not as much.

But I think I've done better at masking. As I grew older, I've learned to be a person who will avoid actions [that flag me as gay] with what is in my power. I have conformed to a certain degree where I think some people don't see me. They see me as unattached. Maybe there's a question about my sexuality, but there's no just like, gay, gay, gay, gay . . .

But I feel that if my partner and I were affectionate somewhere that there could be words approaching violence or words necessitating a response that then encourages conflict, whether it just be verbal conflict or actual physical conflict.

Being able to express affection for your partner should be as easy as breathing. Like oxygen is just here, and we can take it in.

My breathing doesn't affect the way that you breathe. For some reason, the way that people express affection with their partners affects
someone else's existence. It doesn't make sense to me. Why does that
image cause a physiological response in your body, to get angry, and
then what moves you to act out on it? How is your life decreased,
affected, depreciated that you need to do something to "correct" it?
How does that happen?

That gets in the way of community. In forming community in Milwaukee, if you're a Black person living in Black spaces and you're
queer, you want to avoid getting hurt. If you ain't got the safety of
your body, the safety of your person, you don't got nothing. If forming
community or having affectionate moments with your partners puts
that at risk, you are obviously going to choose to be safe.

Charmaine: Ideally, what would you all want a Black queer community
to look like in Milwaukee?

Lynnae: Definitely has to be supportive of the different lifestyles of
Blackness. But not catering to this idea that we are a monolith. A lot
of variation between ages, between socioeconomic status, having the
flexibility for people to exist along the scale of earning potential or
earnings. I wouldn't want it to be a hundred percent queer. I would
want it to be diverse in sexual orientation and sexual identity. And
ideally Black because I feel that those are the spaces that I can be
my most authentic me. Even taking into consideration queerness, I
would advocate for Blackness before queerness.

Charmaine: Really?

Lynnae: Mm-hmm. That may be because I don't operate in queerness
enough to find where it's safe, where it's comforting, where it's nurturing, where it's delicious. In the same ways that I've been able to
experience that in Black-centered spaces.

Charmaine: What is your vision for community?

Kwame: It would include diverse sexual orientations of people of color.
Not just Black people. I would definitely need my own core group
of Black folks to be with, but it's important to me to include other
people. I first mean Latino and then after that Southeast Asians and
people who identify with being refugees. [Community means] a
minimum standard at which everyone can have a civil conversation,
think critically, engage and listen to each other. That would be really
important for my community.

I feel like I was fortunate enough to have a good family and a good community when I was growing up. I want that for myself now. The community that I would form would be distinguished from the community I grew up with in the way that we could have honest, open dialogue and conversation, really being able to discuss [any topic] and redistribution of power. [My community would operate with] a disregard of the old social order rules governing who can do what.
Charmaine: Amen.

From this interview and other gatherings with beloved community, I learned we can do collectively what we can't do in isolation: envision and practice what community needs to be for us and for us to be healthy individuals.

This conversation was just one of many—conducted in multiple homes and restaurants and over board games, or making herbal medicines, or during travel—with my partner and friends. As I was writing this piece, I reminisced over our time together creating, recreating, and maintaining community. Lynnae shared with me that just recently, she and Kwame slowly started coming out to colleagues.

I asked what changed for them both. Her response had me in tears: "I think being in love helps with us being out. We want to celebrate that space. You don't want to hide it. You want the world to know."

Word Is Bond: A Ritual

Taja Lindley

In Echoing Ida, we understand the power of words. They are magic, capable of changing our world, our outlooks, our lives—for better and for worse. Words and stories are dangerous and delicious. Here, Ida Taja Lindley—an artist who defies any one label, such as "performer," "writer," "healer"—taps into the sacred power and promise of the Word. Not in the biblical sense, mind you, but capitalized because the words that we speak, hear, and write create reality. She shares this meditation on the Word and a ritual that you can do to connect with the world and with yourself.

There is power in what we say.

And there is power in what we write.

The word—written, spoken, and in our heads—is a form of energy that makes anything possible.

When legislators write policies, they affect government programs and services. When journalists publish articles, they inform, educate, and persuade the public. When novelists publish books, they invite us into new worlds and spark our imagination.

Ida B. Wells awakened and shifted the national conversation on racism by documenting lynching in pamphlets and speeches. Tina Turner used words and mantras to courageously leave an abusive relationship. Octavia Butler wrote her desires on a piece of paper, and we know that she achieved her dreams—if only posthumously. They all have one thing in common: their word.

Word is bond.

Our words lose meaning, value, and power when what we say and what we do are not in alignment. "I'll call you back in five minutes." "This will take two seconds." "I love you"—when we know things will take longer or we do not authentically express how we (don't) feel.

The alignment of our words with our actions is called integrity. And every time you maintain your integrity, you strengthen the power of your words.

When witches cast spells, they use their words to call in and wield energies. When people speak in tongues, they are speaking the language of their God. And when we write down our goals and our dreams, they come to be.

Spirit and the word are connected, so choose your words carefully. Keep your promises. Follow through on your commitments. Only say what you mean.

It is with the power of the word that we can create.

Thoughts that repeatedly run through our minds and that we say with our mouths become beliefs. We have the ability to shift beliefs with affirmations by thinking and saying affirming words over and over again.

As a Gemini rising, I'm obsessed with words. I place written affirmations on altars, under my pillows, next to candles, above my desk, and on my mirror so that my daily tasks and activities are infused with the power of my words. The dry-erase boards above my desk read: "I expect infinite blessings from unforeseen places to shower over my life." "Every day I create the life I desire." "I am a commitment to my authentic and enthusiastic yes."

Affirmations have saved me from thoughts and beliefs steeped in fear and perfectionism and given me the momentum to pivot toward my dreams with courage and purpose.

I wasn't always so willing to write my words down on paper. When I was twelve, my diary was read without my permission. I was made to read my words aloud, get on my knees, apologize, and beg for forgiveness. While my words were scathing, they were my truth, and I was punished for expressing myself.

I learned then that the written word could be dangerous.

But fifteen years later, when I picked up journaling again, I remembered Audre Lorde's wisdom: "Your silence will not protect you." Best to write anyway, speak anyway, tell the truth anyway.

Infuse your life with the power of words.

*

Create some sacred time for yourself. By "sacred" I mean uninterrupted, with your devices off, no distractions, with the intention to be alone and in communion with your inner self. You need paper and a pen for this activity.

Close your eyes or lower your gaze and take three deep clarifying breaths. You can deepen your breathing by inhaling for as long as you're able through your nose. Then you exhale for as long as you're able through your mouth. Take the time to really breathe.

And continue to breathe.

Take your hands and rub them together, generating heat from the friction. When you've gathered enough heat, bring your hands to your neck. The place where you speak, share your voice, and tell your truth. Feel the energy pulsating from your palms.

And continue to breathe.

With your breath, say something kind about and to yourself. If you're feeling stuck on what to say, here are some words to inspire you:

I am love. I am lovable. I am loving. I am loved.

I am a powerful creator of my life experience.

When I speak, the universe hears me and responds accordingly.

My every word is a prayer.

I speak my truth, even when it may be uncomfortable or inconvenient because I understand that what I have to share and say needs to be heard.

My story is important, and I tell it with peace and ease.

Say what resonates over and over again. It's a mantra. Spend as much time as you need in this repetition.

When you're ready, pick up your pen and bring it to your paper. Spend your time freewriting (writing without forethought or judgment) to the following questions.

You don't have to answer them all but choose the one(s) that you like the most and the one(s) that you like the least. Anything you have a strong reaction to (good or bad) deserves some investigation and attention.

Set a timer for seven minutes to freewrite for each question you choose.

- What story have you yet to tell? Are there family secrets that have gone unspoken? Incidents that have been swept under the rug and have gone unaddressed? Dirty laundry that deserves to be aired and faced? Unburden yourself and write that story now.
- Write a letter to your younger self. What would you tell yourself knowing what you know now? Write your name. Literally write to yourself.
- If our world were free from every form of oppression, how would you spend your time? What would you create? Who would you be? And why?
- Complete the sentence (as many times as you can in seven minutes): I feel most powerful when _____.
- Take a look at the gap between where you are now and where you want to be (this can apply to any area of your life). What encouraging words can you come up with to be the bridge between these spaces?

When you're done, take time to reread your writing and underline words, phrases, and sentences that speak to you and jump off of the page. Think about a poetry reading, when the poet says something that strikes a chord with the audience and everyone says, "Mmmmm!" Find those chords in your own writing.

Did you find any affirmations? Mantras? Perhaps you discovered spaces that need healing or uncovered beliefs that are not serving you well. Acknowledge your "ah-ha moments" and the spaces and places where you still have questions.

Based on your writing and underlined phrases, create a list of what you want to believe, what you want to create, and who you want to become. Speak in the affirmative—stay away from words like "no," "not," and "don't." Place these words somewhere where you can see them and read them every day. Notice how your beliefs and your life begin to change.

ONWARD

Sometimes, the Struggle Isn't With "Them." It's between Us.

Cynthia R. Greenlee and Charmaine Lang

Black women writers have always shared our gifts. This anthology you are holding, in some fashion, is but the latest in a line of late-twentieth-century compilations—collective conversations, really. It exists because Toni Cade Bambara edited *The Black Woman* anthology in 1970. Because the very press that published *The Echoing Ida Collection* also published *But Some of Us Are Brave: Black Women's Studies* by Akasha (Gloria T.) Hull, Patricia Bell-Scott, and Barbara Smith in 1982. It exists because *Home Girls*, a Black feminist anthology that collected the works of feminist and lesbian authors, came a year after that. Ida Charmaine Lang has researched both Audre Lorde's and Toni Cade Bambara's archival collections, which rest with so much love at the Spelman College Archives. She saw the many women of these anthologies—the makers and mothers of the Black feminist canon—in a much more intimate way: through their letters. Their letters are evidence of creativity, conflict, and their unconditional commitment to Black relationship and healing. Their blueprint is simple: it starts with the vulnerability of being seen, of naming and questioning what has brought us to points of difference and discord, then offering a path for reconciliation.

The letters that follow—a correspondence between Lang and coeditor Cynthia R. Greenlee, two Idas who have shared a long friendship and a period of estrangement—use this same blueprint. In the spirit of their writer-ancestors, they explore the collaborative epistolary essay as both a writing tool and terrain for the emotional work of rebuilding a fractured bond. Our work is not just the words.

345

Dear Cynthia,

It was during the Take Root Conference in Oklahoma that we first met. When was that? 2013? 2014? We were in a session together and we shared a bit about our PhD woes and anxieties. You were further along and almost complete with your program. I remembered you shared with me gems that continue to guide me through the intermittently painful journey of PhD study.

"Find a supportive community external from the academy. Make sure you have an advisor of the heart, someone who is in your corner. And understand that this process ain't forever."

That was the beginning of our friendship: you doling out tips to survive the harshness of academe.

If you felt any eyes on you during the conference, you were right. I followed you around, studying you like there would be a test afterward. Wanting to know the secrets that you held, and how you got to be so damn smart, masterful with language.

I listened to every word you said, storing the words that were new to me, to look up its meaning, its root, how to use it in a sentence and add it to my own vocabulary, which always feels inferior next to yours. I'm not comparing. Not anymore at least. I'm expressing just how much you inspire me to do better. To be better.

You are a journalist. And intentional.

You craft sentences into meaning and in the process create worlds.

This is only one of your gifts.

After years of friendship, countless venting about institutional abuse, sharing of more tips (both for success in academic life and love), the end and beginning of significant relationships in both our lives, something shifted. A thing happened that couldn't be chalked up to Mercury in retrograde.

Perhaps I was being reckless in how I imagined love—I abandoned any need to reconcile my yearning to be in a loving relationship, with my carnal desire to be fucked when and how I wanted. My relentless pursuit for both worried you. I know this now because you told me later. But at the time, you called me a sex addict. Almost insistent that I needed recovery from an addiction you diagnosed me with.

    and after the third time you uttered those words
    you began to shape a world that held no space for me

to exist as the messy spirit that I am
seeking: good dick and better love
and capacious friendships
where we use our words to craft worlds
so that we all live satisfying lives.

Dear Charmaine,

I also remember that Take Root meeting and our talk in a table shoved in the corner, so close to the bathroom that odors wafted in our direction. And what I remember most? That the Wi-Fi was spotty. And upon first glance at you, thinking how cute your reddish-blonde locs were. I envied your hair.

But looking back on that conversation, I realize much of my sharing was a release about the hazing people believe is a part of pursuing a PhD—and how good it was to talk with someone who knew a bit of that world. But it also allowed me to give advice (and I'm surprised that you remember it so specifically, in more detail than I did—and those words came from my brain, my mouth, and my experience). That also allowed me to wax forth and be a know-it-all or at least—if I'm being generous with myself—demonstrate my knowledge. And if there's one thing about myself, it's that I like knowing things and showing that I know them. Occasionally. Well, maybe frequently.

And this is where I went astray—and part of my discomfort with my role in Echoing Ida. I started as an Ida needing help and wanting community—and ended as an Ida editor dispensing help and wanting community. But even so, I was always positioned as someone with superior knowledge because I had a professional journalism background and had published a bit. I liked that authority but also knew that it separated me from the group—and while this might not make sense, it derailed our friendship for a time in this setting. The idea that I knew something about the search for love, as I went through a hard marital implosion. The idea that I knew you, after many conversations about the woman who so obviously cared little for you as you flew repeatedly across the country to meet her and were faced with her half-hearted welcome. That we knew each other so well that I could give and you could take unsolicited opinion. And no one REALLY wants advice they didn't ask for—and much of the advice you get when you request it.

Or that, worst of all, I ventured an opinion about the health of your desires. That was the most egregious part of it all. I look back on my words and think "What was I thinking?" I knew, before I suggested that you were looking for sex and companionship in a self-destructive way, that going *there* was a danger zone. And part of my misguided "diagnosis" had to do with my uncertain grasp of polyamory and my own commitment to "serial monogamy."

You said little in response to my tentative question about whether you were looking for love and sex—let's differentiate the two—in the wrong places. I thought I chose my words carefully (so much for self-awareness or "reading the room"). But you were clearly offended. But I didn't know how offended until you stopped communicating. Cold turkey. Full stop. No texts, no phone conversations. Nada.

How long did that stretch on? I can't remember now. Just that it was looong. Months. I felt hurt. Then mad that you obviously didn't want to speak to me.

I stewed in it. Chewed on it.

Was that your intent? Thought about texting—I think I did to test the waters—but no response.

Your silence made me reckon with my stupid mouth and my culpability. Made me roll the words "I'm sorry" on my tongue like something I resisted swallowing. If apologies have tastes, these two words are vinegary and sharp.

The words were so hard to say to myself, I didn't know how I would ever say them to you.

Then, enter Echoing Ida. Kemi told me that you would be attending the Allied Media Conference in Detroit. I was also attending. Kemi chattered about how we could hang together, see Brittany, be Idas together in a sea of thousands. I didn't tell them at first that we weren't exactly friends anymore.

Then, you reached out. You did, right? I'd like to think I am a grown-ass person and could admit my wrongness, but you made the first move. I thought momentarily about not going to the conference at all, skirting the issue and our tattered friendship like a broke-down car stranded in the middle of the street. I resolved to apologize—no matter how defensive I felt.

You didn't make it easy, but neither did you make it hard. As uncomfortable as I was, I admired your tenacity in holding my feet to the fire and not budging under my gaze and fidget. You were like steel and blossoms. Not magnolias, like in that movie about determined Southern womanhood. Steel and frangipani, I thought.

Later, much more recently, I recalled out loud that "You asked my advice." You said quietly but firmly, "I don't remember asking you for advice." Well, damn.

Sisterhood is powerful, but complicated. And I hesitate to even use that word here. Because it's so overused and underpracticed. I'm used to being called "sister" or "queen" on the street by Black men who will call me a "bitch" five seconds later when I ignore them or don't acknowledge their obvious greatness. I'm used to being called "sister" by Black women in the movement, even in Echoing Ida, who come for my neck when I don't play the way they want, when I'm not radical enough, when I edit hard because I want the world to see all of us at our best. Even Echoing Ida, during this tedious process of making this collection, when the editors stood accused of not advocating enough or caring about Black women. That angered and wounded me so. I'm too used to people calling me sister, soon after calling me everything but a child of God, saying "I love you" minutes later. And truth be told, unlike many Idas, I didn't come to Echoing Ida to find sisters. But I did find you.

Dear Cynthia,

Toni Cade Bambara's 1980 novel *The Salt Eaters* requires us to look within, to consider the question "Do we want to be well?"[1] And at what cost? To be healed, whole, and well were human experiences that I hadn't fully imagined before reading *The Salt Eaters.* And now, as I move into relationships with myself and others, I chew on what wellness looks like to me, and how to achieve the wholeness I desire. How to achieve the wholeness I desire, so that I can have thriving relationships of all sorts. So I ask myself a question inspired by Minnie Ransom, the novel's healer: We know we want to be well, but what does wellness look like, and how are we going after the wellness we so desire?

Dear Charmaine,

I know how I am supposed to answer Bambara's question.

But this pandemic season of 2020—losing my father, my dog, my livelihood, my mobility, my sense of safety as the Black body count from police killings grows into a mountain of limbs—has obliterated my wellness. Grief loosened my hair from its roots, unmoored me, and shattered my foundation. People don't tell you that grief can rip you open, leave you with a mortal wound that others can't see, a wound that will leave you breathing but an inch short of death.

I want to be well—but how does one do that in the time of plague and racial peril? I am so fatigued, my body and mind so compromised and overwhelmed with the minutiae of life, that all I can do each day is ONE thing. And that one thing, today, may be pouring milk on my cereal. Or going to the mailbox. Or cleaning the litter box (what a horrific chore, but one that lamentably gets worse the longer you delay).

The only way I know to be well is to allow myself to experience suffering and stillness, with no expiration date. I can't tell you how many times I've found myself mesmerized by the buzzing flight of some insect and lost track of time or what I was doing.

I allow myself the grace to be messy and mistake-full now, to be reflective and better in the future sans self-flagellation. Part of the reason I found it so hard to reengage with you is that I realized the gravity of my error and that I hurt you. I couldn't be blissfully ignorant. I had to reconcile that with myself before I could reconcile with you.

I'm careful to be in community when I want to be—and to disengage when I don't. I guard my time and essence (Tupac said, "Protect your essence!" in that posthumous collabo with Scarface) more closely, and it makes human interaction all the more poignant and Technicolor when I engage because I want to, when I choose the object of my attentions. I can no longer be bothered to trifle with those who do not appreciate me, love me, or respect me—at least one of those three is a prerequisite. And I find my best company is my personal trinity: me, myself, and I.

Dear Cynthia,

Most days I forget that we are even in a pandemic. The world has always been in panic mode to me. It's only now that a global alert exists.

Somewhere along the way of embodying queer Black womanhood, and being steeped in academe, I became an expert at bobbing and weaving with racism. Or at least noticing it from a mile away and detouring accordingly.

My struggle with getting through Toni Cade Bambara's *The Salt Eaters* most likely reflects my personal struggle with wellness. Do I want to be well? Hell yeah. Of course. I want to be well and whole.

Lately, my wellness is getting quiet, getting high, sitting still even for a brief moment, basking in the sounds of crystal quartz bowls, and regular therapy sessions.

How does wellness connect to our relationships? What I love about the letters between Black women writer-activist-cultural workers, scattered across archival collections nationwide, is the unapologetic way that Black women named their experiences and emotions. Not much unlike our own efforts here, to name the hurt that we both caused and felt. And are addressing.

When I think of us now, I am reminded of a letter Audre Lorde wrote to Pat Parker, a Black lesbian mother poet, 35 years ago: "When I did not receive an answer to my letter last spring, I took a long and painful look at the 15 years we have known each other and decided that I had to accept the fact that we would never have the openness of friendship I always thought could be possible being the two strong Black women we are, with all our differences and sameness. Then your card from Nairobi, and I thought once again maybe when I'm out there next spring Pat and I will sit down once and for all and look at why we were not more available to each other all these years."[2]

Aren't we blessed for having a model of how to forge a way through the sometimes necessary messiness of life?

We struggle together against forces seeking to swallow us whole. Patriarchy, sexism, racism, classism, homophobia, transphobia. When the struggle is closer to home, we struggle between wanting what's best for each other, and the projection of our fears, perhaps. Wellness then, looks like us adding compassion to our struggle between us.

I think that's why I'm so close to the letters, for what they teach me about life, loving, and being in relationship. Our Black feminist foremothers were neither perfect nor trying to pretend that perfection was even a goal. Their letters were vulnerable and freely expressed their disappointment in each other as easily as they did in systems meant to demean them. I love them for that. Their closing salutations carried gratitude and forever community vibes.

Beverly Smith, cofounder of the Combahee River Collective, often ended her letters with "I love you."[3] Bambara would sometimes sign off with "Overwhelmed, Toni."[4] And Lorde often closed with "In the hand of Afrekete."[5] Each salutation served as an open invitation for further dialogue between the writer and receiver. For those of us reading the letters, we bear witness to how transformation and love unfolds.

Let's end this note with love.

In Sisterhood and Struggle,
Charmaine

Notes

1. Bambara, Toni Cade, *The Salt Eaters* (New York: Vintage Books, 1980), 3.
2. Audre Lorde to Pat Parker, letter, December 6, 1985; Audre Lorde Papers, box 1, folder 4; Spelman College Archives.
3. Beverly Smith to Audre Lorde, letter, May 23, 1981; Audre Lorde Papers, box 5, folder 125, series 1.1; Spelman College Archives.
4. Toni Cade Bambara to Audre Lorde, letter, September 14; Audre Lorde Papers, box 1, folder 011, series 1.1; Spelman College Archives.
5. Audre Lorde to Evelynn Hammonds, letter, April 8, 1983; Audre Lorde Papers, box 1, folder 4; series 1.1; Spelman College Archives.

Bernie Is Not My Bro and Omarosa Is Not My Homegirl: Idas as Interrupters

Janna A. Zinzi

On a sweltering Saturday morning in Phoenix, hundreds of "progressive" leaders and activists from around the country gathered for the main event of Netroots Nation 2015. It was supposed to be a presidential forum of the Democratic candidates, but only Bernie Sanders and Martin O'Malley attended. Hillary Clinton didn't seem to think it was necessary to show up or even send a video (insert eye-roll emoji). Young white guys lined up all morning to get a seat at the front of this conference center auditorium so they could be close to their beloved Bernie. Folks were even dressed up in Robin Hood costumes to represent the redistribution of wealth and economic equality, Sanders's foundational talking point. Out there looking like it was Comic-Con.

Only a few days earlier, Sandra Bland was murdered by police in Texas. Mourning Black death was no novel feeling, but this hurt differently. Likely because she was a young Black woman, and we saw ourselves in her. She was/is us, our sister, our cousin, our homegirl. While her death and police violence were important topics for the Black attendees, Netroots is typically a very white tech bro space. Her murder went unaddressed in most plenaries or sessions. It was business as usual for white folks—even the "liberal," social justice–minded people who genuinely care about democracy. In response, Black organizers got together and planned an action during the presidential forum. We wanted to know the candidates' stance on police violence against Black people and ask them on the spot to address this very real and overlooked issue.

We wanted to know if they actually believed that Black lives matter.

Several Idas were at that Netroots. We came through as a squad and were busy hosting panels, running workshops, networking, being bosses. And we were most certainly going to participate in any action that elevated the voices of Black women amid a backdrop of white silence.

So when it came time for the presidential forum, a significant bloc of Black folks attending Netroots, as well as local activists, sat together in the back of the auditorium. I felt an exhilarating yet tense energy, currents of adrenaline pumping through us. Although we'd practiced for this action the day before, gathering at a local soul food restaurant to organize, share information, and break biscuits, I wasn't prepared for the reaction we got from the audience. When our group of dozens of Black comrades marched in two lines toward the stage asserting "Black Lives Matter," many people were angry and stunned. Their casual disregard and privileged blind spots were on full display . . . written all over their smug faces. Many a white boy was PISSED that we had the audacity to interrupt their messiah.

I stood on a chair in front of the stage, proudly sporting my marigold-colored Echoing Ida T-shirt, and recorded the whole incident. Idas, including Shanelle Matthews, Gloria Malone, and Amber Phillips, walked to the middle of the auditorium with other Black women activists for the most evocative and gut-wrenching aspect of the action. One by one, they stood on a chair and shouted their response to the prompt, "If I die in police custody . . ."

If I die in police custody, I want you to know I was murdered.
If I die in police custody, tell my daughter how much I love her.
If I die in police custody, keep fighting for justice.
Say my name.
Don't stop until we are free.

In return, our fellow conference attendees yelled at us to shut up, sit down, move out of their way, and let Bernie speak. A Latina dressed in a Robin Hood outfit was chanting, "We hear you," which was ironic and maddening because you can't hear anything if you're yelling over us. A young white woman asked me if I was okay and said she had my back. I wanted to believe her but was shaking with anger. I wonder if she understood how unsafe I felt surrounded by people who refused to acknowledge our humanity. When Sanders continued to try to deliver a stump speech about economic inequality despite being asked about his stance on police violence, we rolled out. Some people in the audience left with us. Some booed at us or clapped that we were leaving. A few people thanked us for educating them.

This event activated many of us in what is now known as the Movement for Black Lives. It also gave us permission to play a dual role as writers and activists. In journalism spaces where objectivity is a foundational principle, many Black writers cannot use their voices in dissent or visibly take a "political" stance.

But what do you do when your life is at stake?

This has become a critical conversation in 2020 public discourse for Black journalists covering the murders of George Floyd, Breonna Taylor, Ahmaud Arbery, and other Black folks who have been killed for minding their own business.

Fast-forward to 2017, another sweltering summer day but this time at the National Association of Black Journalists annual conference in New Orleans. It was the first time members of Echoing Ida attended as a group, and we felt excited and curious about being in a professional writing space as opposed to an advocacy-centered conference. It was certainly a more polished and "respectable" vibe than our typical conferences, but we attended panels discussing advocacy in journalism and Black women's reproductive health and justice. We ate oysters and drank cocktails in the street; it was dope.

But the good times stopped rolling when former reality TV star Omarosa Manigault, the newly crowned director of communications for Trump's Office of Public Liaison, got added to the schedule as a last-minute addition. In the most disrespectful fashion, she was added to a panel titled Black and Blue: Raising Our Sons, Protecting Our Communities, which was about police violence *with* relatives of Philando Castile and Alton Sterling. This after *her* president encouraged police at a rally to rough up suspects even more (translation: fuck up Black and Brown folks). High-level gaslighting and totally on brand. Nikole Hannah Jones of the *New York Times* and Jelani Cobb of the *New Yorker* were supposed to participate but pulled out when Omarosa was added. Shout out to them for not participating in a propaganda shit show.

The panel ends up being in a room that can accommodate maybe a quarter of the conference, making it impossible for a couple of us Idas and dozens of attendees to get in. I was fussing HARD for a moment, but after a smoke break, Jasmine Burnett and I made our way in. We squeezed into a row with fellow Ida Renee Bracey Sherman and sat with some prominent Black women in politics and punditry, including Brittany Packnett. As Omarosa deflected questions about her culpability in the Trump administration's reprehensible support of police violence, Packnett stood up and put her back to her. I'm pretty sure many in that room wanted to do the same but that could have put their jobs on the line. We stood up too with our backs to Omarosa, who maintained a pompous and dismissive attitude toward legitimate questions like, "What have you done for Black people lately?" A few other journalists joined the protest, but what I remember most is facing the audience: a sea of good-looking, smart af, professional Black media folks who were livid. Some were shouting retorts against her lies. Some left the room entirely. Some were furiously typing but pretty much everyone was unimpressed. After it was over, many attendees thanked us, which felt strange because why wouldn't we do that? It was then that I understood the challenge of being a Black journalist tethered to "objectivity" when our lives are literally at the hands of misinformation.

The political moment of 2020 is illuminating all of the hypocrisy within our movements and that anti-Blackness is inherent in all of our systems, whether it's media, politics, entertainment, or social justice. In the spirit of Ida B. Wells, it is our mandate to speak out against injustice and anti-Blackness, whether with pens, laptops, or our bodies. We do not just write about activism or justice for our communities; we also take action, even when we are afraid. When we are called to show up, we also show out. Free speech is a privilege we don't take lightly. We

Suzette Hackney ✓
@suzyscribe

Attendees are standing and turning their backs to Omarosa Manigault's #NABJ17 panel participation. Others are walking out.

1:39 PM · Aug 11, 2017 · Twitter for iPhone

voice uncomfortable truths for our folks who can't due to real threats of retaliation. We protest for our people challenging the status quo from within our toxic institutions. The double consciousness of Black life in America is exhausting. Censorship—even self-censorship—in the name of "objectivity" can no longer eclipse our humanity.

Reverse Haiku for Black Writers
When the Calls for Pitches Are Too Much

Cynthia R. Greenlee

In the summer of 2020, when Minnesota resident George Floyd was murdered by police officer Derek Chauvin kneeling on his neck for nearly nine minutes, it sparked a wave of uprisings around the country. Protests galvanized and paralyzed cities as different and diverse as the nation's preeminent Chocolate City and capital Washington, DC, and the whitey-white reaches of Portland, Oregon. Floyd's death at the hands of law enforcement was just one of many killings of Black Americans, but it also prompted an unprecedented media push and reckoning. Editors sought out Black writers for hot takes, commentaries, and freelance writing gigs. "Please pitch us," editors who'd never evinced an interest in Black writers suddenly tweeted, referring to the industry term for proposals for upcoming articles. The Associated Press revised its long-standing rule and said that when using "black" as a racial descriptor, that it should be capitalized. Call it the Great Black Gold Rush of 2020—in which Black opinions became a priceless commodity for a brief exhilarating moment of extraction. Except prices WERE attached to Black-authored words. And too often, the journalistic mainstream wanted Black creatives to expose our wounds for a pittance, barely a week's worth of groceries or a utility bill. This series of Twitter haiku responded to the editorial feeding frenzy that left many Black writers wondering if we should seize the day when Black pain was in vogue and white editors primed to publish. Or should we recuse ourselves from this latest fifteen minutes of race-based fame when it seemed that almost any Black writer would do?

No. 1

Editors want Black writers
To bleed out neatly
In print so the whites will learn

No. 2

Black death is the rage again.
Black lives and essays
Are cheap. DMs open now.

No. 3

One might think that Black writers
Are as hard to find
As the African quagga

No. 4

Your magazine has one or
No Black editors.
But I should write for it. Why?

No. 5

Don't write "white supremacy."
Too harsh for readers . . .
"Implicit bias?"

No. 6

All the calls for Black writers
Made me check the date.
Is it Black History Month?

Toward Our Black Feminist Future

Kemi Alabi

It's July 2020. America's shattered mask litters the ground. A pandemic blew it down, made kindling. A viral lynching struck a match, made fire. Cities still blaze—coast to coast and further still. A whole globe heating. Our future awaiting claim.

A new and defiant virus, COVID-19, continues to stun the world. Its unhampered spread through the United States revealed all our systemic shams. The Trump regime sacrificed our lives for its economy, protecting business as usual with each late and bumbling move. Everything from housing to employment to media let our people free-fall into the unknown. With health, care, and safety kept beyond what most can afford, we plumb new depths of sick and tired. Only our death toll reigns supreme, far surpassing every nation with over 150,000—and more by the literal minute,[1] with Black folks dying at a rate three times higher than white.[2]

Meanwhile, the old pandemic rages. Police continue to protect property and serve power by killing us, killing us, killing us. We watched George Floyd's last eight minutes and forty-six seconds. Murder taught us Tony McDade and Breonna Taylor's names. Gunned down in the street. Shot dead in her bed. *Her bed.* Reports show twelve Black trans people murdered so far this year: along with McDade, we lost Monika Diamond, Nina Pop, Dominique "Rem'mie" Fells," Riah Milton, Brian "Egypt" Powers, Brayla Stone, Merci Mack, Shaki Peters, Bree Black, Dior H. Ova, and Queasha D. Hardy.[3]

May this monthslong uprising—the largest protest movement to hit this country[4]—grant rest to all our snatched kin, including those whose names we'll never know. Swelling through the spring, radicalizing Juneteenth, and continuing to rage through the summer, demands to defund the police and respect all Black life continue to fill our streets and screens. What home, what workplace, what industry remains untouched by this blaring freedom call? A charge fills the air, and it's the undeniable power of the people. The mutual aid networks we've formed to secure what we need—from groceries to abortions—are up and running, growing fast. No one else is coming to save us. No one can love and lead us like we do.

We're living through a Black feminist prophecy. Didn't Octavia Butler show us? Her *Earthseed* science fiction series depicted the rise of an autocratic American president. Unchecked corporate power, massive wealth inequality, slashed safety nets, and climate disaster bred disease and social devolution. Left to save ourselves, Lauren Olamina, the fifteen-year-old disabled Black protagonist, led the willing into a new world.

Didn't the Combahee River Collective tell us? *If Black women were free, it would mean that everyone else would have to be free since our freedom would necessitate the destruction of all the systems of oppression.*[5] We tried to sound the alarm, but where are they in this house? Once found and ringing, who answered the call? Who delighted in the noise?

No one else is coming to save us. No one can love and lead us like we do.

The chants have changed since the Movement for Black Lives first emerged. *Indict! Convict! Send those killer cops to jail!* The whole fucking system's still guilty as hell, but the demand deepened to the root and its sever: abolition. And didn't Miss Major show us? Didn't Angela Y. Davis tell us?

As prison abolitionist and scholar Ruth Wilson Gilmore says, "Abolition is about presence, not absence. It's about building life-affirming institutions." What would it look like to practice this presence, this life affirmation, so generously with ourselves and one another that our imaginations stretch and swirl with it? Wouldn't it be easier to feel into and build the world that comes after this one? A world where health, care, and safety are within everyone's reach?

When I think of such care, I remember the tender ways Echoing Ida writers have held each other over the years. I've witnessed this community bloom and shift and wither and break. I've witnessed and been complicit in the way institutions—media, nonprofits—gobble up and spit out Black truth tellers. It's a community I've failed. It's a community that's failed me. We are each capable of great acts of care and just as great acts of harm. To practice healing and transformation instead of punishment and disposal is perhaps the greatest call of our time.

We can wait for no one else. We must try and fail and try and fail—with our imperfect plans and imperfect selves—to build a world free enough to hold us.

The media and movement factors that birthed Echoing Ida have shifted countless times, but the call for truth remains the same, and the writers in these pages and beyond will continue to answer—with new stories, in new mediums, through new moments of chaos and triumph. We have no other choice. The Black feminist future awaits our claim. May the wisdom documented in these pages travel to those who seek it. May we hold tight these truths, declared at our 2018 retreat, that helped set our visions free.

We are Echoing Ida, and we believe . . .

In writing as liberatory practice.

In narrative honesty and intellectual boldness.

Black brilliance is not rare or the exception. It is common and necessary.

We locate the possibility of our lives through pleasure.

Abundance and pleasure are our birthright.

The future is borderless, abundant, and in color.

We are a portal, a balm, a forcefield.

Our truth is the key to every locked door.

We will win.

Notes

1. "US Records a Coronavirus Death Every Minute as Toll Tops 150,000," *Aljazeera*, July 30, 2020, https://www.aljazeera.com/news/2020/07/records-coronavirus-death-minute-toll-tops-150000-200730034507419.html.
2. "The COVID Racial Data Tracker," The COVID Tracking Project, accessed July 30, 2020, https://covidtracking.com/race.

3. "Fatal Violence against the Transgender and Gender Non-Conforming Community in 2020," Human Rights Campaign, accessed July 30, 2020, https://www.hrc.org/resources/violence-against-the-trans-and-gender-non-conforming-community-in-2020.

4. Larry Buchanan, Quoctrung Bui, and Jugal K. Patel, "Black Lives Matter May Be the Largest Movement in U.S. History," *New York Times*, July 3, 2020, https://www.nytimes.com/interactive/2020/07/03/us/george-floyd-protests-crowd-size.html.

5. Combahee River Collective, "The Combahee River Collective Statement" (1978), reprinted in *Home Girls: A Black Feminist Anthology*, ed. Barbara Smith (New York: Kitchen Table/Women of Color Press, 1983), 264–74.

Contributor Biographies

Emma Akpan is her mother's daughter, a wayward church girl, and writer whose heart rests with Black girls everywhere. A graduate of Duke Divinity School, Emma currently attends Metropolitan AME Church in Washington, DC, and continues writing on the intersections of religion, race, pop culture, and sexuality.

Renee Bracey Sherman is a reproductive justice activist, abortion storyteller, strategist, and writer. She is the founder and executive director of We Testify, an organization dedicated to the leadership and representation of people who have abortions, and executive producer of *Ours to Tell*, an award-winning documentary elevating the voices of people who've had abortions.

Brittany Brathwaite is a reproductive justice activist, entrepreneur, and community accountable scholar. She has a deep-seated commitment to supporting the leadership, organizing, and healing of girls and women of color. She is currently a doctoral student in critical social psychology at the CUNY Graduate Center.

Jasmine Burnett is a third-generation midwesterner whose Black lesbian feminist identity informs her writing and culture work. Her writing explores topics of midwestern regional identities, race, gender, sexuality, and equity in the cannabis sector. As an herbalist and gardener, she delights in making medicine to sustain her practice of interdependent living and community building.

Bianca Campbell holds network building strategy at Forward Together and has doulaed births, abortions, and personal transformations. Through her holistic mind-body wellness practice, Bianca supports activists of color for the liberation work ahead. You can connect with her on Instagram at @spektrawellness and @caribhealingcollective, the latter co-led with fellow Idas.

The **Carib Healing Collective** is a small and growing group of people across the Caribbean diaspora who seek community and a deeper knowledge of healing practices, handmade medicines, Caribbean history, and culture. To connect follow @caribhealingcollective on Instagram.

Samantha Daley is a Jamaican, queer, Black feminist whose origins in the movement are deeply rooted in reproductive justice. She is a cofounder of the Carib Healing Collective, which aims to heal and connect the Caribbean diaspora through herbalism, affirmation, and political education of Caribbean legacy.

Elizabeth Dawes Gay is a social entrepreneur and thought leader whose life mission is to create a world where womxn of color have what they need to achieve their ideal well-being. Elizabeth's lived experience as a Black woman in the United States drives her to fight injustice and create a more equitable world.

Yamani Hernandez is a Black, intersex, queer, nonbinary mom from Chicago. She is a seasoned parent and nonprofit and reproductive justice leader committed to radical compassion, healing justice, and personal and political transformation. Yamani has led the National Network of Abortion Funds since 2015.

Ruth Jeannoel is a Haitian American cultural organizer, holistic healer, and writer. Currently, Ruth serves as the founder and director of the growing nonprofit Fanm Saj, Inc. in Miami. Ruth believes in the personal being political and has a strong commitment to providing communities with tools to re-create our own stories for the sake of Black Liberation.

Charmaine Lang is a North Carolina–based writer whose work focuses on the intersections of race, gender, and wellness. As a researcher,

Charmaine uses ethnographic methods to examine the social and economic determinants of self-care practices among Black women activists in the Midwest.

Taja Lindley is an artist, healer, memory worker, and activist based in Brooklyn, where she works as the managing member of Colored Girls Hustle. She is also the creator and host of the *Birth Justice Podcast NYC*.

Erin Malone is the communications director at Forward Together and a seasoned communications strategist. She has led communications campaigns to win paid sick days and living wage legislation, secure affordable housing, keep hospitals open, secure strong union contracts, and provide medical relief in Haiti.

Gloria Malone is a digital strategist who highlights changemakers in traditionally homogeneous sectors. When she's not helping people make a splash in the media landscape, Gloria can be found traveling with her teenage daughter, trying out a fitness class, or enjoying her favorite anime.

For more than ten years, **Shanelle Matthews** has helped social justice activists, organizations, and campaigns inspire action through storytelling and communications. She founded the Radical Communicators Network (RadComms) and developed Channel Black, a media-training program tailored to the needs of Black leaders.

Alexandra Moffett-Bateau is an assistant professor of political science at John Jay College of Criminal Justice, CUNY. Her intellectual work focuses on race, urban politics, and political behavior. Through her expertise as a researcher and academic writer, Alexandra works to support organizations in their outreach to local communities.

Jordan Scruggs is a Black, nonbinary, queer southerner born and raised in Tennessee. Proud to share their lived experience of mental health, being queer, owning their awkwardness, and love of Whitney Houston and Prince. They can't wait to welcome y'all to the South they know.

Bishakh Som is an artist, illustrator, and writer based in Brooklyn. Her books include *Apsara Engine* and *Spellbound: A Graphic Memoir*, among others, and her work has appeared in the *New Yorker*, *Boston Review*, and *Brooklyn Rail*.

Quita Tinsley Peterson is a Black, queer femme that writes, organizes, and fights for reproductive justice and queer liberation in the South. As a Black nonbinary southerner, it is through their lived experiences that Quita has come to believe in the power of storytelling and collective resistance.

Alicia M. Walters is a writer, artist, and facilitator on a mission to transform people and society by centering Blackness. She created Echoing Ida in 2009 to uplift Black womxn and our voices in media. She is also the creator of the Black Thought Project. She lives, mothers, and builds community on the land of the Ohlone people in what is also the revolutionary city of Oakland, California.

Raquel Willis is an activist, award-winning writer, and media strategist dedicated to elevating the honor and dignity of Black transgender people.

Acknowledgments

This book would not have been possible without the guides and coconspirators who showed up, threw down, said yes, made room, sparked thought, blazed trails, and became our champions.

We give thanks to Jamia Wilson, Lauren Rosemary Hook, and the entire Feminist Press team.

We give thanks to Forward Together, with special shoutouts to Eveline Shen, Rosa Yadira Ortiz, Adwoa Agyepong, ChaKiara Tucker, Maria Santos, Diana Lugo-Martinez—and all the flowers to Erin Malone, who helped imagine this book into being.

Carla Murphy, Angela Bronner Helm, Olivia Ford, and Lori Adelman touched nearly every piece in this collection, guiding ideas from conception to birth, infancy to full-fledged adulthood. Thank you, beloved editors, for journeying with so many of us.

Regina Mahone (*Rewire*), Emily Douglas (*The Nation*), Jen Baker (*New York Times*), Jamilah Lemieux (*Ebony*), Meredith Talusan (*them.*), Danielle Belton (*The Root*), Kimberly N. Foster (*For Harriet*), Sonya Renee Taylor (*The Body Is Not an Apology*), Dani McClain, Eesha Pandit, and the entire Crunk Feminist Collective graciously shared their time and resources with us for this collection. Thank you.

We give thanks to the Pacific Ocean, Zenju Earthlyn Manuel's Black Angel Cards, Motherpeace Tarot, essential oils, bonfires, s'mores, cannabis, whiskey, and California red wine for facilitating so many connections, revelations, and transformations during our annual retreats.

And we give thanks to the ancestors who light our path, with eternal gratitude to our foremother Ida B. Wells-Barnett.

Dr. Cynthia R. Greenlee is a North Carolina–based African Americanist historian and a James Beard Foundation Award–winning writer and editor.

Kemi Alabi is a poet, teaching artist, and cultural strategy director of Forward Together. They live in Chicago.

Janna A. Zinzi is a communications strategist, travel writer, and burlesque artist and educator based in New Orleans.

More Activist Anthologies from the Feminist Press

$pread: The Best of the Magazine That Illuminated the Sex Industry and Started a Media Revolution
edited by Rachel Aimee, Eliyanna Kaiser, and Audacia Ray

All the Women Are White, All the Blacks Are Men, But Some of Us Are Brave: Black Women's Studies
edited by Akasha (Gloria T.) Hull, Patricia Bell Scott, and Barbara Smith

The Crunk Feminist Collection
edited by Brittney C. Cooper, Susana M. Morris, and Robin M. Boylorn

The Feminist Porn Book: The Politics of Producing Pleasure
edited by Tristan Taormino, Celine Parreñas Shimizu, Constance Penley, and Mireille Miller-Young

The Feminist Utopia Project: Fifty-Seven Visions of a Radically Better Future
edited by Alexandra Brodsky and Rachel Kauder Nalebuff

Go Home! edited by Rowan Hisayo Buchanan

I Still Believe Anita Hill: Three Generations Discuss the Legacies of Speaking Truth to Power
edited by Amy Richards and Cynthia Greenberg

Queer Ideas: The David R. Kessler Lectures in Lesbian and Gay Studies
from the Center for Lesbian and Gay Studies at CUNY

Radical Reproductive Justice: Foundation, Theory, Practice, Critique
edited by Loretta J. Ross, Lynn Roberts, Erika Derkas, Whitney Peoples, and Pamela Bridgewater Toure

Still Brave: The Evolution of Black Women's Studies
edited by Stanlie M. James, Frances Smith Foster, and Beverly Guy-Sheftall